Project managing
change

FT Prentice Hall
FINANCIAL TIMES

In an increasingly competitive world, we believe it's quality of thinking that gives you the edge – an idea that opens new doors, a technique that solves a problem, or an insight that simply makes sense of it all. The more you know, the smarter and faster you can go.

That's why we work with the best minds in business and finance to bring cutting-edge thinking and best learning practice to a global market.

Under a range of leading imprints, including *Financial Times Prentice Hall*, we create world-class print publications and electronic products bringing our readers knowledge, skills and understanding, which can be applied whether studying or at work.

To find out more about Pearson Education publications, or tell us about the books you'd like to find, you can visit us at
www.pearsoned.co.uk

PEARSON
Education

Project managing change

practical tools and techniques
to make change happen

Ira Blake and Cindy Bush

 Prentice Hall

FINANCIAL TIMES

An imprint of **Pearson Education**

Harlow, England • London • New York • Boston • San Francisco • Toronto
Sydney • Tokyo • Singapore • Hong Kong • Seoul • Taipei • New Delhi
Cape Town • Madrid • Mexico City • Amsterdam • Munich • Paris • Milan

PEARSON EDUCATION LIMITED

Edinburgh Gate
Harlow CM20 2JE
Tel: +44 (0)1279 623623
Fax: +44 (0)1279 431059
Website: www.pearsoned.co.uk

First published in Great Britain in 2009

ISBN: 978-0-273-72045-4

British Library Cataloguing-in-Publication Data
A catalogue record for this book is available from the British Library

Library of Congress Cataloging-in-Publication Data
Blake, Ira.
  Project managing change : practical tools and techniques to make
  change happen / Ira Blake and Cindy Bush.
      p. cm.
  Includes bibliographical references and index.
  ISBN 978-0-273-72045-4 (pbk. : alk. paper) 1. Organizational change.
  2. Organizational change--Management. 3. Organizational
  effectiveness--Management. I. Bush, Cindy. II. Title.
  HD58.8.B5496 2009
  658.4'06--dc22
                          2008043491

The opinions expressed in case studies reflect the views of the individual, and
not those of any organisation.

The term 'change prism' is a registered copyright of Ira Blake and Cindy Bush.

10 9 8 7 6 5 4 3 2 1
12 11 10 09 08

Typeset in Melior 9.5/13pt by 30
Printed by Ashford Colour Press Ltd, Gosport

The publisher's policy is to use paper manufactured from sustainable forests.

To James & KJ and our dearest family and friends for their constant love and support.

And to all those change management enthusiasts who said they wanted this book – thank you for helping us make it a reality.

Contents

Acknowledgements

WE WOULD BOTH LIKE TO THANK the following brilliant pioneers, for introducing us to, and whetting our appetites for, all things change management: Professor John Kotter, Dr Hilary Harris, Peter Block, Peter Senge and Darryl Conner. They continue to be the inspiration for our humble forays into the complex and elusive world of change.

To our friends who came through for us in the writing of this book, we would like to sincerely thank Dr Howard McMinn, Fergus Smith, Nimira Harjee, Chantelle Edwards, Dr Phil Lewis and Jane McGeeney.

Ira would like personally to thank Jeff Gray, John Heath, Jim Erskine and Mike Leenders, Bob Kelley and Bill Cowley, Tony Murphy and Javier Garcia, Kevin Flanagan, Julian Fielden-Page, and Professor Chris Brewster for signposting and encouraging her change management journey.

Cindy would like to thank Sheila Legon, Dr Linda Hoopes, Dr Marilyn Laiken, Dr Norm Halpern, Phil Clothier, Sue Adam, Alf Rock and Gerald Wu for generously sharing with her their change management wisdom and courage.

We would like to close this by thanking all our current and past colleagues and clients, co-workers and leaders with whom we have had the privilege to work and learn from over the years. It is because of you and your belief in us that we have had the opportunities to succeed, fail, reflect, try again, gain and refine the experience held in this book.

Publisher's acknowledgements

We are grateful to the following for permission to reproduce copyright material:

Figure 4.9 adapted from Eli Lilly and Company. Note that in no way does Eli Lilly and Company endorse the author or publisher; The Resiliency Questionnaire and Quiz Scoring on pages 188–9 from *The Resiliency Advantage: Master Change, Thrive Under Pressure, and Bounce Back from Setbacks* by Al Siebert, PhD. Reprinted with permission. © Copyright 2005, Al Siebert, PhD; Figure 13.1 from *Fundamentals of Change Management* (ODR 1998), reprinted with permission by Conner Partners; Figure 13.2 from THE FIFTH DISCIPLINE by Peter M. Senge, copyright © 1990, 2006 by Peter M. Senge. Used by permission of Doubleday, a division of Random House, Inc.; Appendix 1 © Alan Chapman, 2005–08. From the free resources website www.businessballs.com. See http://www.businessballs.com/swotanalysisfreetemplate.htm. Reproduced with permission; Appendix 4 from *Organizational Behaviour: An Introductory Text*, 7th Edition (Huczynski, A. and Buchanan, D. 2007), reprinted with permission.

In some instances, we have been unable to trace the owners of copyright material and we would appreciate any information that would enable us to do so.

Foreword

THE PROCESS OF CHANGE is inherent in humans: it happens to us all, all the time, and in general we cope remarkably well. It seems that it is only when humans are combined in organisations that change becomes a real problem. And there it certainly is a problem. Research tells us that most major change initiatives fail and that even smaller changes can be extremely difficult to achieve successfully.

Clearly there is some kind of gap in the market and, inevitably, there has been a rush to fill it. There are a great many books and articles that tell us how we should manage change initiatives. A cynic might ask why things remain so difficult when all that information is available. One problem might be that most of these books tend to focus on the 'big stuff', see the people involved in the change as difficulties to be overcome and are often highly prescriptive.

What is needed is a book that puts people management at the fore of the analysis and provides simple and practical advice and support without preaching a one-best-way to do things. Such a book would analyse the issues, look at making and embedding change as a project and provide tools and support to help project manage the process, whilst at the same time understanding that change is context specific and not every approach will work in every situation. A text like that would be of at least as much use to managers engaged in the many small but practical changes that have to be made in organisations all the time as to managers engaged in major 'culture change' projects.

The book that you are looking at now is precisely that kind of book. Built on years of practical experience, careful analysis and an understanding that simple and straightforward language is of much greater value than 'consultancy-speak' or academic jargon, this book provides clear understanding, valuable tools and practical support that will benefit anyone engaged in any kind of change project.

Chris Brewster
Professor of International Human Resource Management
University of Reading

Preface

Who will benefit from reading this book?

IF YOU ARE INVOLVED, LEADING OR MANAGING a project team that will introduce changes to the people in your organisation, *Project Managing Change* can help you. As well as offering a practical, project-based approach, this book will provide you with a collection of tools, frameworks and 'job aids' which we have developed during our many years of change management, both as internal and external consultants.

This book has been written for three main audiences:

1. new and experienced change managers – to give you tools and step-by-step guidance to deliver successful change programmes

2. project managers and project stream leads – so you can understand what change management does and how it plugs into and is managed as part of an overall project plan

3. consultants or those managing consultants (internal and professional services).

With the above audiences, we assume you have little or no project management experience. If you specifically want to build your project management skills, there are two further books in this series that will help you: *The Definitive Guide to Project Management* (Nokes and Kelly, 2007) and *The Project Manager* (Newton, 2005).

Organisations today are facing a period of great change, innovation and competition. Nokes and Kelly (2007) assert that in such competitive environments, all new growth comes from projects. As part of their research, they conducted an informal survey of experienced project managers and of the top five problems identified, two related specifically to people:

1   understanding people – getting people to 'rub along' with each other and adapting one's approach to allow for individual differences

2   getting highly skilled/technical employees to think outside their disciplines, especially regarding 'people' aspects.

The other problems identified were:

▌ lack of a common approach across the organisation, causing inefficiency and risk

▌ having to deal with unexpected crises that could reasonably have been foreseen longer in advance, if not avoided

▌ selling the benefits of project management to customers, so that they are prepared to make the necessary investment regarding cost, time and planning.

Most of the strategic and major changes businesses have to make are implemented through projects. All projects result in a change that affects someone and could potentially be viewed as possible candidates for change management. Managing the impact of change on people requires a specific skill set and many project managers have little or no working knowledge of this type of change. When properly managed, change activity can easily be manipulated into PMI, APM, PRINCE2 and bespoke project and programme methodologies, but trying to do without change management when it is required will often lead to project failure.

Our approach advocates uniting 'people-focused' activities, for example communications, training, culture and behaviours, into a single area of responsibility within a project. Our experience shows us that this generates synergistic benefits and raises the profile of all affected employees with the project.

Why do *you* need this book?

If you are an experienced change manager embarking on a project, you will have found yourself asking yourself a number of questions. Take a look at the list of questions below. Do they look/sound familiar?

	Know	Don't know
What is changing?		
What and where will it impact?		
Who is critical to the project's success?		
How committed is the business?		
What are the critical success factors we know of? Are there others?		
How do we get authorisation and resources?		
What, how and with whom will we communicate?		
What actions or interventions will optimise the change?		
How will jobs, teams or the organisation change?		
Who is accountable for the success of the change?		
What's *my* role?		
What's the plan?		

If you are new to project and/or change management, you may not yet have reached the point of asking these questions or you may not even know what questions to ask. In both cases, this book will guide you through the process of finding the answers.

The key to delivering an effective change management programme is selection. This book will provide you with the means to assess your organisation's strengths and weaknesses in eight areas, and will highlight the specific topics you need to concentrate on as a project manager or as a project stream lead responsible for change management. This book will enable you to select and apply the tools *you need* to help you deliver the greatest impact or 'bang for your buck'.

How this book is organised

Part 1, Chapter 1 is an introduction to change management and can be skimmed over by experienced change managers who want to get straight into the practicalities of how to project manage change. However, if you are new to the discipline or reading this book out of personal interest or development, this chapter provides a useful overview and summary of the evolution of change management and current thinking.

Part 1, Chapters 2 to 4, are all about preparing for and planning for change. Here we cover how to synchronise your change activities with those in the wider project/programme, how to organise yourself and your resources and how to ensure the right capabilities exist or are developed for the change to be implemented and delivered effectively.

Part 2, Chapters 5 to 12, are your toolkit. All the activities, assessments and outputs you will need to generate during the life cycle of a business change programme are here – each with step-by-step instructions on how to use the tool and many with worked examples and templates to help you get the most out of them.

Part 3, Chapters 13 to 15, answer the question 'What does a change manager do?' Here we look at the day-to-day tasks and areas of responsibility that you will need to focus on to (1) deliver the change plan and (2) create the conditions for successful change. This section also covers what individuals – you especially – bring to the role and the value you create for the project.

Chapters 16 and the summary provide guidance on sustaining the change and useful tips and checklists for change management practitioners.

Where possible, we have included sample documents and worked examples. Many of the examples have been used and tested in real organisations and programmes, but have been adapted for your use in any major organisational change. We have created a series of blank templates referred to in the tools for you to use in your own change projects. As a purchaser of this book, you can access and download these templates from www.pearson-books.com/managingchange.

This book is not intended to be an *oracle* of all things change management, but has been devised by experienced practitioners to share knowledge and tools. There is no such thing as a 'one size fits all' package – it usually means it fits no-one and you end up with a fragmented, aimless set of disjointed activities that no-one understands or benefits from. We would encourage you to think of the tools and materials as a menu from which to choose dishes appropriate to your specific situation or appetite.

The purpose of this book is to provide a structure for you to organise the activities needed to deliver change. The drive and enthusiasm to deliver it must, inevitably, come from the change manager.

1
part

Principles for project managing change

What is change management?

THE TERM CHANGE MANAGEMENT has as many meanings as the number of people who you ask about it. We find this definition to be both practical and useful:

> Change management is the process, tools and techniques to manage the people side of business change to achieve the most successful business outcome.

This chapter is an overview of what we mean by and understand change and change management to be. In it we summarise the evolution of change management and current thinking on the subject. If you are a new change manager or a project manager embracing change management as a new responsibility, getting a firm grasp of what change means will be useful before moving on to the hands-on chapters of this book. This understanding sets the foundation for the building blocks of change – the change prism and eight lenses – that are covered in Chapters 5 to 12. If you already know this information, use it as a quick refresher and move on.

Change or die?

> It is not the strongest of the species that survives, nor the most intelligent, but the one that is most responsive to change.
>
> Darwin, 1859

Picture a warm sunny day and think about what you associate with it. Light and loose clothing, cool drinks, salads, open windows and doors. Slowly, the environment changes and it becomes winter.

What will happen to those who have not noticed the changes in temperature? What will happen to those who do not change their behaviour accordingly? People seem to appreciate the need, and know how to, adapt to these changes. They may not welcome the change but they do adapt their attitudes and behaviours in response to it.

Change in nature, or evolution, can be seemingly unstructured and chaotic to those being affected. It is only when viewed retrospectively that purpose and direction are revealed. Staying competitive in business doesn't allow for the luxury of evolution – it takes too long. Only by approaching change in a structured way can you shape and achieve a predefined future and realise benefits to the business.

> those organisations that choose not to adapt, will not survive

The objective of change management is to guide people through change so they can adapt to and appreciate 'the new'. Corporate change is no more complex than any other change we may encounter in our lives, but the process of accepting and adapting to change is not as well understood. Growth is based on an organisation's ability to survive, which is in itself a function of the ability to change. Adaptability to change is preceded by the ability to 'let go' of what was before and is based on employees understanding the changes and adopting the right behaviours. Those organisations that choose not to adapt, will not survive.

The change equation:

Change management = sustained change in human behaviour

The most important thing for you to understand right away is that change is all about people and the purpose of change management is to bring this intrinsic human behaviour to the forefront of corporate life.

People are *the* bottom-line business drivers, so their capabilities and needs must be fully integrated into business processes and planning. Every organisation should prioritise building the people dimension into strategic thinking and programme development to get the best return from their employees' energies, knowledge and creativity.

People and change

Organisations must constantly change and adjust their strategies and the way they conduct business to stay in the competitive game. For employees this can feel like a seemingly never-ending series of initiatives and projects that impact their day-to-day jobs and roles in an organisation.

People are at the heart of change, their personalities, values and behaviour all work for and against change in organisations. People issues have proven to be the mitigating factors in most change programmes and often it is the employees that ultimately determine success or failure. This is especially true in the majority of businesses where 60 per cent of the operating costs to run a business are tied to the people, for example salaries, benefits, hiring and redeployment.

The Gartner Group found that 'without the appropriate change implementation support, a company spends $3–$10 for every dollar invested in technology to retrofit it to the culture'. In 1995, *Computer World* also demonstrated that nearly half of all major technical initiatives failed because of fear and anxiety in the organisation and resistance from key managers.

A project may have a significant impact on employees and managers alike, and individuals will go through 'ups and downs' during all the project phases: it will be a very unsettling time. The whole organisation will reflect this transition and there will be dips in performance as people adjust to new ways of working. Figure 1.1 illustrates the range of optimistic and pessimistic emotions that will be experienced by those impacted by change throughout the project:

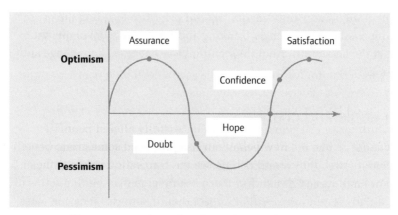

FIGURE 1.1 Change curve: 'emotional reaction to change'

People change only when they are led and supported through the 'change curve'. The change curve is a series of normal and to be expected stages. These stages involve both emotions and reactions. To the untrained eye they are the behaviours of people who ought to 'know better' and 'behave reasonably'. The role of change management is to help the organisation move through the change curve more rapidly by creating a change receptive environment in which to implement the programme.

Change can be difficult for employees to accept, but understanding why the change is happening and what the changes mean for them can dramatically improve their receptiveness to the change. In addition, the confusion and fear experienced by the organisation's employees during and after a major change can be significantly reduced if it is managed well. By actively managing the change, the end result is that employees become productive in the new environment more quickly.

Myth: *People change their behaviour based on facts and logic.*

Mythbuster: *People are more likely to change when they are shown a truth that influences their feelings more than when they are given analysis intended to shift their thinking. The reverse can also be true when dealing with very technical or scientific-thinking employees.*

In most change projects, the amount of actual change is less than what is perceived. Much of the old may be compatible with the new. Change management quantifies the change, grafts the new practices onto the old roots while removing the inconsistent or unworkable pieces. If the new practices are inconsistent with the cultural DNA of the organisation, the challenge is far greater. Culture changes when you have successfully altered people's actions, when the new behaviour has produced some group benefit for a period of time and people see the connection between the new actions and the performance improvement.

> employees become productive in the new environment more quickly

When a change is managed well, the day it goes into effect (i.e. goes 'live') becomes a non-event. People are already accepting and while there may be initial problems in the early days these are accompanied by conversations about managing through the difficulties and not by screams of hostility.

Background – 'the history bit'

Change management is hardly a new concept. Over the past 20 years, programmes to improve organisational efficiency have become prevalent. Their success, or lack of it, is a function of the organisation's ability to persuade all of their stakeholders to change and act together for a common benefit. Successful organisational change occurs when the organisation has convinced employees not only to absorb change but to become committed to it.

There are four conditions required before this can happen.

1. Employees will alter their mind-sets only if they see the point of the change, can see what it means for them and agree with it.
2. The surrounding structures, processes and reward systems must be in place to support the change.
3. Employees must have the skills to do what is required.
4. They must see their role models actively modelling the change.

In the past few years, change management has evolved from being the domain of psychologists, academics and 'touchy-feelys' who talked about intangibles and lacked any accountability to becoming a recognised business discipline. Even more recently change management has experienced a paradigm shift – away from the bolted-on 'change consultant' model towards the creation of an integrated, structured approach to change management that delivers tangible and measurable value to strategic and tactical business programmes.

According to Jeff Hiatt and Tim Creasey (2008) change management is the application of 'two converging and predominant fields of thought: an engineering approach to improving business performance and a psychologist's approach to managing the human-side of change'. The convergence of thought from both the engineering and psychological school of thought is essential for successful business change.

Organisational change can take many forms and can be operational, tactical or strategic in nature. Each of these types are explored in more detail in Chapter 2. Whatever the type of change, it is an emotional experience for those affected, not a cerebral one. Persuading and influencing people to absorb and accept change because they want to do things differently is critical. This is discussed more fully in Chapter 3 where we introduce the 'commitment curve'.

Change management is not a 'soft option'. Having one's attitudes challenged is not comfortable; on the contrary, it leads to discomfort, often as a result of having less control. In organisations where 'groupthink' or consensus is prevalent, it can also lead to temporary disharmony and conflict. Change management anticipates and manages these reactions ensuring the effect on day-to-day business and individual performance is minimised. In change management, you must balance your delivery responsibilities to the organisation against the performance and well-being of employees.

Summary of the different models of change

Much has been written on the subject of change and various models of change proposed (CIPD, 2007). In sharing these models, our purpose is not to provide an academic evaluation but to add to your knowledge of what else is out there should you wish to explore the more theoretical approaches to change management. The application of different models has implications for the way organisations and their leaders regard change, the way they manage change and even the effectiveness of any change initiative. The three main, contrasting models are from Lewin, Beer and Shaw.

Lewin's model

This model considers that change involves a move from one static state to another static status quo via an interim state of activity. Lewin (1951) specifies a three-stage process of managing change: unfreezing; changing; refreezing.

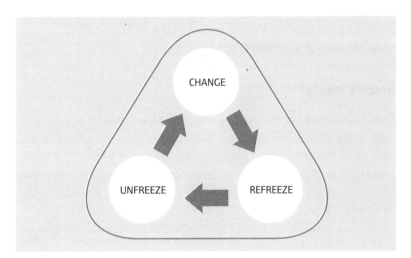

FIGURE 1.2 Lewin's change model

The first stage involves creating a level of dissatisfaction with the status quo, which creates conditions for change to be introduced. The second stage requires organising and mobilising the resources needed to bring about the change, and the third stage is about embedding the new ways of working into the organisation.

Beer's model

Beer and his colleagues (1990) advocate a model that recognises complexity in change and hence the requirement that a complex, but still uniform, set of responses are needed to ensure effectiveness. Beer *et al.* prescribe a six-step process to achieve change focusing on 'task alignment', in which employees' roles, responsibilities and relationships are critical to bring about changed ways of thinking, attitudes and behaving. The stages are:

Stage 1: Mobilise commitment to change through joint diagnosis

Stage 2: Develop a shared vision of how to organise

Stage 3: Foster consensus, competence and commitment to a shared vision

Stage 4: Spread the word about the change

Stage 5: Institutionalise the change through formal policies

Stage 6: Monitor and adjust as needed.

Shaw's model

This model looks at change in a different form. Change is seen as both complex and evolutionary. The starting point for this model (and more recent models) is that the environment of an organisation is not in equilibrium. As such the change mechanisms tend to be 'messy' and may operate in reverse to the way outlined by Lewin. Shaw (Higgs and Rowland, 2003) advocates that the forces for change are already inherent in the system and emerge as the system adapts to its environment.

Summary of alternative approaches to change management

While the models look at change as a concept, there are several approaches to change management we wanted to mention. In contrast to our approach to change management as aligned with project management, the other schools of thought below show the breadth of thinking in the field and give you a taste of other ways of understanding and managing change that may work for you.

> there are several approaches to change management

Engineering approach

This looks at how to make changes to the operations of a business as a mechanical system. It focuses on observable, measurable business elements that can be changed or improved. Change can be gradual, as seen in continuous process improvement, or radical, as in business process reengineering. Historically companies with a mechanical view do not value change management concepts. They have a tendency to ignore or apply quick fixes to the 'people problem' interfering with the improvement initiative.

Psychological approach

The emphasis here is how humans react to their environment and to change. According to the psychological approach, change management is concerned with helping each individual 'make sense of what change means to them'. Business practices such as human resources and organisational development follow this approach.

Process approach

John P. Kotter, a world-renowned expert on leadership at the Harvard Business School, has written widely and is considered seminal on how the best organisations actually change. His international bestseller *Leading Change* (1996), which outlines an actionable, eight-step process for implementing successful transformations, became a key change reference for managers around the world. The eight steps Kotter identifies in the change process, in summary, are: establishing a sense of urgency; creating the guiding coalition; developing a vision and a strategy;

communicating the change vision; empowering broad-based action; generating short-term wins; consolidating gains and producing more change; and anchoring new approaches in the culture.

Being v. doing approach

In *Powerful Conversations: How High Impact Leaders Communicate*, Phil Harkins (1999) says that leaders influence cultural change not just through memos and meetings but also through the many one-on-one conversations that they hold throughout a day. What makes a conversation powerful is that all those involved in the conversation share important feelings, ideas and beliefs. There are clear expressions of wants and needs. At the end of the conversation, there is a real commitment to what was explicitly stated and shared with those who were part of the conversation. Conversations must be planned and managed with the focus on 'being the change', and the doing of the change will happen as a result.

Skills-based approach

Rosabeth Moss Kanter (1999) in *The Enduring Skills of Change Leaders* states:

> Change-adept organizations share three attributes: the imagination to innovate, the professionalism to perform, and the openness to collaborate. The most important things a leader can bring to a changing organization are passion, conviction, and confidence in others. Too often executives announce a plan, launch a task force, and then simply hope that people find the answers – instead of offering a dream, stretching their horizons, and encouraging people to do the same.

Storytelling approach

In *The Story Factor*, Annette Simmons (2006) notes that stories make points in less confrontational ways than arguments. The message can be put out and left for the individual to ponder. Stories are also powerful because they touch the emotions as well as the mind, in a memorable way. She states:

Changing a diametrically opposed opinion demands that you move in baby steps. A story gives you the perfect format to gradually and indirectly move someone from one side of a conflict to the other side. Quoting research statistics, presenting philosophical arguments, and delivering elegant rhetoric aim too high. You need to aim lower – underneath rational thought – and take smaller steps.

Change management is not a linear process and, as you uncover more information and as issues and assumptions are challenged, you will need to revalidate and update what has gone before. Ambiguity is lessened with each iteration, but you should always be aware that it may never be completely resolved. Your own experiences can immeasurably enhance your organisation's change capability and we encourage you to regard this book as a starting point to be improved on and added to as you build up your expertise and experiences.

Change projects – types and effects

AN OFTEN REPEATED JOKE is that the only thing you can rely on is change. Whether it is small, large or somewhere in between, unless you are repeating something you know over and over *ad infinitum*, there will be a degree of change involved. In Chapter 3 we talk more about the importance of planning, but in this chapter we look at the importance of preparing for and anticipating the impact that change has on organisations, and more specifically on people and behaviour.

Understanding the nature of the change you wish to effect and the context in which you are working are important in determining an appropriate change strategy. Entering uncharted change territory without some idea of the landscape puts you at an immediate disadvantage from the start. One of the first stages in charting the territory is to understand a little more about the type of change you wish to effect, where you want to go and how you plan to travel there.

Types of change projects

Everything you do in an organisation, in your job or in your personal life, is subject to and influenced by change. However, not all change will require the level of planning, preparation or investment of resources that our approach recommends. The level of change management effort depends on two dimensions: (1) the complexity or scope of the change (i.e. how much will be changing in the organisation) and (2) the scale of impact of the change (i.e. how many people/functions/offices will be affected). Both dimensions will directly influence how much energy will be required by the organisation to absorb the change and are an early indicator to you of how much change management will be required to drive behaviour change and realise benefits. (For an alternative list of scope descriptors, please refer to Appendix 4.)

the level of change management effort depends on two dimensions

Figure 2.1 shows a common classification and the relationships between the change types: operational, tactical and strategic. The boundaries are somewhat artificial in that there are areas of overlap between the types of change.

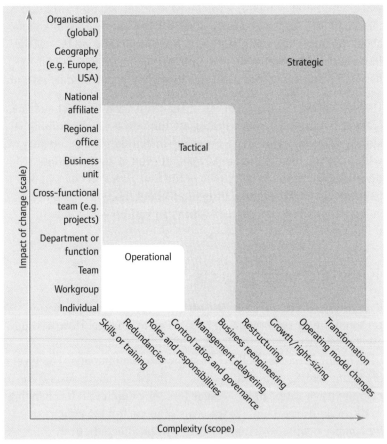

FIGURE 2.1 Types of change

Some changes will be relatively simple or affect only one or a few individuals. In these instances, change is dealt with on an *ad hoc* basis and the focus of any change management effort will be directed towards dealing with the individual's reaction to the change, and changes to local processes and behaviours. This type of change is classified as 'operational'. In general, changes at the individual, workgroup and team levels can be addressed through communications and training and do not necessarily require project change management as detailed in this book. However, the principles and techniques of change management can be useful at any time that even one person is required to do something differently.

Tactical change is probably the most commonly occurring type of change as businesses look continuously to improve their performance and process efficiency. Strategic change is radical and requires a large shift in assumptions made by the organisation and its stakeholders. Transformation is the most extreme and far-reaching form of strategic change and can result in an organisation that differs significantly in terms of structure, processes and culture from the existing one. Strategic change often involves lots of changes, small and large, bundled together, and these projects tend to have longer timelines. It is in the larger tactical and strategic change where project managing change is most needed and could make or break the success and long-term benefit of these large undertakings.

At work, change is either proactive (let's improve) or reactive (let's fight back), or a combination of the two. Some typical changes that may require people to do something differently are as follows.

Change driver	Description
Technology	Using new or upgraded software, hardware, systems or equipment
Process	Following different steps to completing a task or activity
Product	Developing new or improved products or services
Money	Staying competitive in the market, managing with less or increased funding
Marketplace	Changing demographics or customer requirements

All of the above examples can drive change that is small or large, and the change management activities you choose to do will be relative to what you are trying to achieve. A smaller amount of activities will be needed for operational changes; larger and broader activities for tactical and strategic change or large transformation programmes.

How do I assess my change management need?

Until you sit down and try to wrap your head around a change it can seem bigger or smaller than you first anticipate. The simplest way to figure out the scope of the change (How big is the change from what we do today?) and scale of the change (How many people, processes and other resources will it affect?), is to construct simple *from/to* statements. Think of it as before/after behaviour. What does someone or a group of people do now, and what will they do after the change takes place?

CASE STUDY

Sizing up change at a Canadian bank

During a change at an investment bank, a large project was gearing up, pulling the usual resources into a team to do a change – with representatives from IT, from HR, from finance, etc. However, once some from/to statements were drafted, it was apparent that the impact of the project for HR and finance was much smaller than originally anticipated, and their roles and involvement in the project were reduced accordingly.

Doing from/to statements helps to bring that first bit of clarity to what needs to happen, by whom and by when. For example, a change scenario could be that Bob will go *from* doing *ad hoc* reports on progress *to* producing bi-weekly reports using a template.

What will help Bob successfully make that change? This is an example of a small-scale change, but it would be a mistake to underestimate how far that journey may be for Bob! This would be the *scope* of the change. Perhaps he requires IT skills to use the templates, or the bi-weekly reports will be added to his job description. Or he will need to interact with different people to gain the information for the reports, or his boss will need to learn how to do the reports first, so that when he and Bob meet to discuss progress they are using the same template.

In large-scale change, there may be groups of people who will need to do something differently – groups of 'Bobs' who will have changes to their jobs. Those groups of people can be inside or outside your organisation, and how many there are will affect the *scale*. In the example we are using, let's work through the scale:

All other employees at Bob's level will go *from* doing *ad hoc* reports on progress *to* producing bi-weekly reports using a template.

The finance department, who requires the report, will go *from* asking for *ad hoc* reports *to* monitoring that the bi-weekly reports are received.

Managers of the employees at Bob's level will go *from* not reviewing the reports *to* requesting and reviewing the bi-weekly reports before they are sent to finance.

The CFO will go *from ad hoc* requests *to* submitting a final overall report bi-weekly to the CEO.

As you think a bit about what would need to happen in the above scenario to make it successful – constructing a new template, issuing it to everyone involved, conducting some training sessions, sending out a memo from the CFO that this is now required, etc. – these are all activities that would need to be carried out in the project. This will become clearer as you start to work with the tools in this book, such as the change impact assessment (CIA). From/to work can be done as part of the formal 'future vision' work (see Chapter 13) or it can be used as an input into the strategy and future state (see Chapter 5).

The effects of change on people and organisations

Why spend time learning about people? I just want to get on with things!

In our action-oriented business culture, spending time planning, developing understanding or thinking about people is sometimes not recognised as valuable. People are at the heart of change, their personalities, values and behaviour all work for and against change in organisations. Without people, change does not occur. Technology does not rewire itself (yet), processes are not conducted or improved on their own, and developing a vision for the future is not something that draws itself on paper.

> people can make or break any organisational change

People can make or break any organisational change – and this can happen at any level or role in the organisation. People react differently to change, some love it (we call these the change-junkies, their common cry is 'Let's change it!') some hate it (we call these the resistors, whose common cry is 'I'm not changing!'). These two extremes and all the glorious reactions inbetween make up any given organisational environment.

Fear and control

Many studies about why people react so differently to change have been conducted and, essentially, people's reactions can be boiled down to one thing … the basic emotion of fear. Fear of the unknown, fear of failure, fear of success, fear of hurt, any fear you would like to label. How a person manages that fear can be based on their personality, their cognitive capability, their family upbringing, the country's culture they were raised in, their beliefs and attitudes, their abilities and skills, and influenced by the specific situation they find themselves in, experiencing the fear.

People are control freaks. We may not go around introducing ourselves at parties as such, but we are. We want to be in control of our own destiny, our day, our time, and when others get in the way of how we want things to unfold, watch out! We become fearful, annoyed, frustrated: 'What's wrong with people?'; 'What can they be thinking?'; 'Where is the world going to these days?'

Dr Elisabeth Kübler-Ross (1969) conducted work with terminally ill patients, and observed their reactions as they discovered and grappled with their illness and impending death, arguably the biggest fear anyone faces. Her model described five stages of emotional behaviour as follows:

Denial: *'It can't be happening.'*

Anger: *'Why me? It's not fair.'*

Bargaining: *'Just let me live to see my children graduate.'*

Depression: *'I'm so sad, why bother with anything?'*

Acceptance: *'It's going to be OK.'*

Dr Kübler-Ross applied these stages to any form of personal loss such as job, income, freedom, the death of a loved one, divorce or infertility. She noted that these stages do not necessarily come in the order noted above, nor are they experienced by all patients, though she stated a person will always experience at least two.

In organisational change, as with personal change, it is not a linear process. Moving forward and back along the stages is quite common as more information becomes available or as the physical environment or others' behaviour around you starts to change.

Change and stress

Any significant change that is introduced at work means people may go through the same emotional cycle as above. Just because we are at work does not mean we are robots functioning without emotion. Our emotions accompany us into the workplace, and whether changes in our lives are work-related or not, all the changes bombard the emotional coping capacity that people have overall. Organisational change can trigger a sense of loss and bewilderment, initiating the cycle and inducing stress.

Certain life events are more stressful than others, and as they don't occur one at a time, people are often managing a number of events at once. There is only so much that one person can do to manage all the stressful situations that occur simultaneously in life – and the fear, loss and lack of control that come with them. If the stress becomes too much, then it is felt not only at home but at work, and measurably so in areas like employee turnover or absenteeism. Too many events at once can lead to emotional breakdown, illness or accidents.

A famous test conducted by Drs Holmes and Rahe (1967) asked people to rate the amount of stress they feel in 'life change units' when certain events occur. Below is a sample of their list and the scale of associated stress that goes with it. Try scoring yourself on how many of them you are currently experiencing, and add up the total number of points.

Event	Points	Event	Points
Death of a spouse	100	Divorce	73
Marital separation	65	Detention in jail or institution	63
Death of a close family member	63	Retirement	63
Major personal injury or illness	53	Marriage	50
Being fired at work	47	Marital reconciliation	45
Change in health of a family member	44	Pregnancy	40
Sexual difficulty	40	New family member through birth, etc.	39
Major business readjustments	39	Major change in financial status	38
Death of a close friend	37	Change to a different line of work	36
Major increase in fights with spouse	35	Taking on a mortgage	31
Foreclosure on a mortgage or loan	30	Major change in responsibility at work	29
Son or daughter leaving home	29	In-law troubles	29
Outstanding personal achievement	28	Spouse seeks work outside the home	26
Go back to school	26	Major change in home living conditions	25
Revision of personal habits	24	Troubles with superior, boss	23

Event	Points	Event	Points
Change in working hours/ conditions	20	Change in residence	20
Change to a new school	20	Major change in or amount of recreation	19
Major change in church activities	19	Changed number of family get-togethers	19
Major change in social activities	18	New car or other big purchase	17
Major change in sleeping habits	16	Major change in eating habits	15
Vacation	13	Christmas or holiday observance	12
Minor violations of the law	12		

- Score 300+: Be extremely careful – you are at a greatly increased risk of serious illness (reduce stress *now*).

- Score 150–299+: Be cautious – your risk of illness is moderate (reduced by 30 per cent from the above risk).

- Score 150 or below: Be glad – you only have a slight risk of illness (but still need to take care of yourself).

Note: Individual responses will vary greatly, so your score is only a crude measure of your level of stress – at this particular moment in time. What this may help you understand better is *why* you are stressed and take control of it.

How many of the above events are related to working in organisations? It could be about one quarter, depending on how you interpret the statements and their impact. Compare your score with how you perceive your stress levels in relation to your colleagues – are you more or less stressed than they are? Even a simple comparison such as this can give you an insight into the general level of stress within your organisation.

The American Institute of Stress (2003), a research group, estimated the annual cost of stress to US business to be $300 billion. Job stress is the cause of:

▌ accidents

▌ absenteeism

▌ employee turnover

▌ diminished productivity

▌ direct medical, legal and insurance costs

▌ workers' compensation awards as well as tort and FELA
judgements.

Control and change management

What does this have to do with change management? When change
is introduced at work, people will feel afraid and experience a loss
of control. This is stressful for most of us as we thrive on control
and predictability, and any upset throws us off for a while. This
upset can lead to stress, and overloading changes on employees
could result in a serious cost to the organisation.

> we thrive on control and predictability

Change management seeks to smooth the process of introducing
change to people, so that it is absorbed and accepted willingly and
readily. This has the overall impact of reducing the stress
associated with change and the risks that come with it.

Essentially the tools and techniques of change management are
about helping people make sense of the change for them, and
finding in it what they can control. This regaining of control is
what motivates employees to start the journey from awareness to
commitment, described more fully in Chapter 3.

Resilience and readiness to change

Change management seeks to give control to those experiencing
change. For some, just a little bit of control is enough, but for
others, they need more. What if the situation does not allow you to
have control – for example a confidential restructuring or a hostile

takeover by a competitor? You may not know a change is coming until the day it arrives. Change management can help prepare employees to bounce back from unexpected change by building the skill of resiliency.

The characteristics or skills associated with resilience (Kelly *et al.*, 2003) are:

▌ positive world view

▌ positive self-concept

▌ focused sense of purpose

▌ flexible thinking

▌ social flexibility

▌ organising ambiguity

▌ proactive experimentation.

Resiliency is an individual's ability to cope with whatever life throws at you. How resilient are you? How quickly do you bounce back when things change? How strong is your change muscle? (There are tools to help you measure resilience later in the book.)

CASE STUDY

Building resilience to make change happen

Resilience, the ability to cope with significant change constructively, creatively and productively, is often overlooked. Resilience is not just coping, it's rebounding stronger. It is vital during relentless change and I felt it was a crucial skill for over 4,000 employees impacted by a multi-year large transformational project at a Canadian bank. My role was to drive the strategic change and, in order to do so, building resilience one employee at a time was key.

Through 90-minute sessions I conducted with employees, we discussed building resilience by:

▌ learning to adapt, being goal oriented and proactive

▌ developing strong relationships

▶

▌ maintaining perspective, being hopeful and optimistic

▌ channeling your attitude, efforts and energies on what you can do

▌ having a positive view of yourself and others

▌ recognising and building on strengths

▌ reframing – turning negatives into positives

▌ learning from setbacks.

In these sessions we used role-modeling and examples to illustrate how to regain control in your personal and work life by being focused, determined and flexible, and had participants create action plans.

By focusing on resilience, I learned that: (1) you could shift the emphasis to what was possible and provided a common framework and language for crucial discussions; and (2) talking about resilience energised and empowered individuals, encouraged ownership, built a mindset for change, and increased the capacity to handle more as the pace accelerated. I knew this because as more change activities were introduced there was increased acceptance and adoption of the new ways of working, both in the time it took and in reaching the target KPIs.

Nimira Harjee, Independent Change and
Organisational Development Consultant

Capacity

The final area we need to consider as an effect of change is capacity. For change to be accepted (and by that we mean a sustained change in human behaviour that allows an organisation to realise the benefits of that change), space for the change to be absorbed needs to be present. This space has to exist both at the individual and organisational levels. This is closely related to levels of stress and what you can take on in a given day, how you bounce back or how often you resort to ignoring a change, hoping it will go away.

Change capacity can be viewed in two ways:

1 how much can be implemented, and

2 how much people can absorb.

How much can be implemented?

Capacity impacts productivity at the individual level and, cumulatively, the capacity of the organisation to change. This can be illustrated with a simple capacity planning model commonly used in manufacturing (see Figure 2.2).

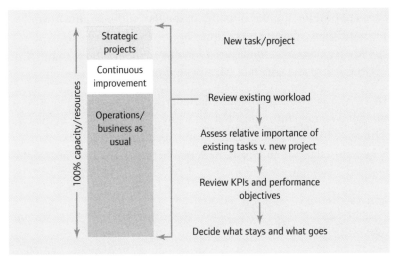

FIGURE 2.2 Capacity planning model

This model starts from the assumption that everyone is working at 100 per cent of their capacity if they are (1) working their contracted hours and (2) not on any sort of performance improvement programme. This is a potentially contentious statement, but it is a fallacy to think there are 'empty vessel' resources sitting around waiting for work – especially if the resources you require for the project have specific skills or experience that are in demand by the business. Somehow space or capacity must be created, and the only way to do this is to be clear on what is to be stopped or not done by an individual anymore. When individuals are assigned new tasks or projects, they go through an internal assessment similar to the one on the right-hand side of the model. However, the model is rational, and makes no assessment of the political or emotional aspects or value of the activities being performed.

space or capacity must be created

We have worked at organisations where the capacity for change is measured in the number of hours in the day and how much can be accomplished in each one of those hours. Projects are executed quickly and success is measured by how much has been done or the number of changes that have been implemented.

There is, however, an obvious shortcoming to this approach. You can put a change into place but, in many instances, there is then a time-lag while the change is fully absorbed by individuals, their behaviour changed and sustained, before any of the benefits can be realised (see Figure 2.3).

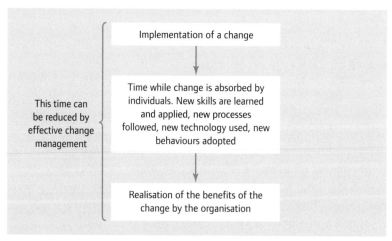

FIGURE 2.3 Relationship between implementation and benefits realisation

Understanding the scope and scale of what you are introducing before embarking on a change will help you to manage that time-lag between implementation and realisation.

An innovative approach to managing the pace of change

One hospital undergoing major transformation used a system of 'change points' to determine if it was reaching capacity in a particular month. It wanted to make sure it was not overloading its staff and that it realised its financial investment.

Small changes, such as trying a new supplier for gowns, required little staff behaviour adjustment and was allotted 10 points. Large changes, such as changing shift rotations for nurses, required more behaviour adjustment, and were allotted up to 100 points. No particular stakeholder group was allowed to reach more than 200 points in a one-month period, therefore managing the pace of change and increasing the likelihood that it would be absorbed.

How much can people absorb?

Consider the second measure of capacity – absorption. According to research, during transformational change each employee loses an average of two hours of productivity per day trying to process the change and what it means for them. Just over 40 per cent of employees who scored low in personal resilience reported feeling drained and depleted at the end of most days, not having enough energy to complete the tasks at hand (Smith, 2002).

This may seem like a lot, but our experience has shown this to be the case. In extremes, employees can almost stop working altogether, unable to focus on continuing business as usual. In one public sector client, the project manager had to revise the plan to reflect the reality of resources being productive for only three hours per day. This drop in productivity can last for days, weeks or even months, depending on the complexity and scale of the change, the level of ambiguity and the magnitude of the perceived threat to jobs and security. As people's understanding increases, so does productivity but the rate of improvement will depend on the rate and frequency of changes that will deliver the benefits. It also depends on the levels of individual and organisational resiliency.

If employees are in a state of 'overcapacity', either real or perceived, this will negatively impact the project in the following ways: inertia; unfavourable prioritisation of other tasks; and resistance to the change or programme. This is commonly known as 'change fatigue'.[1]

EXAMPLE

You are at your desk and you hear that the computer monitors will be upgraded next week to a new, ergonomic-style monitor. Obviously the company wants to save money on neck strain injuries and people being off work. The day arrives, the old monitor goes out and the new one comes in. After some brief adjustments to your chair height, a chat with the health and safety consultant, you get on with your day. You have absorbed that change relatively quickly, and six months later the company sees a 20 per cent reduction in the number of claims.

Later that same afternoon, you find out that the work your department does has been tagged for outsourcing, and your job will be taken over by someone in India. You will be offered a new role in another department, if you qualify for it, or you will receive a redundancy package. Obviously the company has not saved enough through health claim reduction, and is looking to gain more savings through outsourcing.

This change is not absorbed as quickly. What does this mean to your pension? To your stability, to your home life? What does this mean to your salary, the promotion you were working toward, to your co-workers? On top of all that, your kid is sick at home that day, you have the in-laws coming for the weekend, and your mortgage is up for renewal.

1 Change fatigue also occurs if there is recent history of similar failed implementations in the organisation.

That day you do no work at all. You can't stop talking to your co-workers about what has happened, the rumours on e-mail are spinning out of control, there is talk about a group lawsuit against the company. You tail spin for a good month while you work out all the answers to the questions, and then spend another six months trying to come to grips with what this means to your life. The rest of the year is spent adjusting to your new job, boss, co-workers, commute and, good heavens, you still have not got your head wrapped around hot-desking. You are nowhere near the level of productivity you were at in your previous job, and are spending hours every day surfing the internet looking at other companies and sending out your CV.

In the end, the company did save money with outsourcing, however, with the disruption and anguish the outsourcing caused, sickness and absenteeism went through the roof. This nullified any anticipated overall savings.

Understanding how much one person is able to absorb in a given day is an indicator of people's receptivity or readiness to change. Readiness is an individual trait and can manifest itself in group situations or organisations when it is (1) not stretched or absent and (2) when it is stretched to the limit. When it is not stretched, it can be invisible, other than perhaps you observe the odd bored-looking person wandering aimlessly around the office. When readiness to change is stretched, it is often seen in increased levels of accidents, absenteeism and stress. Conducting a change readiness assessment will provide you with information about how the change is being received by the organisation. (More tools are available to help you later in the book.)

readiness is an individual trait

Questionnaire: do you need a change manager?

If some of your current work feels like it warrants change management activity, and you are concerned by the impact of the change on people, accompanying fear, control, stress, and the existing levels of capacity and resilience, you may need a change manager to step in and drive the change activities.

Picture in your mind a project at your work that is currently underway. Ask yourself the following questions to decide if you need a change manager.

Question	Answer
Do employees have the opportunity to provide input into the planning process?	Yes/No
Does the implementation plan focus on both the technical and human aspects of change?	Yes/No
Can managers clearly and specifically describe how the change improves the organisation?	Yes/No
Do managers share the implementation plan with employees?	Yes/No
Throughout the change, do employees receive status or progress reports?	Yes/No
Do implementation plans include a review of the performance and recognition process, to make sure we reward new behaviours?	Yes/No
Does the implementation plan contain activities that reduce confusion, misunderstandings and conflict?	Yes/No
Does the implementation plan take into account building commitment with stakeholders?	Yes/No
Are all the changes introduced integrated into one overall implementation plan?	Yes/No
Is the plan updated and approved frequently as unexpected events occur?	Yes/No

If you answered no to more than five of the questions, chances are you need a change manager. If you answered no to less than five, your implementation plan may just need some tweaking to include what's missing and critical. The discipline of project managing change is built on solid methodologies and they can be readily incorporated into any existing project plan.

Project management approach to change

MOST TYPES OF PROJECTS covered in Chapter 2 will require change management. Project managers respect the need for a range of specialist disciplines on their project and a change management skill set is quite different from a project management one. However, all change managers must have at least an appreciation of project management and experienced change managers may even be expert project managers in their own right.

This overlap between skills may cause some confusion, but the essential difference between a project manager and a specialist change manager is obvious when you look at their respective priorities with regards to the project.

▌ The priority and purpose of the project manager is to achieve the project objectives assigned by the organisation within specified constraints of time, budget and resources.

▌ The priority and purpose of the change manager is to manage the people-side of business change to achieve the most successful business outcome.

The ironic thing about project managing change is that not all change is deliberate or can be predicted. The key is to plan what can be planned for whilst allowing yourself the capacity and flexibility to react to unplanned change when it emerges.

Overview of project management

Let's start with a definition of project management. Many organisations have their own definitions of what a project is – and you should always check if that is the case – but for the purposes of having a common understanding, we have used the PMI (Project Management Institute, 2000) definition to avoid any misunderstandings regarding terminology. The PMI defines a project as:

> A temporary endeavour undertaken to create a unique product, service or result.

Confusingly, the term 'programme' is sometimes used interchangeably as a synonym for project. Although these terms are related, they do not mean the same thing. A programme is actually a set of related projects, sometimes called a portfolio, and requires different handling and skills in its management. A project manager is focused on making their project succeed; delivering the project is everything. A programme manager has other criteria, such as organisational or political dimensions, to consider, along with the overall portfolio.

a typical project starts with someone having an idea

A typical project starts with someone having an idea. This idea can come from anywhere in an organisation, for example from a leader through formal strategy-setting sessions, from a front-line worker who sees an opportunity for improvement, or from an external body such as the government introducing new policies. These ideas gain acceptance informally through discussion with colleagues and/or through a more formal process involving senior management, management committee or board. A funding model and process must then be agreed before the project can start, staff appointed and work begin. This work has to be planned, managed and problems dealt with, until the project concludes and is wound up.

All projects have at least three phases which represent the time or duration of the project: start-up, run and close-down. Commonly, the middle or 'run' phase is divided up into several chunks, so projects can realistically have four, five or more phases.

Figure 3.1 represents how programmes are made up of groups (a portfolio) of projects and how projects are broken down into component phases or stages that make up the project life cycle. The phases are comprised of project stream plans (such as change management), that need to be in alignment with the phase time-line. This is fairly common terminology and if you are not already familiar with it, you will be soon.

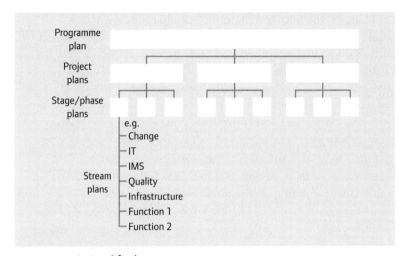

FIGURE 3.1 A simplified programme structure

Formal methods of project management offer a framework to manage this process, providing a series of elements such as templates and procedures to manage the project through its life cycle.

There are lots of different project management methodologies available, each promoted by its owner as having some special advantage or suitability to your project – and each comes with its own unique language. But when you look at the different systems it quickly becomes apparent that they are all variations on the same theme and have a lot in common.

Many systems are proprietary and project management consultants sell them as a package of services that will include training sessions and consultancy alongside documentation that will include templates and guidance notes. PRINCE2 has been adopted as standard by the UK government, and its use is mandatory for most central and local government projects. We are not recommending PRINCE2 as the best, just using it as an example of an established project management system. A definite advantage of PRINCE2 is that it is effectively non-proprietary in that you can buy the system (or a 'light' version) from the Stationery Office without a requirement to buy training or consultancy.

Project management systems with their checklists and templates, processes and procedures can reek of rigidity and bureaucracy. On a smaller project, involving perhaps two or three people, formal project management is less essential. In a small team, communication can be a less-structured agreement on objectives and the scheduling of work can all be done informally, especially if the team members work closely together. The challenge for smaller projects is to make use of project management techniques at an appropriate level. It makes little sense to produce copious documentation for a tiny project; the effort has to be justified by the result. Documentation can be quite useful as an historical record and a way to share information with a wide audience, so you will need to apply your own judgement as to what is appropriate and useful.

Project management methods provide useful tools and techniques that represent accumulated best practice and the same basic principles apply whichever system you use. The different systems have much in common and none of them will manage the project for you. They provide a framework, but the success of a project depends on the skills and intelligence of the people running it.

Change management in projects

Change management helps those leading the project to identify what is likely to change. It identifies potential barriers, risks and issues based on the understanding and learning from previous initiatives, and the concerns held by employees in the organisation today. Rating the findings, based on the likely impact each of these issues may have on the current programme, will prioritise the areas of focus for the change plan to address.

After you decide on implementing a change, immediately jump into the planning process – the better your plan, the better your foundation for a successful change. Every successful change starts with good planning. No matter how hard you work on your change, you can't overcome inadequate or faulty planning: 'They didn't plan to fail, they simply failed to plan.'

But, with the best will in the world, you will not be able to anticipate or plan for all the issues and reactions to the change.

Planned v. unplanned change

Unplanned change results from a change in the business environment (external) or as the result or repercussion of a set of decisions that affect the programme (internal). Unplanned change puts a drain on resources and also a strain on budgets. It not only undermines the change plan, but can also reduce the value of the project to the business as a whole. The work required to address unplanned change is known as 'fire-fighting'. Fire-fighting is often what causes a change programme to spiral out of control. Constant fire-fighting consumes resources, which means that planned work that provides value to the project does not get done.

> give yourself room for manoeuvre

The question isn't about how to avoid the bumps and bruises that come with change (because you can't), but more about how you respond when things don't go as you expected. Thorough project planning and involving the right people in the development of your change plan will reduce the risk of any serious oversight, but give yourself room for manoeuvre (aka contingency) so that you can be flexible enough to deal with potential areas of ambiguity or additional or reprioritised work if they arise.

So if planning is so important, why are so many change managers tempted to skimp on it? Well, there are a number of reasons. Firstly, in today's business culture, the emphasis is on the 'doing'. Secondly, society (and customers) has developed a 'want it now' mentality so it is sometimes hard to resist the sense of urgency this generates. Planning is also not a 'sexy' activity – it takes time and there are no quick wins or immediate returns. So, while life makes short-changing the planning process easy, it also takes away the safety net when you are finally faced with the realities of managing change in a project.

Project management of organisational change is enabled by a robust process, but you must not ignore the most critical enabler of all – the employees.

Figure 3.2 illustrates a typical change project life cycle. The diagonal line represents the progress of the project from inception to completion (100 per cent), at which point, the benefits are delivered. Overlaying this line is a dotted curve known as the employee commitment curve. This curve links a series of 'states' or levels that employees experience in response to, or as a reaction to, the change.

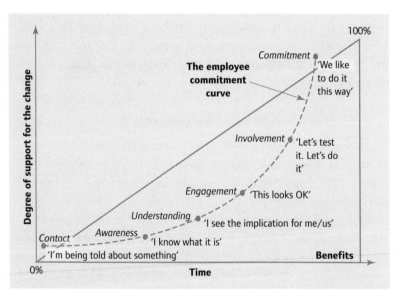

FIGURE 3.2 Supporting employees through change creates commitment and delivers benefits

The following table describes each level in the commitment curve and lists the characteristic questions that employees and stakeholders need to have answered before they can be ready to proceed to the next level of commitment. The employee involvement activities must work on the rational level (by providing information), emotional level (by building trust by being transparent and honest in communications) and on the political level (through sponsorship and role modelling). Perhaps, most importantly, our activities and communications must also ensure that momentum is being actively managed.

Level of commitment	Definition	Characteristic stakeholder questions
Contact	Encounters change; realises change is imminent	▌ What is the project? ▌ How will it affect me? ▌ When will it be introduced?
Awareness	Has high-level knowledge of the context and content of the change	▌ Why do we need the solution? ▌ What do the new services do? ▌ Will it change my job? ▌ Will there be job losses?
Understanding	Accepts the nature and intent of the change	▌ Will I have to learn to use different or new technology? ▌ Will I have to learn new procedures? ▌ How will it simplify my job and increase efficiencies?
Engagement	Works towards change, invests time in change and articulates commitment to goals of change	▌ What are the benefits of the solution, to the organisation and for me? ▌ When will I receive training? ▌ Will my job be easier with the changes? ▌ What support will I receive?
Involvement	Articulates the change as an accepted norm, articulates their personal ownership of the change	▌ When will I start to use the new services? ▌ How will I be continuously supported and how can I support the project? ▌ What are the actual benefits and results achieved?

The line linking these 'states' reflects the task of change management – that of managing the journey employees will go through during the period of change to get to the destination – commitment. Whether the change is perceived as positive or negative, the communication plan will ensure that relevant, accurate and consistent information is provided to the right people in the organisation at the right times.

Global Energy's approach to change

In 2006, as part of a wider business transformation programme, we spoke to a number of Global Energy's stakeholders and found that in previous programmes and initiatives, Global Energy was effective at managing the employee to the 'I know what the change is' point, but then the cycle was broken and employees felt that they had been left in the dark until the project was completed. This perception was reinforced in the results of their 2006 Employee Opinion Survey.

If the change is to be positive, and profitable, should we lead or manage change? And does it make a difference? The answer is 'yes' to both. The need for action must be clear and there must be clarity and a shared understanding of the vision – especially among sponsors and senior management. The change manager must paint the bigger picture and 'join the dots' to put the change or project into the organisational context. Developing and managing delivery of the change plan will define how the project change team will lead and support employees through this period of transition.

Project planning and organisation

The production of a project plan is a key part in the development of any project. Project plans are generally organised in phases with the number of phases dependent on the complexity and scale of the project. The plan sets out the work or 'work packages' to be completed during the project, with their start and finish dates, the resources required and a cash flow profile which will show at what stages of the project money will be spent.

There are many ways to produce this project plan. It could be done with pencil and paper, be a word-processed table or a spreadsheet, or be held in a dedicated application like MS Project or Clarity.

The phases in the project plan are broken down into activities and deliverables, which are allocated to teams (project streams) who define and own the tasks. In reality, what often happens is that each stream will define its own activities, requirements and resource needs and then the project manager or PMO (project management office) will splice them all together with a common time-line. A whole bunch of trade-offs are made as dependencies, priorities and budgets are decided.

> trade-offs are made as dependencies,
> priorities and budgets are decided

Reliance on one piece of work finishing before the next can begin (a dependency), becomes visible as the plan is developed and so a reasonably accurate timescale for the whole project can be set. A project is like a car engine – all the streams, activities and tasks need to be synchronised with each part performing the tasks it has been designated: IT, Business Processes, PMO (planning and reporting), Information Management, Governance and Communications, Finance, HR, etc. Progress can be monitored against and reported on for each stage until the project reaches completion.

In most projects some tasks will be dependent on each other – you can't paint a wall until the bricklayers have finished building it, for example, or you can't run an event until you have found a suitable venue. The project plan should make these dependencies clear – if the wall is not built on time, or if you cannot find a venue for the event, other tasks in the project may be delayed.

Planning brings other more subtle benefits. The planning process can be a very effective tool for communication. Throughout the planning process, from setting objectives to deciding on tasks, you will need to talk to all those people who can bring knowledge to the project or are likely to be involved in its implementation. Objectives and roles must be clear so people will know where the project is going and what they have to do. If it's handled well, the planning process will set up channels of communication and draw participants into involvement in the project.

Change management methodology – the 4Ds

As our understanding and experience evolved, we constructed our own change planning methodology – the 4Ds – from our years of implementing change projects, as internal and external consultants. Our methodology unites the 'people-focused' activities into a single area of responsibility within a project, which can then be broken down into project modules or phases. In this respect, change management can be viewed as a competency in its own right – like management information, process definition and project management.

Myth: *Organisations realise the importance of change management in projects.*

Mythbuster: *In reality, most organisations don't provide their project managers with the support or resources to help them manage change effectively. Often projects are into the 'run' phase before the pain is felt and the omission realised.*

The 4Ds are:

▍ Diagnose – i.e. what is the problem that needs solving?

▍ Design – i.e. what treatments are available and best suited to the problem?

▍ Develop – i.e. what needs to be done to prepare for treatment?

▍ Deliver – i.e. implement the treatment.

The important thing about these phases (and why we've differentiated them with a distinct terminology) is that they are flexible. If the overall project is three-phased, you can combine diagnose and design, for example, into the first or planning phase, or design and develop into the second phase. The main reason for categorising in this way is to give the activities a sense of order and chronology. When you are developing your change plan, don't focus too much on matching project phases to stages but be guided by the activities and the outputs you need to generate, and make a call on what makes the most sense.

Diagnose

This first phase is usually a quick evaluation of performance, either in a specific functional area or wider against benchmarks and best practices. The result is a baseline analysis showing the strengths, weaknesses, improvement potential and key development areas. The diagnose phase concentrates on answering the question 'What are the real or specific problems?' and differentiating between symptoms and root causes. This phase can also be viewed as your organisation's healthcheck.

As you turn organisation detective and look at previous programmes and initiatives, you may find that similar issues and problems keep recurring. Recognising when and where they occur, and correctly identifying issues and problems, will give you a diagnosis, or at least a working hypothesis, on which to build and execute your change plan.

Trying to climb the mountain in one go is a daunting task. Our experiences in issue diagnosis have led us to a way of breaking the mountain into manageable chunks. Each of these chunks represents a different element of change and encourages us to look at the problem from different angles or through different lenses to get a more comprehensive understanding of the whole. These lenses are covered in Chapters 5 to 12.

In our experience, the most common 'people' or change management problems in projects are:

- defining success as 'technology/process is live' instead of 'employees have adopted desired behaviours'
- expected benefits are not delivered or have not been defined
- insufficient change management capability and/or resources in the project team
- stakeholders and employees are not involved or participative in the change process in the early stages (e.g. diagnosis and design)
- an imbalance between the common approach and unique requirements (business area, segment, geography)
- lack of unity or insufficient engagement from leaders
- involvement from HR left too late or HR processes misaligned to change
- an imbalance of change effort between transformation and day-to-day operations
- business processes do not support how the business delivers products and services to customers

▮ employee and manager resistance to change is not openly recognised or addressed.

If you find your project ticks more than three or four of the common problems in this list, try ranking them in terms of importance or impact and tackle the top three or four. Only when you find yourself with spare capacity should you turn your attention to the other, less important issues.

The diagnose phase is dominated by strategic change activities, for example:

▮ development of 'future state' or vision

▮ organisational analyses and assessments

▮ development of a change strategy

▮ stakeholder mapping and communications audit

▮ establishing change governance and a charter.

These are some of the non-change management project activities that will let you know you are in the diagnose phase:

▮ programme business case or feasibility study

▮ programme plan and baseline assessments

▮ programme governance established

▮ PMO and programme standards established

▮ quality, risks and issues processes defined

▮ requirements gathered.

The purpose of the diagnose phase is to confirm or create a shared view about the future: vision, strategic objectives, scope of the project and how much resistance the project is likely to encounter.

Design

This phase is about defining the solution to get the organisation to its future state. There is no magic formula or cookbook that will automatically lead to the best solution, so it is important to generate and explore possible opportunities and options before going into designing the solution. This is usually done through a series of workshops with key stakeholders and subject matter experts (SMEs). The purpose of these workshops is to validate the changes identified by the project's customer needs assessment or requirements gathering process and assess the suitability of different solution options to deliver those requirements and the strategy. Your project may be associated with a change in technology and it is important that you understand what business requirements will be met and what will not be delivered by the new system so that expectations can be managed.

there is no magic formula or cookbook

Workshops are the key milestones/deliverables in this phase and are sometimes called conference room pilots (CRPs) because they have a standard structure and to distinguish them from any other workshop activity. There are gaps of some weeks between CRPs so that the design can be progressed and customisation of the solution to the organisation's specific needs can be carried out.

Conference room pilot (CRP)	Change managers' agenda/checklist
CRP 1	✓ Understand 'as-is' or current state ✓ Identify key issues and barriers ✓ Review and validate requirements ✓ Validate future process maps ✓ Build mutual trust and dialogue ✓ Review available options
CRP 2	✓ Comparison and assessment of shortlisted option(s) ✓ Demonstrations or scenarios by internal and external providers ✓ Gap analysis and risk assessment of option(s) ✓ Selection of preferred solution ✓ Identification of high-level benefits
CRP 3	✓ 'Model office' demonstrations re: 'look and feel' of the solution ✓ Scenarios (pr ocesses) are run through the solution ✓ Test connections and hand-offs with suppliers and customers ✓ Requirements checked and signed off re: the solution ✓ Identify implications for process measurement, skills and competencies, technology, capabilities, organisation structure/design, behaviours and culture

Also in this phase is a change readiness assessment which will help you to identify what stakeholder management will be required, and development of the benefits element of the business case including quantifiable improvement opportunities.

The design phase is dominated by strategic and tactical change activities, for example:

▌ development of a high-level business case

▌ definition of change milestones and deliverables

▌ change leader development

▌ communications strategy

▌ definition of organisation design principles and macro design

▌ definition of values and behaviours

▌ resilience, capacity and training needs assessments.

These are some of the non-change management project activities that will let you know you are in the design phase:

▌ achievement of phase 1 exit (programme control/gate 1) and phase 2 entry criteria

▌ sponsor engagement and management

▌ solution definition and standards

▌ product/vendor/partner selection.

The purpose of the design phase is to identify as many improvement opportunities as possible – focusing on one business process at a time and the identification of a preferred solution or future state model.

Develop

Selection of the preferred future state model is followed by detailed design activities including end-to-end process delivery and measurement, skills and competencies, organisation structure, culture and behaviour change. This third phase is about defining and developing the detail of the solution to address the people, process and technology needs of the future organisation. Each activity or 'work package' is broken down into individual tasks so that the effort, timescale and resources can be allocated. This is how you produce your detailed change plan.

The develop phase is when the detailed change plan is produced, following final scope and cost–benefit decision making. It is also when the implementation and transition plans are put together, supported by a communications plan, and when change networks and stakeholders are mobilised and toolkits developed and deployed to ensure the organisation is ready to take on the change.

The develop phase is dominated by tactical change activities, for example:

- development of change plan
- building the change network
- stakeholder management
- roadmap development (communications and culture)
- micro (operational) organisation design
- review of HR policies and processes
- development of training courses and materials.

These are some of the non-change management project activities that will let you know you are in the develop phase:

- achievement of phase 2 exit (programme control/gate 2) and phase 3 entry criteria
- scope management and project change control
- solution testing
- solution acceptance
- post-delivery support requirements.

The end of this phase is marked by a significant milestone – testing. In IT terms this can be testing of the system functionality (unit testing), how the system performs (end-to-end process testing) and system response times (load testing). The final activity is testing by the actual employees who will be using the system (user acceptance testing). In business change terms, testing usually takes the form of simulations or a pilot of the new ways of working.

Deliver

The fourth phase focuses on how and when you deliver the solution into the organisation. The emphasis here is on the deployment of tools and interventions and capability development. Benefits realisation is also a feature of this phase, as are change sustainability planning and transition activities.

This phase sees the acceptance of the implementation and transition plans which define the way in which the solution will 'go-live', including logistics, cut-over arrangements (such as interim metrics, parallel processing etc.) and the identification of quick wins to build momentum and receptivity to change.

> this phase sees acceptance of implementation and transition plans

The main concern for the change stream in the deliver phase is to enable and support behavioural change. As well as leaders and champions demonstrating or role modelling the new ways of working, there are four other levers you can employ:

1. operational support
2. motivators
3. systemic compliance
4. process reinforcement.

These levers are covered more fully in Chapter 16.

The deliver phase is dominated by operational change activities, for example:

- communications roll-out
- training programme delivery
- feedback loops
- transition planning and execution
- alignment of HR policies and procedures with new ways of working
- coaching and support.

These are some of the non-change management project activities that will let you know you are in the deliver phase:

■ metrics collection and programme accounting

■ sponsor sign-off

■ programme review/lessons learned

■ project staff appraisals.

At the end of this phase, the changes become reality, the solution is rolled out, training is given, the planned benefits start to be realised and behaviours change. The 4Ds will take you to a certain point, for example midnight on the day before people will start doing things the new way. Figure 3.3 shows how the 4Ds or phases align to set the organisation up for sustainable change.

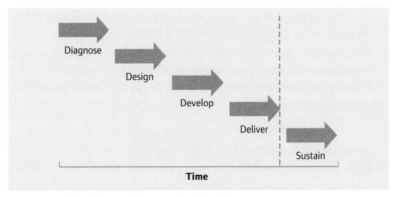

FIGURE 3.3 The 4Ds enable sustainable change

As soon as the change becomes operational in this way, your focus will need to shift from getting people to try the new way to answering the question 'How do I make this change stick and become the way we do things around here?' Sustaining change requires a different focus and different activities to implementation and these are covered in Chapter 16.

Benefits of integrating project management and change

Project managed change increases the likelihood that a project will be completed successfully and that anticipated benefits will be delivered.

CASE STUDY

Benefits of project managed change

I was leading a project to implement an Oracle system in a large manufacturing organisation. The workforce was extremely diverse, from PhD scientists, to highly trained engineers and manual workers. The workforce was extremely safety and security conscious and displayed a high degree of cynicism towards large systems implementations and particularly towards the benefits of the 'soft' elements of change.

We tailored our change and stakeholder plans to focus on the effects and benefits (outcomes) of the work we would do. We made direct links between changes in stakeholder perceptions and the realisation of tangible and intangible benefits, and for each project stage we tracked the attitudes of stakeholders against the commitment curve. We described their positions in positive and negative indicators (i.e. competency definition style) and rescheduled the change impact assessments (five during life of the project), to target and track progress on these indicators.

The attention to detail in the planning of our approach paid off in spades. We were able to plan change interventions and communications with a much higher degree of acuity – specifically the WIIFM (What's in it for me?) message was much easier to define earlier for each stakeholder group. Credibility with senior client and project staff was much improved as the link between change management activity and the success of the project was established early.

Other learnings from this situation were: (1) establish a strong link between benefit realisation and change management activity very early in the project life cycle; (2) demonstrate your value by developing indicators (positive and megative) to determine that your activities are having the desired effect; (3) don't allow change impact assessments to be a lag measure; and (4) be prepared to put your money where your mouth is!

Dr Howard McMinn – Vice-president, Deloitte Consulting

Change management has a contribution to make to any business transformation programme and can complement or be integrated with business performance improvement techniques such as Lean, Six Sigma, Business Process Re-engineering or Total Quality Management. When change management milestones are integrated into the overall plan and aligned with other projects within the organisation, this sets expectations around likely people issues and allows project and line management to anticipate, and prepare for, employee reactions to those issues.

Assessment and analysis of change

OUR CHANGE MANAGEMENT APPROACH, the 4Ds, is built on project management principles so that it can be integrated with existing projects and programmes which use methodologies such as PRINCE2 or PMI. We have developed our learning into a proven, structured approach that consolidates lessons from our previous successes and also from our failures (and if you haven't failed, then you've never really tried!).

The change prism (eight lens framework)

Practical experience of applying this approach on major transformation programmes, our research and that by the major management consultancies has shown us that there are eight key factors that affect the success of change implementations. The change prism is a model we have developed which acts as (1) a checklist for what is likely to change and what the level and type of impact the change is likely to have and (2) a framework for planning.

A checklist for change

The change prism acts like an optical prism: white (or complex) light entering the prism is a mixture of different frequencies, each with their own properties or characteristics. Where an optical prism breaks up white light into its constituent spectral colours, the change prism provides a categorisation structure for your analysis during the diagnose phase, helping you break down sometimes complex issues and problems into manageable pieces.

Working through all the constituent elements or lenses of the change prism during the design phase will identify a range or spectrum of people-related issues and activities that will need to be planned into the project for you to manage.

The eight lenses to consider when project managing change are shown in Figure 4.1.

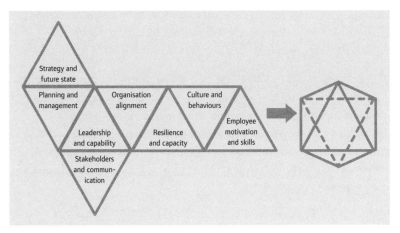

FIGURE 4.1 The change prism

If light inside an optical prism hits one of the surfaces at a sufficiently steep angle, *total internal reflection* occurs. Each lens within the change prism focuses on a particular emphasis or angle, focusing your analysis and assessment of the change to identify specific issues and actions that can be taken to address them. When you combine all the viewpoints through your own process of *internal reflection*, you will get a truly holistic understanding and insight of what needs to be done and the issues that the organisation or project needs to address.

> each lens within the change prism focuses on a particular emphasis

A framework for planning

The application of a project management methodology will help you to prioritise change management activities and resources throughout the life cycle of your project. Applied to your own analysis, the lenses can help you to decide which changes are most important. Remember, you should focus on the changes with the biggest potential benefits, not the most obvious changes or the easiest ones to implement.

The changes you have identified will break down into a sequential set of activities. These activities are the building blocks, but they must be organised into a timeframe within specific project phases. If you follow the framework and project-based approach we recommend, your change plan will reflect the order and dependency of tasks and activities represented by each of the lenses and identify the deliverables and milestones in alignment with the overall project plan.

Usually only large-scale transformations or 'deep' change will require all eight lenses to be incorporated into a change plan. An example of a high-level transformation plan is shown in Figure 4.12 later.

A structured approach to change

In business terms, a process is the structure by which the organisation physically does what is necessary to produce value for its employees and shareholders. A process is a specific ordering of work activities across time and place, with a beginning, an end, and clearly defined inputs and outputs. The eight lenses within the change prism can be interpreted as processes because the ultimate objective of any business process is to deliver products or services to either internal or external customers. A simple process is shown in Figure 4.2.

Inputs → Activities → Outputs

FIGURE 4.2 A simple process

Inputs These are the materials, capital, resources and information that a process receives and acts upon in order to generate output. In manufacturing these are the 'raw materials', in cookery, the ingredients, that are combined and subjected to heat, cold or mechanical treatment to create an end product, or dish. Some inputs will exist already in the organisation but others will need to be created or adapted. This can be done before the 'activity' part but in most cases timeframes are pretty tight and new inputs have to be developed in parallel with the activities.

Activities These transform the inputs through a series of tasks, actions, analysis or synthesis into a refined product or output. This can be done by applying tools, techniques and learning from past experiences (e.g. best practice benchmarking).

Outputs These are documents, information, plans or decisions produced by the application of activities on inputs that deliver value to the organisation. An output must either be internal (such as an input into another process or activity), or external and so be the end point of the process (completed or resolved). An output should always be subjected to the 'so what?' test. If the output is a piece of knowledge or information, for example, it needs to be 'actionable'. Knowing something that can't be used as the basis for improvement or for the creation of value, has little or no worth.

Outputs can differ from deliverables, in that deliverables are tangible or intangible products (documents, services, decisions) that are identified and agreed on in advance with the sponsor and project manager. You may have many more outputs than deliverables, in fact a series of outputs may yield a deliverable, and not all outputs will be converted to deliverables. All outputs still need to have value and contribute to the overall change progress.

The next section of this chapter will give you an overview of each of the eight lenses – their purpose, timing, key activities, inputs and outputs. This will form the basis of your high-level change plan. In Chapters 5 to 12 we will focus on the activities themselves using step-by-step guides and worked examples to take you through each process. This will enable you to develop your detailed change plan, revealing how the inputs and outputs link together between activities and across lenses.

The eight factors affecting change

As we have shown, the eight lenses of the change prism are the basis of a useful diagnostic – helping you define the scale of the people change and its impact. This framework, when used as a planning aid, provides a 'scope check' so that the change activity required is not underestimated regarding the people-related issues and impact on employees. It also ensures that all the success factors are being proactively managed and greatly reduces the risk of project failure.

This section introduces each of the eight lenses and gives you an overview of what their area of focus is, when in a project effort will be required and some of the issues, tools and activities that characterise each one.

1 Strategy and future state

Question: What do we want to achieve and what will it look like when we get there?

When we do it: Diagnose and design phases.

Why we do it: A change management strategy must be compelling and consistent with future context and direction. It should be outcome and process-oriented, actionable and focus attention on decisions that need to be made about what is in and out of scope. Creating a change direction or strategy for the future of the business co-ordinates collective effort and provides guidance to employees throughout the organisation so that they can make informed decisions and plan more effectively. It is critical to capture this early because it provides a reference point or base throughout the change. It is inevitable that you will feel lost at some stage, wondering what you are doing and why. This will remind you.

CRM in Pharmco, Europe

Customer relationship management (CRM) was the biggest programme in the recent history of the European operations of this mid-sized pharmaceutical company. The Programme Manager had been pushing the sponsor and European Lead Team to define the core vision, but although everyone understood the business reasons for moving from a product-focused organisation to a customer-focused organisation, they seemed unable to put this into a compelling statement. The leadership team seemed to be struggling with a raft of independent projects that was either not being managed as or had not been cascaded as a cohesive programme. Numerous and sometimes conflicting priorities meant that the loudest voices were heard rather than the most deserving and projects requiring attention were often overlooked. Ultimately this led to 'fire-fighting' behaviours and crisis management becoming the norm.

The lack of a communicable vision was impacting the CRM project: communications seemed too generic (i.e. based on non-pharma industries' experiences such as banking, retail, airlines etc.); stakeholders were not engaged; and employees felt distanced from the project and unable to share what was happening with customers. A facilitated session run by the change manager was a turning point, focusing leadership attention on the negative consequences of their behaviour. The solution was framed as a potential 'umbrella' statement applicable to a number of projects, effectively linking them together in a makeshift programme portfolio. Recognising the value of such an approach, the leadership was happy to collaborate, producing a vision – 'Pharmco Knows Me' – and a mission statement. This was the necessary call to action employees had been waiting for.

What are the inputs?	What are the outputs?
SWOT (strengths, weaknesses, opportunities and threats) analysis	Change management strategy
	Guiding principles for change
Strategic business goals	Scope and scale of change
Definition of end state/vision	Programme sponsorship map

Project funding model

High-level business case

Identification and appointment
of change manager

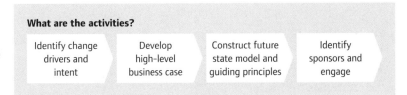

What are the activities?

Identify change drivers and intent → Develop high-level business case → Construct future state model and guiding principles → Identify sponsors and engage

FIGURE 4.3 Strategy and future state lens

Description: At the beginning of projects, we sometimes only have limited information about why we are undertaking the change. We need to determine what the changes will be in terms of what is likely to change and what the level and type of impact the change is likely to have on the business. Defining this will determine which processes and how many people will be affected, the new corporate and process objectives (guiding principles) and the alignment of the project strategy with the organisation/business strategy. A change management strategy needs to be emotionally appealing so that employees can associate with what is to be achieved and be energised by it.

> a change management strategy needs to be
> emotionally appealing

The change management strategy should be a succinct document containing the following information/elements:

- summary situational analysis
- review of implementation history
- organisation/business model and drivers
- identification of programme/project executive sponsor
- programme vision and objectives
- guiding principles

▌critical success factors

▌change management focus and the role of the change manager

▌change roadmap

▌assumptions.

It can be extremely challenging to capture, create and organise all of this into a meaningful and accessible format. Individual research, interviews, workshops and brainstorming sessions may be key activities in this phase.

2 Planning and management

Question: What needs to be done and what benefits do we want or expect?

When we do it: Diagnose and design phases.

Why we do it: Change planning provides a rigour for the identification of activities and a framework to prioritise and schedule them. This is particularly valuable in reducing duplication and confusion if responsibilities for different activities are split between project streams or individual roles. Planning activities in this structured (and phased) way allows you to align your change plan to the project plan and overall reporting requirements. If these plans and reports don't exist then, at the very least, you have an organised approach to manage the change that can be shared and discussed with others.

What are the inputs?	What are the outputs?
Change management strategy	Change management plan
Programme high-level plan	Governance structure
Scope and scale of change	Change management charter
Programme sponsorship map	Change management dashboard
Assumptions	

What are the activities?

Develop governance and project charter	Determine milestones, deliverables and products	Construct change plans and reporting	Conduct risk management

FIGURE 4.4 Planning and management lens

Description: The change management plan gives details of the activities, deliverables and timeframes to deliver the change management strategy. The plan must be developed based on the needs of the project (either global or regional) and must also incorporate local business needs and priorities at the business unit level. Ideally, the change management plan should be developed in parallel with the overall project plan. In reality, what often happens is that the change management plan is created some time after the project plan. This can be a constraint, but in a more positive light it can also be a helpful framework for you to hang your own activities and deliverables upon. Don't worry if that is your situation, do what you can within the limitations and negotiate the rest with your project manager. If you can justify your requirements or need to do something, it will be in their interest to listen – and compromise if necessary.

In the same way as a project plan, the change plan should contain the following information in addition to the change management section:

▌ high-level activities

▌ milestones

▌ dependencies

▌ start and end dates for activities

▌ schedule (order and timing)

▌ resources

▌ delivery accountability

▌ risk assessment.

This approach and discipline in defining the above will ensure the change plan and project plan are in alignment. Progress should be reviewed as part of the overall project planning and tracking process (usually owned by the PMO). Regular or even standardised progress and risk/issues reporting is a necessary discipline for change managers, just as it is for the other project streams.

Planning for complexity

It is not uncommon to have several projects within an overall programme at different stages of maturity or phases running at the same time because different business units are 'going live' at different times. This was certainly the case at a City and County Council regarding their CRM (Oracle) programme. If the overall programme plan is structured to deliver 'waves' of implementation (i.e. a series of distinct implementations interspersed by weeks or months) the change plan must be constructed to deliver the same schedule. This 'wave' approach is commonly adopted in IT systems implementations to either reduce the risk of people accepting new technologies or to synchronise with existing system releases or upgrades.

3 Leadership and capability

Question: Who will we need to make the change happen and what will be required of them?

When we do it: All phases.

Why we do it: Effective leadership is the ability to influence a group of people to achieve extraordinary results. Change leadership is a set of leadership activities and characteristics which enable a programme specifically to meet its change management objectives.

Identifying key roles and individuals to act as leaders and agents of change improves a project's chances of success by building a groundswell or 'bottom-up' support for the change, both in the project and in the business. Our experience has shown that even if the idea started in the middle of the organisation, acceptance and drive for the change must start at the top to get the groundswell going. Managers and employees look to the executives to demonstrate commitment to the change or project and without a visible change in individuals' behaviour or style, employees will question how serious the change really is or whether it is just the latest fad.

What are the inputs?

Change sponsor selection

Mobilisation events

Terms of reference

Change leader profile

What are the outputs?

Change team roles and responsibilities

Change agent profile

Programme team development plan

Change network development plan

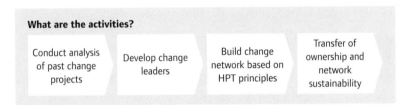

What are the activities?

Conduct analysis of past change projects

Develop change leaders

Build change network based on HPT principles

Transfer of ownership and network sustainability

FIGURE 4.5 Leadership and capability lens

Description: Many organisations find the skills and competencies required of leaders are different during major change than those they rely on in a 'business as usual' state. It is likely that the leadership team will undergo a degree of conflict that affects the organisation whilst being required to support the implementation of change in their areas.

Business leaders should be involved in vision and strategy development and be clear about their roles and responsibilities in the change. They also need to be encouraged and supported to demonstrate their commitment through actions and behaviours. This is not limited to board members, or even to senior executives, but also to their direct reports and even middle management.

A CIPD survey, *Reorganising for Success* (2004) found that 60 per cent of change programmes were associated with substantial changes in leadership styles and only 7 per cent of change programmes were associated with little or no change in leadership style.

In times of significant change, leaders need support to take personal accountability for achieving successful change outcomes and benefits. The change team must focus on developing leadership for change *through* people – building capability (like a change network) and alignment for the future. Change leadership depends on assessment to understand individual and team performance against current and future demands, and employs coaching and other support mechanisms to accelerate behaviour change. It is focused on building commitment, cooperation and capability within the leadership team, project team and the extended change network.

Project leaders often need development to accelerate through the stages in team development from forming to performing. A high-performing project team delivers results beyond what can be expected of a group of individuals, but time must be invested in developing the team, working with them to build their change capability across the four key quadrants of: competencies, relationships, discipline and ownership.[1]

4 Stakeholders and communication

Question: Who needs to be involved or kept informed and how will we communicate with them?

When we do it: Design, develop and deliver phases.

Why we do it: A critical element of any change project is the effective management of project stakeholders to ensure they are fully on-board and actively participating in the change. The stakeholder management process achieves this by delivering the right message, to the right people, at the right time, using the most appropriate communication method. Stakeholder management increases effectiveness, clarifies expectations and reduces

---

1 Taken from the high-performing team methodology, covered in Chapter 14.

resistance against changes. Project progress is swifter when stakeholders are engaged early in the change, often resulting in reduced project costs. Time invested with stakeholders at the start of the project brings huge gains in the quality of dialogue, feedback, sustainability and ownership of change.

Effective communications are critical if programme objectives are to be realised. The *Reorganising for Success* survey by the CIPD (2004) indicated that change programmes involving greater emphasis on communication with stakeholders external to the project/programme lead to better financial performance, and increased communication with financial stakeholders is associated with improved share price performance post-change.

What are the inputs?

Stakeholder analysis and map

Scope and scale of change

Change management charter

Communications audit

Change impact assessment

What are the outputs?

Stakeholder management plan

Stakeholder review process

Communications strategy

Communications plan and roadmap

What are the activities?

Conduct stakeholder analysis and mapping	Develop stakeholder action plans with owners	Actively manage stakeholder groups	Establish management process and governance
Conduct communication audit	Develop communication strategy (tools, message and channel)	Construct communication roadmap	Roll out communications

FIGURE 4.6 Stakeholders and communication lens

Description: Stakeholders are individuals or groups that have an interest or 'stake' in the outcome of the project. They are the ones who must actually change or be aware of the change in skill set, procedure, attitude or behaviour. There are different types of stakeholders and they are defined or categorised by their roles, networks or seniority in the organisation. Stakeholders are also evaluated by their level of commitment to the project or programme. The purpose of stakeholder management is to assess the attitudes of stakeholder groups and individuals at all levels within the organisation, and identify opportunities and activities to effect a positive change, resulting in movement up the commitment curve. The most important lever in achieving engagement and adding value to the project is a structured communications roadmap and plan.

the project needs to answer the 'What's in it for me?' question

The project needs to answer the 'What's in it for me?' (WIIFM) question and be clear how the organisation will benefit. Communication is critical to prepare stakeholders – to inform, educate, motivate and call them to action. The communications developed must be meaningful, relevant, targeted and use appropriate language and media.

The statistics below are often quoted in support of this:

- 100 per cent of organisations rate good communications as a key success factor in implementing change
- 70 per cent of projects fail because there is ineffective communication
- 34 per cent of organisations rate poor communication as the key barrier to implementing change successfully.

However, we recommend that you take these findings with a degree of caution. We have found that communication can be the 'whipping boy' for project failure. That is to say, people often blame communications to cover up other problems or because they fail to recognise what the real problems are.

There is an old expression, 'you can take a horse to water, but you can't make it drink'. Applied in this instance, you can have the best communications in the world, but without the necessary levels of readiness, willingness and ability in the organisation to achieve the change, your communications will not have the desired effect.

5 Resilience and capacity

Question: How ready, willing and able are we to absorb the changes?

When we do it: Develop and deliver phases.

Why we do it: Resilience is the ability to recover quickly from setbacks and adversity. Resilient people stay committed and increase their efforts when the going gets tough. Resilience is a major driver of productivity and, as such, a key factor affecting the capacity of an organisation for change. A lack of capacity leads to stress, and people lose the ability to be resilient and bounce back quickly. At the organisational level, capacity issues can lead to employee-specific problems such as reduced productivity, stress-related health issues, high turnover and absenteeism, and an inability to adapt to and execute change – all of which will reduce the likelihood that benefits will be realised.

What are the inputs?

Change impact assessment

Organisational capacity review

Resilience assessment

What are the outputs?

Capacity and resilience mitigation plan

What are the activities?

| Assess impact and capacity for change | Conduct resilience assessment | Identify barriers and opportunities | Develop capacity mitigation and resilience plan |

FIGURE 4.7 Resilience and capacity lens

Description: Resilience is the ability not only to survive life's challenges, but also to learn from them and find a way to move beyond them. Resilient people are energetic, curious, seek to learn and explore, work together, take risks and want to solve problems. Resilient people are able to realise the new reality more quickly and come through change and reach new levels of productivity faster. Assessment of the indicators of resilience provides an insight in determining how people will respond to change. Developing these skills can help individuals and organisations deal more effectively with the stress associated with change.

Assessing the organisation's capacity for change will tell you if there is too much else going on and indicate that your change may fail – you have to find space for it. Putting the proposed change into context, reflecting on previous change initiatives and how successful or unsuccessful change has been before, will help you to position the project and increase employees' receptivity to the change.

6 Organisation alignment

Question: How will we need to be organised to make the changes work?

When we do it: Design, develop and deliver phases.

Why we do it: Organisation alignment encompasses all the building blocks of a business – how organisations arrange their formal and informal structures, internal processes and systems, relationships, people capabilities and knowledge. Organisation alignment is an essential part of any transformation project and can originate from a range of strategic drivers including mergers and acquisitions (M&A) or implementation of a new business operating model, cost reduction programmes, technology implementations, outsourcing or shared services.

Every change effort has some implication for the organisation architecture, people and processes, from a simple redefinition of department roles and responsibilities through to a global restructure following a merger.

What are the inputs?

Change impact assessment

Future organisation look and feel

Guiding principles for change design

Future process maps

What are the outputs?

Organisation design principles

Strategic (macro) organisation design

Operational (detailed) organisation

Role profiles

Transition plan

What are the activities?

| Review future process maps | Identify design principles | Develop macro design | Define roles and organisation | Transition planning |

FIGURE 4.8 Organisation alignment lens

Description: Organisations have both a physical structure in terms of roles and hierarchies and an infrastructure that includes all the mechanisms and pathways that products and information flow through. In almost every type of change, elements of the organisational architecture must be adapted or transformed for the organisation to achieve and sustain the strategy and vision.

For employees, organisation alignment raises the most concerns regarding the change. Typical questions such as, 'Who will I sit with?' 'Who will I report to?' 'Where will I be working?' are probably the most important considerations for employees after 'Will I still have a job?'

> organisation alignment raises the most concerns regarding the change

Organisation alignment is the process of designing and developing the structure, processes, systems, governance and people that the organisation requires to deliver its strategy. It must consider the harmonisation of six key elements – structure, process, people, governance, systems and culture – that make up the organisation architecture.

Figure 4.9 shows a representation of the elements of organisation architecture and their mutual relationships.

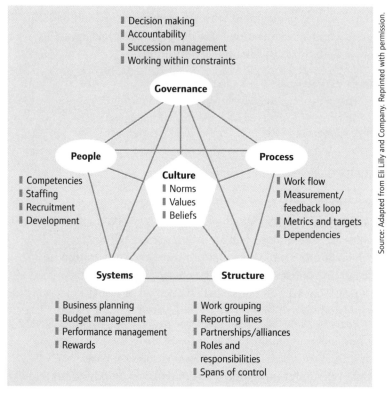

Source: Adapted from Eli Lilly and Company. Reprinted with permission.

FIGURE 4.9 Organisational architecture model

The organisational architecture model is familiar and well-used by us, but there are very similar models such as the CIPD's 7Cs model and the McKinsey 7S model (see Appendix 3) that are better known. If you have used either of them before, and they work for you, they can easily be substituted for the organisational architecture model.

Organisation alignment (OA) is one of the most complex and challenging of the eight lenses and working in this space may require specialist HR and organisation design skills. Whether or not you choose to employ specialists, organisation alignment work should not be undertaken in isolation (based on a desire to design a new structure, for example) but needs to be set within a broader context of change management. It is not possible to realise the full potential of a new or different way of working if the business processes are not integrated with the systems or aligned with the structure of the organisation, or if the proposed changes are in conflict with the culture of the organisation.

Culture can make or break change. Aligning the architecture with the culture is acheived by manipulating the other levers in the OA model. Because culture is an outcome and cannot be directly manipulated, and because of its complexity, culture is dealt with in a separate lens.

7 Culture and behaviours

Question: What values and attitudes do we want employees to embody and what behaviours will we need them to adopt?

When we do it: Develop and deliver phases.

Why we do it: At its simplest level, culture is commonly defined as 'the way we do things around here'. Project and change managers need to appreciate culture as an expression of the values of the organisation. According to Edgar Schein (1992): 'Organisational culture is the key to organisational excellence.' Understanding how culture influences business performance and how changes to culture impact individuals (as well as the organisation) is essential so the change manager can target specific aspects and identify which interventions to use.

Culture is made up of many different elements: some are reflected in the way an organisation is run and others are the assumptions and beliefs that drive behaviour within the organisation. Culture can stall or swallow an initiative with which it conflicts or is not aligned, so efforts must be made to (1) either revise the change to fit the culture or (2) alter the culture to better accommodate the change. We call the latter 'making room in the culture' for the change.

What are the inputs?

Culture assessment

Culture audit

What are the outputs?

Future organisation look and feel

Culture action plan

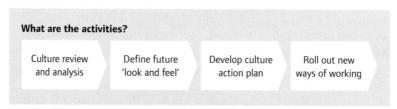

FIGURE 4.10 Culture and behaviours lens

Description: The values, beliefs, assumptions and style of individuals and groups within an organisation form the overall culture. Every organisation has its own unique culture, built up throughout its existence which is underpinned by these collective values, beliefs and assumptions. Trompenaars and Hampden-Turner (1997) define culture as, 'the way in which a group of people solve problems and reconcile dilemmas' and 'the collective programming of the mind, which distinguishes one group from the other.'

> every organisation has its own unique culture

However, this is really only scratching the surface. Culture is remarkably complex, not least because so many of the drivers and factors influencing culture are often hidden or intangible. Every individual brings their own unique 'view of the world' into an organisation and how they think, feel and act is a result of a lifetime of experience and learning. Much of what people believe and value is acquired in early childhood from the social environment in which they grow up.

According to Sholtz (1987):

> Corporate culture is capable of being consciously created and managed by leaders to make it achieve corporate objectives.

However, another school of thought, championed by John Kotter in *Leading Change* (1996) says that:

> Culture changes only after you have successfully altered people's actions, after the new behaviour produces some group benefit for a period of time, and after people see the connection between the new actions and the performance improvement.

It is this latter view that we subscribe to, that culture is an outcome – that it cannot be directly intervened with or be the target of direct actions.

By changing the factors that feed into the culture, we can influence it, but not necessarily control or predict what the actual change to the culture will be.

The CIPD survey, *Reorganising For Success* (2004) found that 96 per cent of change programmes were associated with either substantial or some changes in organisational culture. Only 4 per cent of change programmes were associated with little or no change in culture.

If we cannot directly change the culture, it is critical that we actively plan and manage our interventions from a cultural perspective. Interventions must be identified and delivered with the primary purpose of bringing about culture change, and co-ordinated with other project activities that may have a cultural impact.

Culture change assessments and action plans tend to focus on a number of key levers (usually between four and six) which are essentially:

- behaviours – includes visible behaviours; potential motivation; treatment of employees; peer relationships; attitudes to roles and the organisation
- symbols – includes items representing belonging or purpose, principles, status and position
- reward and measurement – includes benefits, performance, awards, recognition, progression

▌ business and management systems – includes processes, reporting, hierarchies and reporting lines.

Culture manifests itself in different ways: modes of dress, attitudes to work and colleagues, style of office and layout, buildings, employee types and style of working. Culture is inextricably linked to employee motivation and skills, which is covered in the next section.

8 Employee motivation and skills

Question: What motivators, processes and skills need to be in place to enable employees to do their jobs effectively and achieve the future state?

When we do it: Develop and deliver phases.

Why we do it: Leaders and change managers must engage the workforce to build commitment. Getting and keeping employees motivated can help to boost productivity, company loyalty and levels of engagement during periods of change. While the overall organisation's culture and quality of management are key drivers of motivation, focusing on all aspects of HR and people management can deliver benefits in terms of cost savings and performance, for example improvements in your recruitment and retention.

The CIPD survey, *Reorganising for Success* (2004) found that when employees were involved in the change process there was a 12 per cent improvement in the relationships between management and staff and a 16 per cent improvement in the retention of essential staff.

People are not only motivated by personal gain, they can be motivated by feeling part of the organisation and contributing to its goals. To gain loyalty and commitment you need to do more than just pay well, you need to consider people's social and psychological needs. In a business environment, this can motivate employees to improve the volume and quality of their output.

There is now substantial evidence (Tamkin, 2005) that investing in people is one way in which organisations can make positive gains in productivity and other business outcomes. One of the most obvious forms of investment is in the skill levels of the workforce. Investment in skills development can have greater impact than investment in IT, machinery, or research and development.

What are the inputs?

Change readiness assessment

Resistance assessment and approach

Role profiles

What are the outputs?

Training strategy and plan

Training course design

Measuring training effectiveness

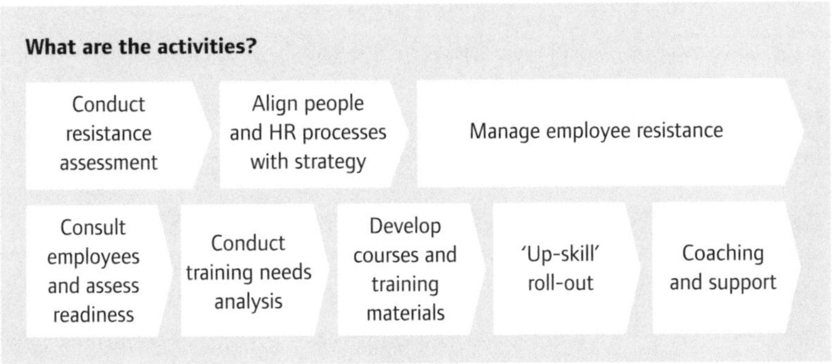

What are the activities?

Conduct resistance assessment

Align people and HR processes with strategy

Manage employee resistance

Consult employees and assess readiness

Conduct training needs analysis

Develop courses and training materials

'Up-skill' roll-out

Coaching and support

FIGURE 4.11 Employee motivation and skills lens

Description: An individual's appetite and potential to be motivated changes from situation to situation and project to project. People are motivated towards something they can relate to and something they can believe in. Conducting an employee survey can be helpful in establishing whether the people in your organisation are motivated and so performing to best effect. In addition to the actual findings of the survey, the process of involving and consulting with employees can be hugely beneficial and motivational in its own right.

consulting with employees can be hugely beneficial

The most fundamental aspect of motivation is the alignment of employees' aims, purpose and values between peers, teams and the organisation. The better the alignment and personal association with organisational aims, the better the platform for motivation.

Get the alignment and values right, and motivational methods, such as those listed below, work better:

▌ communicate a vision of what the business stands for and where you want it to be

▌ communicate values and priorities across the organisation

▌ ensure the work is challenging, with a variety of tasks

▌ establish a friendly, collaborative work environment

▌ consider more flexible working practices

▌ delegate tasks and allow others to take responsibility.

Motivational methods of any sort will not work if people and organisational values are not aligned.

We also need to ensure people have the necessary skills and behaviours to perform in their roles and so generate the benefits expected from the project. The approach to skills development and learning needs to be based on the business reasons for change. The best results are achieved through a learning and development approach that is iterative, participative and builds both understanding and skills.

A properly skilled and trained workforce will have implications for many HR processes, including hiring, development, reward and recognition, industrial relations, and performance management and appraisal. These processes will directly affect the way people work and how they feel about their jobs.

A lack of motivation and/or skills can lead to greater employee resistance to change, to the project or to the programme. Resistance can either be to the actual change or its impact, for example to a specific change in technology, to the introduction of a particular reward system, or to the process of change. The latter concerns the way a change is introduced rather than the change itself, and could be because of poor communication or because the change is imposed. It is important to diagnose the cause and type of employee resistance so that effort can be focused to try and reduce or remove the issue.

Making change operational

At this point you should have a good understanding of the underlying principles that drive the development of a change plan and be aware of all the factors that will provide you with a range of options from which to create your own high-level plan. A generic plan is shown in Figure 4.12 overleaf, with each of the eight lenses mapped to the 4Ds.

In Chapters 5 to 12, we will be unpacking the inputs and outputs of each of the lenses – giving you step-by-step guides to the detailed tasks that you will need to manage and deliver. Every guide follows the same structure and many include worked examples and useful templates that you can use to build your own detailed change plan.

Remember the key to success is in your ability to choose and prioritise those lenses or groups of activities that will address your specific programme issues. Don't try to do everything – do what will work for you and your specific situation.

Blank copies of the templates and document examples are available for you to download and use in your own projects and organisations (see www.pearson-books.com/managingchange).

	Diagnose	Design	Develop	Deliver
Change strategy and future state	Identify change drivers and intent	Develop high-level business case; Construct future state model and guiding principles	Identify sponsors and engage	
Change planning and management	Develop governance and project charter	Determine milestones, deliverables and products; Construct change plans and reporting	Conduct risk management	
Change leadership and capability	Conduct analysis of past change projects	Develop change leaders	Build change network based on HPT principles	Transfer of ownership and network sustainability
Stakeholders and communication	Conduct communication audit	Conduct stakeholder analysis and mapping; Develop communication (tools, message and channel) strategy; Construct communication roadmap	Develop stakeholder action plans with owners; Actively manage stakeholder groups; Roll out communications	Establish management process and governance
Change resilience and capacity	Assess impact and capacity for change	Conduct resilience assessment	Identify barriers and opportunities; Develop capacity mitigation and resilience plan	
Organisation alignment	Review future process maps; Identify design principles	Develop macro design	Define roles and organisation	Transition planning
Culture and behaviours change	Culture review and analysis	Define future 'look and feel'	Develop culture action plan	Roll out new ways of working
Employee motivation and skills		Conduct resistance assessment; Consult employees and assess readiness; Construct training needs analysis	Align people and HR processes with strategy; Develop courses and training materials; Manage employee resistance	'Up-skill' roll-out; Coaching and support

FIGURE 4.12 Change prism transformation plan

part

2

Tools, techniques and templates

Introduction

Having the right tools for the job

IN CHAPTER 4, EACH LENS of the framework listed the inputs, outputs and activities associated with change management. Part 2 is your kit-bag or 'toolkit' and contain information on each of the assessments and instruments that you may need to deploy during your project. In Part 3, we explore what a change manager does and refer to specific tools and techniques that may be deployed to progress change stream deliverables.

Tools, techniques and templates

In Chapters 5 to 12 we lay out the change tools and techniques, organised by each lens in the change prism, to help you locate what you need more easily. We have gathered together a wide range of resources to create a change management toolkit that will provide a reference and source of guidance to inform your planning and thought processes as a change manager. It is a collection of interrelated instruments which we have used and found helpful in project managing change and that together provide a strong rationale and framework for the activities and deliverables in a project change stream.

Each item in the toolkit provides you with step-by-step recommendations and suggestions for execution, based on our experience of using the tools with different clients and in different types of change projects. Each guide follows the same format:

▌ What is it?

▌ Why do it?

▌ When to do it.

▌ How to do it.

In addition, it contains a list of templates available for you to download and populate as you conduct each task or activity in your organisation.

the key to success is selection

As we have said before throughout the preceding chapters, the key to success is selection. Don't feel you need to do everything and don't be seduced by the tools – just because you can do something, doesn't necessarily mean that you should! Choose the tools that will give you the greatest insight or benefit, and at every step you should still be questioning if this is the right thing to do at a particular time.

The project environment, objectives and priorities often change, so even after you've made your selection, ask yourself, 'When or why should I *not* do this?', 'Has anything changed to make this activity or assessment inappropriate or not worth the investment of time and resources?', 'What trade-offs might I need to make for the good of the project or for the employees of this work?'

For those of you who have been itching to dive into the application and delivery of change management, this is the bit you have been waiting for.

A change management toolkit

Change prism lens	Step-by-step guides
Chapter 5 Strategy and future state	Change manager role profile
	Change management strategy
	Guiding principles for change
	Scope and scale of change
	Programme sponsorship map
	High-level business case

Change prism lens	Step-by-step guides
Chapter 6 Planning and management	Change management plan Change governance structure Change management charter Change management dashboard
Chapter 7 Leadership and capability	Change sponsor selection Mobilisation event(s) Terms of reference Change leader profile Change agent profile Change team roles and responsibilities Programme team development plan Change network development plan
Chapter 8 Stakeholders and communication	Stakeholder analysis and map Stakeholder management plan Stakeholder review process Communications strategy Communications audit Communications plan and roadmap
Chapter 9 Resilience and capacity	Change impact assessment Organisation capacity review Resilience assessment Capacity mitigation and resilience plan
Chapter 10 Organisation alignment	Organisation design principles Strategic (macro) organisation design Operational (detailed) organisation design Role profiles Transition plan
Chapter 11 Culture and behaviours	Future organisation look and feel Culture assessment Culture audit Culture action plan
Chapter 12 Employee motivation and skills	Change readiness assessment Resistance assessment and approach Training strategy and plan Training needs analysis Training course design Training effectiveness measures

Strategy and future state

Change prism lens	Step-by-step guides
Strategy and future state	Change manager role profile
	Change management strategy
	Guiding principles for change
	Scope and scale of change
	Programme sponsorship map
	High-level business case
	Downloadable templates
	Summary Strategic Analysis and (SWOT)
	Focus Area Identification and Recommendations
	Change Roadmap
	Scope and Scale of Change
	High-level Business Case for Change

Change manager role profile

What is it?

A CHANGE MANAGER ROLE PROFILE IS USEFUL when a potential incumbent or sponsor is deciding who to task with the challenge of leading change management work. It describes the characteristics, skills or attributes of a change manager, and helps with selection and potential for professional development.

Why do it?

Identifying early on if you need a change manager and then finding the best person to do that role will have a direct impact on the success of your project.

When to do it

Diagnose phase.

How to do it

Step 1: Decide if you need a change manager

First, you must decide if you need a change manager. Here are some questions to help you decide:

▌ Will the change require a significant number of people to do work differently?

▌ Will the change affect a number of people from different departments or business units?

▌ Will the change derive from a larger corporate strategy, with objectives such as increasing growth, reducing costs or reacting to new required legislation?

▌ Will the change be likely to involve introducing or changing a combination of things, such as new technology, different processes to follow or products to sell?

▌ Will the change be likely to require any new customer interactions or a change in how employees think about customers?

▌ Will the change require new knowledge and skills to be learned?

▌ Will the change require leaders/managers to assess people's performance differently?

If you have answered 'yes' to any of the above questions, then you need a change manager. In a world of degrees, you may not need a change manager full-time every day, depending on the scope and scale, but you will need someone to take responsibility for creating sustained change and realising the benefits.

You don't need a change manager if the project does not introduce new working behaviours, technology, processes or skills. For example, if the project goal is to replace all the old back room servers with new ones, and there will be no effect on people's desktops, then there is no need for a change manager.

Step 2: Select the right candidate

Once you have decided there is a need, then you have to find the right person. Good change managers are adept at the following.

- **Understanding and refining scope** – They have the ability to work within and refine the parameters set by the project and sponsor.

- **Understanding the psychology of change** – They understand how individuals and organisations react to change, and how to manage these reactions to increase the likelihood of success.

- **Able to see different perspectives** – They identify, relate to and respect the diverse perspectives of all the people involved in the change.

- **Able to plan for and deliver results** – They gather information, analyse it and convert it into a plan. They are able to drive the plan to completion and achieve results, even in situations of ambiguity.

- **Act flexibly and are organised** – They are able to adapt quickly to changing circumstances, replan and mobilise seamlessly.

- **Build effective relationships** – They are capable of developing and sustaining relationships with and between groups, leaders, and co-workers and in leading a change team.

- **Communication** – They are able to flex personal communication style to suit the situation, business context or personality.

- **Manage resistance** – They are skilled at dealing with resistance to change, removing obstacles that inhibit the change and realising results. They show tenacity, can foresee problems and overcome them quickly.

Step 3: Get on-board the change manager, clarify the role and development plan

Now that you have identified a change manager, it is vital to set them up to be successful. Give your change manager unfettered access to documents, people and technology. Make sure the role, scope, expectations and reporting relationships are clearly agreed, documented and understood, and that there are planned, regular progress and development conversations.

Change management strategy

What is it?

The change strategy is the first deliverable in the change management work stream. In its simplest form, it is a synopsis of the people-related elements of a programme strategy. It is usually presented in either a word document or a presentation. Generally, our preference is for a presentation format as it focuses on the major points, challenges woolly thinking and is more easily communicated to others. A change strategy answers three main questions: 'What are our reasons for doing this?' 'What do we want to achieve?', 'How will we get there?' Within these questions you would expect to cover the following:

What are our reasons for doing this?	What do we want to achieve?	How will we get there?
Situational analysis (e.g. SWOT)	Programme vision and objectives	Programme sponsorship
Review of historical implementations	Guiding principles	Role of change management
Organisation/business model and design	Critical success factors	Change roadmap

Why do it?

It is hugely beneficial for a project to link clearly its objectives and activities to achieving an overall direction that has been set for the organisation. A strategic cascade is often assumed when, in reality, employees find it difficult to see the 'big picture' from the multitude of interventions and programmes they see going on around them. In some cases this clarity does not exist and must be created.

The change strategy aligns the change management approach, objectives and proposed activities with both the project strategy and the business strategy. It acts as both the baseline and anchor point for the change management plan, setting boundaries for the 'as-is' and the desired 'to-be'.

When to do it

As early as possible in the diagnose phase.

How to do it

Step 1: Conduct an 'as-is' review and analysis

You will need to collect internal and external documentation from different sources to review and discover how change has been introduced in the past, and understand why the organisation is where it is today. Typical documents might include (but should not be limited to): business strategy and plans; SWOT analysis; project proposal or RFP (request for proposals); programme steering group minutes; programme/project business case; high-level business process analysis; employee surveys and focus group data; customer survey and focus group data; industry and market analyses; competitor benchmarking data; and wrap-up reports from previous programmes.

If you are confident and experienced working with business and programme strategy, you will probably have developed your own approach to strategic analysis. If you are new to strategic analysis, you will need to review each piece of data with a set of 'filters' or dimensions specifically looking at how the change was managed, how the change was introduced, what the lessons learned were (what went well and what could have been better) and how the change was received, and reacted to, by employees. Use the change prism as a checklist or set of dimensions for doing this.

You will need to identify which themes are recurring and which issues are likely to be the 'show-stoppers'. These will make up the summary analysis you will use to develop recommendations and form the categories in your change roadmap.

Download template: *Summary Strategic Analysis (SWOT)*

Step 2: Define the future state

In most cases, 'future state' is usually a statement of purpose and is embodied as a 'vision' or 'to-be'. It is often accompanied by guiding principles which describe more fully how living the vision will look and feel. Guiding principles are the critical drivers for the change project and describe how we want to make it happen; they can be called the 'code of conduct', covered in a separate tool (see page 96).

A good vision and guiding principles will reflect the three aspects of the change being proposed – rational, political and emotional. An example of the objectives, vision and guiding principles for a global pharmaceutical company's CRM programme is shown below:

CRM objectives

▌ Increase sales force efficiency and effectiveness
▌ Integrate customer information across all marketing channels for a more complete and actionable view
▌ Improve our ability to understand and leverage customer information (analytics)
▌ Use a standard platform with 0% customisation and >5% local configuration only

CRM vision

▌ Improving customer focus and profitability

CRM guiding principles

▌ 'Pharmco Knows Me'
▌ To share what we learn about the needs of our different customers and to harmonise the answers that we provide, ensuring that the experiences we create for our customers will be mutually rewarding and beneficial

This activity is usually achieved by means of a workshop, where the business leaders and project sponsors identify a set of principles or goals which are then concentrated into a vision statement. It is critical that all of the leadership team and programme sponsors agree and sign up to the vision and guiding principles they create. If possible, we would recommend that you have a symbolic 'signing' of the agreed 'future state' with each participant putting their signature to the statement.

Step 3: Define the change approach and success criteria

The approach defines the philosophy and methodology you will use and the scope and scale of the change management work stream. You will need to apply the project management approach and change prism methodology to your specific programme and organisation. (A good start will be a bit of cutting and pasting from Chapters 3 and 4.)

The success or effectiveness of change management will be assessed through people or behaviour-based measures. Such measures can be quantitative, such as reduced headcount in a restructure or improvements against team performance targets following the introduction of cross-functional teams. Measures can also be comparable, like how quickly or effectively this change was implemented compared to other programmes. Measures may also be qualitative – what was the employees'/customers' experience of how the change was managed? You may want to run a survey or hold focus groups to assess this and provide evidence. Benchmarking can also be a useful tool to give you some idea about 'what good looks like', and how much improvement is possible. Before deciding which criteria to use, cross-reference with the programme business case to see what benefits are expected.

In many instances it can be difficult to isolate measures that are attributable only to change management. Process or technology improvements and measures may overlap with change management, so to avoid double-counting benefits or disappointing expectations, you should agree with all parties what proportions are likely to be attributable to each work stream and only document what you are able to influence/control. Refer to Chapter 13 for more information regarding benefits measurement and KPIs.

Step 4: Identify focus areas for change

If you can do it, a change readiness assessment can provide huge insight into issue identification. If this is not an option, based on the strategic analysis in step 1, you will need to decide what you and your colleagues think the major issues/barriers/risks/opportunities are. You will then need to outline recommendations as to how you intend to solve them. Your life will be much easier if you can categorise the risks, issues and/or recommendations according to the eight lenses.

The best-quality recommendations are those produced by collaboration, through a workshop or team brainstorming session. If you know other change managers through your business or personal networks, consult them. And don't forget, look to other similar programmes because if something has worked before it may work again.

Download template: *Focus Area Identification and Recommendations*

Step 5: Identify change roles and responsibilities

Your change management responsibilities are defined by the areas of focus and recommendations you outlined in step 4, which will basically become your KPIs. Your role as change manager should be scoped in terms of delivering the recommendations, the organisational level you will be operating at and your line reporting structure. In smaller projects you may be doing everything, from strategy and working with the leadership team to delivering workshops and performing analysis. In larger or more complex projects there may be a number of change management resources and the different roles will need to be identified and profiled as part of the strategy. If you are planning to use external consultants or third parties this should also be stated in the change strategy.

At this point it would be a good idea to start drafting your change charter. This will help you focus and document where your responsibilities stop and others begin. Do you expect or want to be involved in redesigning the performance management process or will you just share the new KPIs with HR so that they can adapt the process themselves? Will you be involved in job application/ matching or just provide HR with the high-level role profiles? Who will run any consultation process with the trade unions? Who will track and monitor benefits realisation?

Step 6: Change roadmap

This is a visual representation that plots the capabilities and milestones required to achieve the future state. The roadmap highlights focus areas, priorities and enablers. It is a powerful tool to communicate how and when things will be changing and gives the project and employees a common framework and vocabulary to talk about the change.

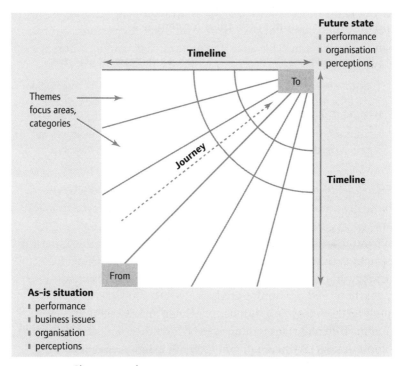

FIGURE 5.1 Change roadmap

Download template: *Change Roadmap*

Step 7: Positioning

Once all the preceding steps have been completed, you should include a list of your assumptions and a management summary.

Guiding principles for change

What is it?

Guiding principles for change describe how living the change vision
will look and feel. They are how we will achieve the vision by the
'code of conduct' – observable activities and behaviours such as
managing customer data, creating cross-functional teams or a shared
service centre, or by business process re-engineering (BPR).

An example of the objectives, vision and guiding principles for a
global pharmaceutical company's CRM programme is shown below,
along with the guiding principles for change.

CRM objectives	Change management objectives
▌ Increase sales force efficiency and effectiveness ▌ Integrate customer information across all marketing channels for a more complete and actionable view ▌ Improve our ability to understand and leverage customer information (analytics) ▌ Use a standard platform with 0% customisation and >5% local configuration only	▌ Increase transparency of contribution between employees and customers ▌ Establish concept of 'One Pharmco' ▌ Prepare and support employees and the regional organisations that are implementing the global CRM technology platforms

CRM vision	Change vision
▌ Improving customer focus and profitability	▌ To develop and support the culture and behaviours needed to realise the brand

CRM guiding principles	Change guiding principles
▌ 'Pharmco Knows Me' ▌ To share what we learn about the needs of our different customers and to harmonise the answers that we provide, ensuring that the experiences we create for our customers will be mutually rewarding and beneficial	▌ To provide common tools, frameworks and shared learning to enable affiliate implementations of the new technology systems. Remove existing barriers to customer centricity and provide conditions for employees to challenge inappropriate business models, processes and behaviours

Why do it?

Defining guiding principles for change provides boundaries for what is within and outside the responsibility of the change manager. It is a 'stake in the ground' against which incoming activities or responsibilities can be compared and expectations managed. Guiding principles are useful to prevent scope creep and reduce the risk of change management becoming a 'dumping ground' for work that no-one else wants to do.

When to do it

Early in the diagnose phase, in parallel with change strategy development.

How to do it

Ideally through a workshop or brainstorming session with your project leadership team. In reality, this is not always possible and you may also encounter a degree of resistance as your colleagues may feel this is out of their comfort zone or area of expertise. If you know other change managers through your business or personal networks, consult them. And don't forget, look to other similar projects for ideas or inspiration. If you are forced down this solitary route, it is vital to get validation, preferably in writing, of the vision and guiding principles for change from your project manager, executive sponsor and change sponsor.

Scope and scale of change

What is it?

A scope and scale exercise provides an indication of the extent of change the project may bring. It is made up of the collective thoughts and understanding of the key people in the project and is generally conducted as a 'quick and dirty' measure ahead of a more detailed change impact assessment.

Why do it?

To inform the change approach and the number of resources, skills and roles needed to deliver the change strategy.

When to do it

Early in the diagnose phase, in parallel with change management strategy development.

How to do it

Step 1: Workshop preparation

You will need to schedule and conduct a short workshop (1–2 hours) or brainstorming session with your project leadership team to discuss and capture collective thoughts and understanding about the project scope and scale. This can be done as part of or as an extension of an existing team meeting or as a dedicated activity. You will need to prepare your colleagues in advance, telling them what you are planning to do and why. You can even send out the scope and scale template in advance so that colleagues can familiarise themselves and come to the meeting focused on the task ahead.

Step 2: Conduct the workshop

Review the following list (column 1 of the template) with your colleagues either as individual copies or, better still, printed poster size and up on the wall of the meeting room. The question you will need to consider for each item in the list is 'Will this change or be different as a result of the project?' Against each item that has received a 'positive' assessment, complete the additional columns to the right to the best of your collective knowledge.

Download template: *Scope and Scale of Change*

Will this change or be different as a result of the project?		Level of impact (H,M,L)	Number of people impacted	Perceived risk to programme (R,A,G)
	Y/N			
Leadership style				
Vision, priorities, goals				
Accountability				
Values and behaviours				
Operating constraints				
Work flow/processes				
Metrics and targets				
Dependencies/sub-processes				
Organisation structure (groups/departments)				
Line relationships/reporting				
Partnerships and alliances				
Roles and responsibilities				
Location/proximity				
Behaviours and attitudes				
Planning and budgeting				
Performance measurement and rewards				
Decision-making process				
Competencies				
Staffing and recruitment				
Training and development				

Programme sponsorship map

What is it?

A sponsorship map documents the relationships and level of support among people in the organisation who have been selected to play a 'leadership' role. Starting with the organisation chart, showing reporting lines, the sponsorship map also shows known allies, personal influence networks and political allegiances. The purpose is to represent how well leaders are aligned to the proposed change and also gives an insight into the organisation's culture.

Why do it?

Successful change implementation is dependent on the understanding, commitment and drive of key individuals. Their perceptions of project credibility *(do-ability)* and positive/negative impact on the organisation's capabilities are a good indicator of buy-in. By considering such variables we can identify the 'go to' people who will be needed to leverage their influence on behalf of the project and prevent concerns from developing into project problems.

When to do it

An initial map should be created in the diagnose phase, but regularly reviewed and updated throughout the project life cycle.

How to do it

Step 1: Identify sponsorship roles

Using a recent organisation chart, identify the executive(s) who have the real power and authority to drive the change through the organisation. Then, identify the next relevant layers of change leaders who must work with them to drive the change successfully.

Step 2: Categorise the sponsors and leaders by their support for the programme

Through focused team discussions, targeted interviews and review of a risk assessment, determine the sponsors' level of understanding and personal support for the proposed change (i.e. executive sponsor, change leaders, advocate, target and blocker) – and where the project fits in their priorities.

An example sponsorship matrix is shown in Figure 5.2.

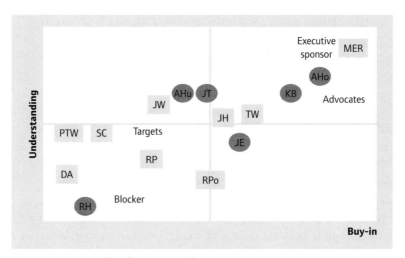

FIGURE 5.2 Example of a sponsorship matrix

Change roles are as follows.

▌ Executive sponsor – authorises, legitimises and demonstrates ownership for the change; possesses sufficient organisational power and/or influence to commit resources.

▌ Change leaders – possess sufficient organisational power to reinforce the change by legitimising, demonstrating ownership and otherwise showing visible change leadership.

▌ Targets – people who will need to change or be most affected by the change.

▌ Agent – understands the changes and has the skills and desire to help the change proceed. Well-respected, and influential with peers/others. Not necessarily in a formal leadership position, but will become your change network if needed.

▌ Advocates – want the change and are supportive. Can be those who sit outside the formal and informal relationships driving the change, but who have influence. Best used to help win over highly-resistant change leaders, agents or targets.

▌ Blockers – a level of buy-in and understanding needs to be obtained from blockers – those who are negative or resistant to the change. Blockers may be active or passive.

It is possible for someone to play more than one type of role. If that happens choose the dominant one and place them according to their current level of buy-in and understanding.

Step 3: Create the map

See Figure 5.3.

Step 4: Validate with trusted allies

The map will probably be the most sensitive document you produce. It should be treated as highly confidential and shared only among the most senior two or three project team members and either the executive sponsor or change sponsor. Copies should not be printed and after sponsorship review meetings any documentation should be destroyed.

High-level business case

What is it?

The change business case is a tool that documents and assesses the contribution of a project or other change in quantitative and qualitative terms. A typical business case contains a number of elements: strategic summary, issues, opportunities, recommended solutions and delivery approach, financial impact or implications, non-financial benefits and timeframe or phasing of when benefits will be realised.

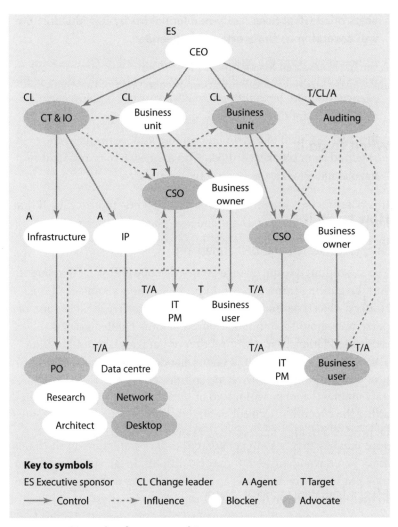

FIGURE 5.3 Example of a sponsorship map

Why do it?

A high-level business case identifies costs and financial benefits of a business change or project and, from a practical standpoint, can really help you justify and secure the resources you need. Typically an organisation's biggest single cost is its people (i.e. salaries, benefits, recruitment, training). Consultancy benchmarks show that savings of 20–40 per cent are possible in areas by introducing new ways of working and/or workforce capability.

A business case can also support planning and decision making and clarify business or organisation expectations of the change project.

When to do it

Diagnose phase.

How to do it

Step 1: Research and benchmarking

You should review the change strategy, scope and scale document, and the guiding principles, and produce a short summary of the strategy, objectives and key drivers for change. The next section or paragraph should list the focus areas, people challenges and recommendations. The third section or paragraph should outline your approach to deliver the recommendations, which will drive how you are going to deliver the solution(s).

You will also need to conduct some individual research and analysis to gauge what is good practice in the industry and how your organisation is faring compared to its competitors in the focus areas you have identified. It may be difficult to get specific data, so look out for proxy measures and indicators. As well as information in the public domain (e.g. annual reports and analyst reports) we suggest you also explore information from professional bodies (e.g. CIM, CIPS, CMI, CIMA), professional survey organisations, market research companies and people management experts such as CIPD or Personnel Today.

Step 2: Identify benefits

Knowing where to look for benefits can be a challenge. Generally, people-related benefits are found in, but not limited to, the areas shown in Figure 5.4.

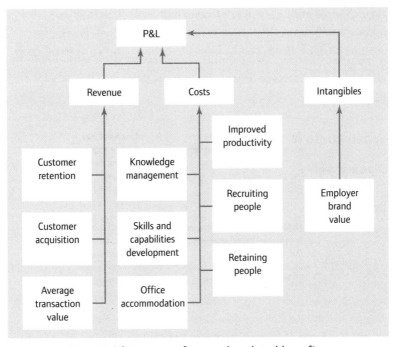

FIGURE 5.4 Potential focus areas for people-related benefits

You will need to ask yourself if savings or efficiencies from each of these sources could result from the recommendations you have identified. If so, your next step will be to find a means of establishing what the current status is (the baseline) and how you will measure any improvement or benefit.

You will need to select measures or KPIs (see Figure 5.5) that will show any improvements as a result of the interventions or solutions the change team put in place. These measures can be financial or non-financial, quantifiable or qualitative. Ideally you should aim to put together a 'scorecard' across all four segments.

Step 3: Define benefit opportunities

Based on your research you will need to do a gap analysis on the data to see the extent or value of the benefit opportunities. Before you get too excited by some of the big numbers, be cautious – you may not have the insight or detailed knowledge behind the 'best in class' figures and there may be contributing factors that you are unaware of behind the numbers. Be pragmatic too – use the best in class as an aspiration, think about the context and culture of your organisation and set your sights accordingly.

	FINANCIAL	NON-FINANCIAL
QUANTIFIABLE	**Financial impact is clearly identified and measurable:** Increased sales Increased availability Reduced handling costs	**Non-financial but measurable impact:** Customer satisfaction Service quality More stable field force Employee morale
QUALIFIABLE	**Financial impact that cannot be estimated accurately:** Customer retention Store alignment with strategy Effective work processes	**Non-financial benefits difficult to measure:** Improved communication Increased teamwork Enhanced reputation with suppliers and customers

FIGURE 5.5 Types of benefit measures or KPIs

Opposite is an extract from a culture change project benefits case (from the public sector) which presents the opportunity gap but sets different targets.

Everyone will be delighted if you exceed expectations, but disappointment may damage the credibility of change managment in your organisation for years to come.

Step 4: Benefits delivery schedule

Some benefits are realisable in the short-term either during implementation or just after, such as reduced duplication of effort because of a new process. Others may take several months after implementation, for example reducing the headcount must allow for legal and terms and conditions requirements or employee consultation periods. Some benefits like closing or moving offices could even take years. This is why you need a benefits realisation timeframe or schedule, so the business knows what value it can expect and when.

Download template: *High-level Business Case for Change*

Issue/contract group	Indicator type or measure	As-is baseline	Sector benchmark	Proposed solution	Realisable benefit (%)
Respect for leadership	Staff perception rating	14.9% (2005)	31.80%	Open board meetings 'Back to the floor' Fill permanent posts Induction for temporarily promoted staff	>10% improvement points (to 24.9%)
	Staff perception rating	First month average of exit interview card sort	None	Role model leadership behaviours Admit mistakes and discipline re: hiding mistakes Roll out (and training) on leadership model	
Strategic planning	Staff perception rating	First instance of BRS survey	None – suggest 60% positive response target	Own the plan and hold our nerve Implement common decision-making framework Implement scenario planning at board level Embed continuous improvement approach	>5% improvement each subsequent survey
Training and support	L&D investment	(New) unknown	£440 public sector excl. employee remuneration (£896 inc. remuneration)	Revise induction process to include culture, stress, support etc.	>15% improvement points (to 54.7%)
	Staff perception rating	39.7% (2005)	54.80%	Timely training for temporarily promoted staff HR/people process training programme Coaching clinics on HR topics for managers	
Knowledge management	Staff turnover (admin and junior management grades)	19.8% (1.6% pcm)	10.1% public sector	Share best practice between teams Standardise processes (maps) Share successes Recognise and reward expertise	>5% reduction (to 14.8%)

6 Planning and management

Change prism lens	Step-by-step guides
Planning and management	Change management plan
	Change governance structure
	Change management charter
	Change management dashboard
	Downloadable templates
	Detailed Change Activity Planner
	Risk Register
	Change Management Plan Document
	Change Management Charter
	Change Management Dashboard

Change management plan

What is it?

THE CHANGE MANAGEMENT PLAN DEFINES what you need to do to achieve the change management strategy. The plan identifies the order and dependency of tasks and activities and the resources required to deliver them. The plan also provides the structure so that work streams for each of the lenses in the change prism are integrated across the phases and tasks/activities are aligned to the overall project plan. The application of a project management methodology facilitates the prioritisation of activities and resources throughout and links them to deliverables and decision gates. The change management plan typically contains the following sections:

- summary of intent and change objectives
- change governance and sponsorship

■ definition of activities and tasks

■ high-level schedule of activities

■ resource case and plan

■ risk and issue management

■ assumptions.

Why do it?

Developing a change management plan ensures that all aspects of change management are adequately covered and everyone involved in the project has a common understanding of what the change team will be doing.

When to do it

Design phase.

How to do it

Step 1: Summarise intent and objectives

If you have developed your change management charter, you can cut and paste the objectives and focus areas into this section along with the project goals and definition of the 'to-be' organisation. It merely sets a context for the change, and will save you flipping between multiple documents as you develop the plan.

Step 2: Review analysis and scope

During pre-project planning, analysis will have been conducted to identify what is likely to change, what the level and type of impact the change is likely to have, and what activities need to be planned into the project to manage the people-related issues identified. If you have completed a change management strategy, this will just be a summary of the information you generated in steps 1, 2, 3 and 4. In general these activities are defined simplistically as follows.

■ **Change management** – identifying the new ways of working and behaviours required, how ready staff are to adopt them, and defining the activity needed to ensure that that change happens.

▮ **Stakeholder management** – targeting individuals or groups who can influence project success and defining how they should be involved.

▮ **Communications** – understanding who the key audiences are at project level and designing the messages that are going to support the change needed.

▮ **Staff transition** – ensuring that changes to roles are managed consistently and in a way that is fair, transparent and in line with HR policies.

▮ **Training** – making sure that those members of staff who need to take on new roles receive training that is timely and tailored to their needs.

You will need to break down each of these categories into component activities based on your own issue identification analysis, your findings or learnings from previous change implementations and using the change prism as your checklist. An example of this is shown below.

Category	Objective	Activity/ activities	Tasks
▮ Change management *(organisation alignment/ employee motivation and skills)*	▮ To understand who will be impacted and their preparedness for the change	▮ Change impact assessment	▮ Identify target groups or roles ▮ Profile each group ▮ Define and communicate CIA approach ▮ Identify and train resources ▮ Create materials ▮ Schedule and conduct events ▮ Identify impact level and timing for each group ▮ Identify specific issues for each group ▮ Create report ▮ Monitor, track and review
	▮ To understand the levels of willingness and ability to accept the change	▮ Change readiness assessment	▮ Identify target groups or roles ▮ Profile each group ▮ Define and communicate CRA approach ▮ Identify and train resources

▶

Category	Objective	Activity/ activities	Tasks
			▌ Create materials
			▌ Schedule and conduct events
			▌ Conduct analysis
			▌ Identify specific issues for each group
			▌ Share findings
			▌ Input to stakeholder action plans
			▌ Monitor, track and review

Step 3: Overview of change governance

In this section, you will need to summarise the change governance structure. This is the definition of appropriate structures, committees and processes with the remit to make authoritative and timely decisions on the change initiatives associated with a change project. If you have already completed the tool on change governance structure, you can cut and paste that into this section. For completeness, you may want to include a summary of the key sponsors or a copy of the sponsorship map, keeping in mind who will have access to your change plan and the confidentiality and sensitivity of the sponsorship map. If you have not completed it already, the tool is located in the strategy and future state lens (see Chapter 5).

Step 4: Define project infrastructure requirements

Once you have defined the change workload for the project, you will need to consider which additional project activities you will be required to execute or participate in. For more information on this refer to the 'considerations checklist' in Chapter 14. Your responsibilities as change manager will be at several levels, from planning and tracking task progress, to project management of change milestones, deliverables and governance, and as a member of the project lead team. Project management activities you may be required to include are:

▌ attend programme board team meetings

▌ give presentations to project teams and sponsors

- complete progress tracking and reporting
- maintain risks and issues log
- conduct project planning (and replanning)
- engage sponsors
- develop change training and education.

Step 5: Consider 'other' activities

In addition to the change and project responsibilities, it is also likely that you will pick up some *ad hoc* activities. We would urge you to try and anticipate what these could be and factor them into your plan. If they do not transpire, you will have built in some (much needed) contingency. As the 'people' stream, you may be asked to manage and resource activities such as team development (to develop a high-performing team), social and team-building events, HR liaison, on-boarding new project team members, meeting and workshop facilitation, sourcing promotional items, staffing kick-off events, coaching, etc.

Step 6: Scheduling activities

When you have defined the activities (both change and project), you will need to align the timing of the activities, and any outputs or deliverables, to the overall project timeline. This may have an impact on the order and duration of the change stream activities by providing end dates and highlighting dependencies. You will also get a sense of what activities can be done in parallel and what must be done in sequence. Figure 6.1 shows an example of a change plan.

Alignment to the project timeline may also have implications for other project streams that have dependencies on change deliverables (e.g. job-to-role mapping, access levels, CRP participation). This will require you to negotiate and possibly make trade-offs of time against resources. However, you must be clear about which activities have minimum constraints that you cannot compromise on: for example, a survey must allow time (minimum two weeks) for people to receive, complete and return it.

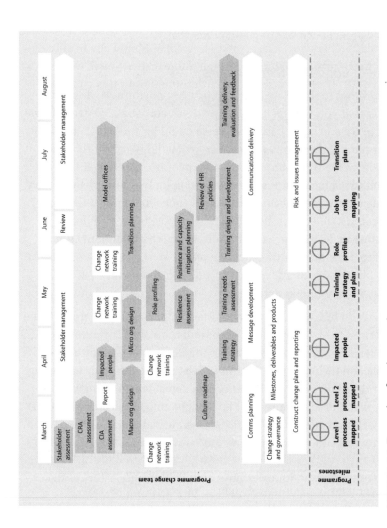

FIGURE 6.1 Example of a change plan

Step 7: Resource case

When you have clarity over what is to be done and by when, you should calculate the resource needs to execute the change plan. You will need to make an assessment on how many person-days are required to complete each task. This will enable you to calculate how many resources you will need. It is wise to make this calculation based on a five- or six-hour operational day to allow for time inevitably spent on breaks, telephone calls, e-mail, etc. Figure 6.2 shows the change activities, the duration to complete them, and at the bottom the number of resources required on any given week.

Your resource and skill requirements may be significantly different in each of the programme phases. You should think about how you will manage this. You have a number of options such as temporary help, contractors, consultants, flexible working arrangements or secondments. If you are dealing with anything but full-time continuous resources, you must allow time for training and handover of responsibilities. A spreadsheet is a very useful way to map out the duration, tasks and peaks of activity, and can easily be extended or adapted to take you from the high-level planning stage to the detailed or operational change plan.

Step 8: Resource planning

To make the change plan and resource case operational, you will need to define all activities to the task level (as recommended in step 2) and map them against the programme calendar. Make sure you block out all public holidays or dates that cannot be used for change activities (e.g. company days and conferences) and include non-change and non-project activities that will reduce the number of resource person-hours or days available. Figure 6.3 takes the above resource plan to the next level by including the 'other' activities at the bottom and the resource required.

Download template: *Detailed Change Activity Planner*

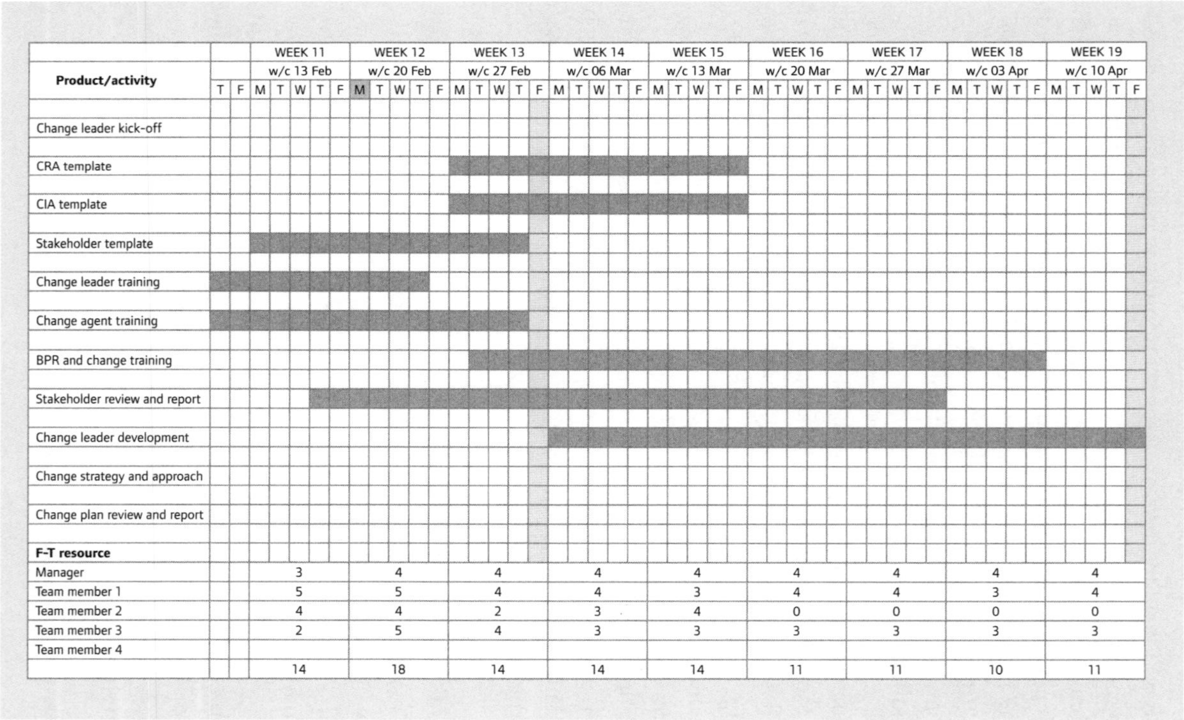
Product/activity
WEEK 11 w/c 13 Feb
WEEK 12 w/c 20 Feb
WEEK 13 w/c 27 Feb
WEEK 14 w/c 06 Mar
WEEK 15 w/c 13 Mar
WEEK 16 w/c 20 Mar
WEEK 17 w/c 27 Mar
WEEK 18 w/c 03 Apr
WEEK 19 w/c 10 Apr
T F M T W T F M T W T F M T W T F M T W T F M T W T F M T W T F M T W T F M T W T F M T W T F
Change leader kick-off
CRA template
CIA template
Stakeholder template
Change leader training
Change agent training
BPR and change training
Stakeholder review and report
Change leader development
Change strategy and approach
Change plan review and report
F-T resource
Manager 3 4 4 4 4 4 4 4 4
Team member 1 5 5 4 4 3 4 4 3 4
Team member 2 4 4 2 3 4 0 0 0 0
Team member 3 2 5 4 3 3 3 3 3 3
Team member 4
14 18 14 14 14 11 11 10 11

FIGURE 6.2 Example of a change resource case

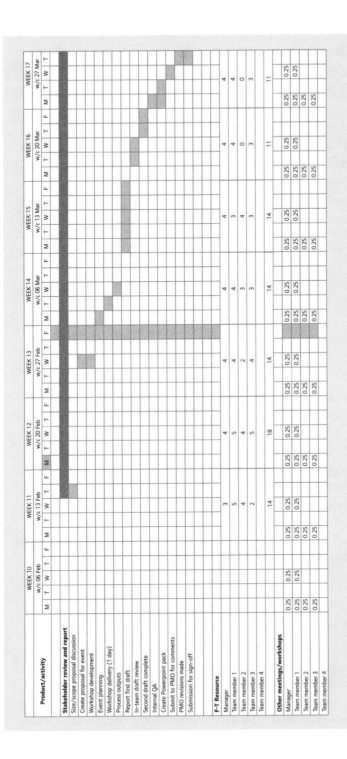

FIGURE 6.3 Extract from a change activity planner (stakeholder review and report)

Step 9: Management of risks and issues

In this section you should define the process that you will use for managing risks and how you will be capturing and reporting the information. A risk is an unplanned event or situation that may occur but has not yet occurred *and,* if it does occur, would have an impact on the project/programme's ability to achieve its objectives, i.e. cost, benefits, timescale, quality. The change manager is responsible for ensuring that change-specific risks are identified, recorded and regularly reviewed.

A risk register is a widely accepted format and is essentially a spreadsheet, as shown below:

Ref/ID number	Description	Impact	Likelihood	Due date	Owner

A risk becomes an issue when it reaches its due date, when what you anticipated might happen actually happens. You will also need to define how you intend to record and track issues. The basic procedure usually requires you to inform the PMO[1] of the status change from risk to issue and this will need to be authorised by the project manager. You will then need to propose a solution for the issue raised and modify your change plan to include the agreed actions to reduce the impact on the project. It is good practice to review and update progress of risks and issues as a standing agenda item during your change team and project team meetings.

Download template: *Risk Register*

Step 10: Assumptions

This final section requires you to document any prerequisites, expectations or gaps in the information you used to build your change plan. Documenting these could trigger the generation of

---

[1] Issues are managed centrally by the project management office (PMO) that releases copies of the issue log to issue owners for review and progress updates.

additional information or clarification that may require you to modify your plan.

Download template: *Change Management Plan Document*

Change governance structure

What is it?

Managing change is essentially about managing people. In a change project, you may have a change team, a change manager, a change network, change leaders, sponsors and steering groups. Each group requires a discipline of management, including terms of reference, progress reporting and a clear decision-making remit. There should already be a project governance structure in place, and the change governance structure will augment and be aligned to it. If there is no project governance structure in place, you should raise this with the project manager or executive sponsor, and work with them to put one in place.

Why do it?

Defining and agreeing the change governance early will allow you as the change manager to run the change in an effective and efficient manner, providing clear accountabilities for decision making, product approvals and a route for escalation of risks and issues.

When to do it

Diagnose phase.

How to do it

Step 1: Research what governance already exists for the project and organisation

Gather information regarding current project governance plans, and also operational governance. The project will need to link in with 'business as usual' at a number of levels, and the change governance will need to do the same. Make sure you understand how decision making happens daily, what decisions need to be taken at what level and, if possible, read the terms of reference for each group.

Step 2: Determine the groups involved in change that will need to be governed

From the change plan, have you identified that there will be a change network? Have you identified all your change leaders? Have you considered the change team? Depending on when you complete this activity, governance may need to be regularly reviewed and adjusted to meet changing project and business needs.

Step 3: Outline early terms of reference for each group

Each change group will require management and structure to run it. Sketch out a draft terms of reference one-pager for each group, outlining how often you think they should meet, who the membership should be, who will lead/chair the meetings, what kinds of decisions would be expected and how progress will be reported.

Step 4: Align the change groups to existing project and organisational governance

Draw an organisational chart of the governance groups and ensure there is overlap at the membership and lead leadership levels. Figure 6.4 shows an example which makes the most sense if you start reading at the bottom (with the weekly meetings) and work your way up.

Review the structure of the known and proposed governance groups, bearing the following in mind.

▌ At what level does the project manager have exposure to senior leadership? (This person needs the highest hierarchical exposure possible.)

▌ At what level does the change manager have exposure to senior leadership? (This person needs the highest hierarchical exposure possible.)

▌ Where are the overlaps between membership of the change leaders and the senior executive team? (There needs to be at least one person who attends both.)

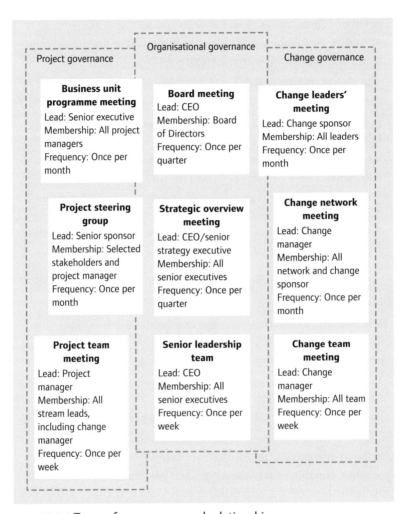

FIGURE 6.4 Types of governance and relationship

▌ Where are there overlaps between the project and the overall strategy decision makers? (There needs to be at least one person who attends both.)

▌ Where are there overlaps between the change manager and project manager? (There needs to be at least one person who attends both.)

▌ If needed, how does the CEO and Board of Directors gain understanding and make decisions regarding the project and the change? (There needs to be overlap between the CEO, senior executive team, change leaders, change sponsor and ideally the programme and project steering groups.)

▌ The change manager will need to be present at all the change group meetings, effectively as lead or to support the lead.

▌ In the terms of reference, decision-making processes and remit need to be clear. Decision making for the change governance can take place in two ways: (1) have a pre-meeting with a small subset of selected members to determine decisions, then communicate these to the wider group at the large meeting or; (2) conduct decision making at the large meeting. This mainly depends on the project culture, change manager style and the culture of the organisation.

Step 5: Agree the change governance structure with the project manager

Once you are comfortable with the overlaps, alignment and augmentation of existing governance with the change governance, agree the proposed structure with the project manager or sponsor if possible.

Step 6: Assemble the teams, schedule meetings and draft terms of reference

For the identified change governance, determine membership, frequency and duration of meetings, and plan to kick off each one. During the kick-off, an agreed terms of reference should be one of the deliverables for each group. For more information on constructing terms of reference, use the tool located in the leadership and capability lens in the next chapter. Circulate the final terms of reference to the project team, change team and senior sponsors.

Change management charter

What is it?

The change management charter is an agreement between the change stream and the project and/or business. It is a one-page blueprint that summarises the key points in the change strategy, sets boundaries regarding scope, clarifies roles and identifies team members and resources.

Why do it?

The main benefit of a change charter is bringing clarity at the beginning of a project. A charter aligns expectations and helps develop relationships within the change team and will minimise misdirected effort. It will also facilitate interaction between sponsors and change team members to increase understanding and buy-in.

When to do it

Design phase.

How to do it

Step 1: Change team workshop

You will need to schedule and facilitate a workshop or brainstorming session with your change team to discuss and capture collective thoughts and understanding about the change project and work stream. You should ensure that all team members have read the change strategy, scope and scale document, guiding principles and project objectives.

All decisions and outputs should be captured either on flip charts or brown-paper working documents. Nominate a team member responsible for capturing outputs.

To encourage discussion you may want to use the following questions:

▌ What people challenges will the programme raise? (Define the 'problem statement'.)

▌ What are the drivers for the project or change?

▌ What are the objectives for the change work stream?

▌ What processes or business areas will be impacted?

▌ What are the boundaries or exceptions that are 'off limits'?

▌ What are the specific issues for each target area?

▌ What are the expected outcomes of the project?

▌ What are the business or project expectations of the change stream?

▌ What level of investment are you expecting to make?

▌ Who are the appropriate people (e.g. subject matter experts) that need to be involved?

Step 2: Charter development

After the workshop, you need to collate and synthesise the outputs into the charter template, which should be no longer than one page in length. An example of a change management charter is shown in Figure 6.5.

You will need to validate this with your team and subsequently with the project manager and change sponsor – all of whom should sign it to signify their agreement with the content.

Download template: *Change Management Charter*

Change management dashboard

What is it?

A change management dashboard (see Figure 6.6 for an example) is a visual reporting tool you can use to track and display key information about the change management plan and its delivery. The main purpose is to show in an easily digestible format what is going on in a change stream and track progress against (1) the plan and (2) the deliverables or products.

Why do it?

A dashboard has the benefit of doubling up as an external communication tool as well as being an internal tracking mechanism. Most project reporting requirements are standard, mandatory (so you will have to comply too) and contain huge amounts of information. As a result, reports tend to be long and

Objectives	Key activities	Scope	Resource requirements

■ To ensure the design and delivery of the defined change activities in the change strategy and plan
■ To manage dependencies with the overall programme to achieve successful business change and delivery of benefits
■ To ensure that the key stakeholders are informed and involved and are providing the required support for the change
	■ Work with change network to review and update stakeholder analysis
	■ Creation of stakeholder handling plan
	■ Quarterly checkpoint meetings to assess the quality of stakeholder management and identify actions and lessons learnt
	■ Produce stakeholder report
	■ Run change strategy review meetings with programme team and document
	■ Facilitate change sustainability session and document
	■ Capture lessons learnt and document
		In scope
		■ HR
		■ Finance
		■ Purchasing
		
		Out of scope
		■ Core operations
		■ Field-based services
		■ Corporate communications
		■ Organisation design (except for implications raised by CIA and design work)
		■ HR process and policy
			■ Project duration: 8 months
			■ People:
			  3 change consultants
			  1 change manager
			  12 change leaders p/t
			  (1–2 days/wk)
			■ Change sponsor or steering committee

Deliverables	Key activities (cont.)	CSFs	Dependencies
■ Change strategy and plan ■ Assessment of change readiness and impact ■ Change management training for programme team and leadership ■ Stakeholder analysis and management plan ■ Stakeholder development plan ■ Operational change network ■ Communications strategy and plan	■ Create CRA, CIA and stakeholder templates ■ CRA and CIA reports (post CRP 2) ■ Design and deliver training (1 day for change leaders; >5 × 1hr sessions for meetings; 1 day training for change agents ×2) ■ 13 week change activity rolling plan for review at change network meetings ■ Conduct and document time-based hot-spot analysis (post CRP 2) ■ Review outputs of design work and CIA for OA indications. Conduct meetings with change leaders and business to agree proposals and document opportunities	■ Delivery of programme objectives to achieve a shift in organisational priorities and ways of working ■ Understanding and deployment of change management approach and benefits across completed by knowledge transfer and transfer of skills	■ Communications plan to include stakeholder handling content ■ Availability of key staff for training and meeting participation ■ Availability of business process maps ■ Provision of team area and meeting room facilities

FIGURE 6.5 Example of a change management charter

wordy, requiring a significant effort by the reader to extract specific information. A regularly updated dashboard becomes a focal point and hung on the wall as a poster attracts other programme streams looking for information about the change stream. It also contributes to project alignment of inter-work stream communication and collaboration.

When to do it

Design/develop phases.

How to do it

Step 1: Establish a method for collecting data

This can be done either through existing change team meetings or an e-mail prompt for updates across the team. Weekly updates are the norm, but you should plan the frequency of updates depending on the pace/phase of the project. This may be daily in a large-scale complex implementation.

Step 2: Ownership

Nominate a dashboard owner in the team who will be responsible for collecting regular updates and revisions to the dashboard. It is good practice to include the revision date and the date when the next version is due.

Step 3: Communication

The owner should send the dashboard first to the change manager, change sponsor and other members of the change team for final validation and a check for accuracy. Subsequently, copies should be shared with the project and a poster-size copy printed off and put on a wall in the team area.

Download template: *Change Management Dashboard*

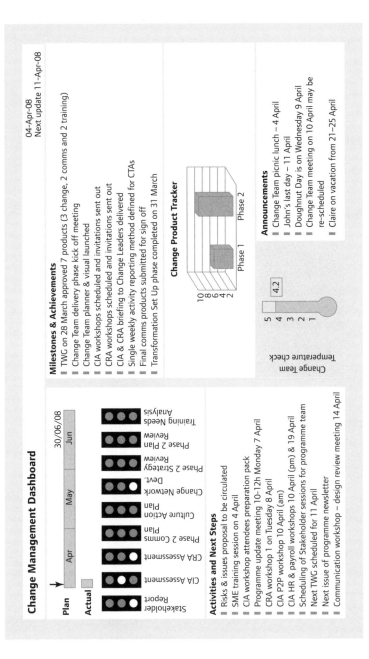

FIGURE 6.6 Example of a change management dashboard

7 Leadership and capability

Change prism lens	Step-by-step guides
Leadership and capability	Change sponsor selection
	Mobilisation event(s)
	Terms of reference
	Change leader profile
	Change agent profile
	Change team roles and responsibilities
	Programme team development plan
	Change network development plan
	Downloadable templates
	Example Terms of Reference Presentation
	Change Agent Profile and Assessment
	Programme Team Development Plan
	The Really Fiendish Teambuilding Game

Change sponsor selection

What is it?

CHANGE SPONSOR SELECTION IS THE PROCESS of identifying the change sponsor (not necessarily the same as the project sponsor) and agreeing the roles and responsibilities of the change sponsor during and after the project. The change sponsor will be a 'go-to' executive for the change manager, and will provide day-to-day assistance, guidance and escalation in completing the change strategy.

Why do it?

Agreeing responsibilities with the change sponsor sets expectations early so that the project team understands the role and how to work with the change sponsor. Using specific criteria to select a change sponsor will improve your chances of identifying the most suitable person for this role, as your decision-making process will be more objective and supported by facts rather than based purely on perception.

When to do it

Diagnose phase.

How to do it

Step 1: Identify candidates

Using a recent organisation chart, identify the executives who have strong credibility and personal leadership in the organisation. If you do not have the organisational knowledge or length of service to identify these people, you can ask HR for a list of potential candidates.

Step 2: Assess the candidates against sponsorship criteria

Assisted by your project colleagues and/or HR, discuss the candidates based on the following criteria and create a ranked list.

Element	Characteristic
Vision	Sees and clearly communicates the future state and the path for getting there.
Commitment	Sees and clearly communicates a compelling business case for moving from the status quo. Has the power to sanction or legitimise change.
Influence	Possesses hierarchical or positional power and influence over key players, has personal credibility and commands respect.
Accountability	Has overall accountability for delivery of change and must hold those responsible within the project team and affiliate for execution and implementation.

Step 3: Assess candidates against role requirements

You will also need to discover if the candidates will be available to carry out the responsibilities of change sponsor. This should be done in the same meeting as step 2. However, if you do not have HR representation at the meeting, it is advisable to validate your assessment before making any approach to secure the resource.

Activity	Involvement
Project scope	Sponsors decide which changes will happen, communicate the new priorities to the organisation and provide the proper support.
Mobilisation	▌ Chair progress and change leader meetings ▌ Provides kick-off and interim communications ▌ Guidance and clarification on scope and vision.
Role model	Sets an example for new behaviours – 'walks the talk'.
Staffing and finance	Prioritises and authorises release of resources/budget.
Governance	Decision making and conflict resolution (including escalations) within the project scope, change governance and guiding frameworks (e.g. charters, statements of practice etc.).

Step 4: Select sponsor and set expectations

Once you have selected your change sponsor and gained their agreement to take on the role, the following list of items/questions may be useful. In the first sponsor meeting set expectations of the role of the sponsor and also provide a 'menu' for future or follow-up meetings to discuss progress of the change or project.

▌ Review/discuss the roles and responsibilities of the sponsor (start by sharing the table in step 3).

▌ Discuss project management with respect to:

- level of involvement
- frequency and form of updates and feedback
- governance structure

- review responsibilities for reporting successes to the business (organisational governance)
- tracking progress – dashboards, reports etc.
- communications.

Mobilisation event(s)

What is it?

Also known as a 'kick-off' event, this is usually the first face-to-face communication event of the project. Its purpose is to unite the project community and to share the objectives, roadmap and challenge ahead. A mobilisation event is hugely symbolic – effectively launching the project and welcoming people into the project team.

Why do it?

A mobilisation event has several benefits:

▌ it provides momentum to the project

▌ it introduces project team members to each other

▌ it raises awareness of the project in the business

▌ it creates a common level of understanding about the project.

When to do it

Diagnose phase (usually within the first two weeks of the project life cycle).

How to do it

Step 1: Appoint an event manager (often the change manager)

Designing and delivering a mobilisation event can be a huge task and potentially involve tens or hundreds of people from the business. Approaching this as a project in itself will ensure the necessary co-ordination of activities and delivery on time and to budget. Early activities for this person or team will be as follows.

- Draw up a list of expected attendees.
- Establish the budget available for the event.
- Schedule a date and time and book venue (including refreshments, facilities etc.).
- Identify and involve key resources like the communication and PR departments.
- Define the first communication tools (e.g. intranet site, newsletter, e-mail) where details of the event can be found.

Step 2: Determine event objectives

The event manager will need to consult the project leadership to understand what the objectives and communication priorities are for the event, such as what topics should be covered. They will also need to manage the inevitable trade-off negotiations about what is nice to have and what is achievable.

Step 3: Design the event

A mobilisation event typically covers some or all of the following:

- an exercise to encourage participation (e.g. an ice-breaker or energiser)
- an introduction to the event and an overview agenda
- a sponsor or keynote address ('big picture' view of the project and solution approach)
- project objectives and outline/roadmap
- project roles and responsibilities
- project work stream presentations: who we are and what we do
- key questions and challenges for the project
- next steps after the event.

Step 4: Design the agenda

The next stage is to create a running order for the event sessions which follows a natural flow, either chronologically or taking account of information dependencies between topics.

For each session the event manager will need to determine the style or nature of the session (e.g. plenary presentation, tradeshow, workshop, small group exercise), the time needed or available to deliver the session, materials and facilities required, and who will be accountable for delivering each session.

Step 5: Create master materials pack

The event manager needs to have copies of all the materials collated into a single source or pack several days before the event. Small changes may be acceptable up until the day before, and so version control becomes very important. Project branding of the slides and additional formatting can be minimised by issuing templates in advance.

Step 6: Set up and run the event

The event team should arrange access to the venue for several hours before the event to make sure that tables and chairs are arranged properly and any posters or tradeshow materials are put up on the walls. Finally, make sure name badges are available for everyone and registration procedures are understood (e.g. checking off names from a list, handing out information packs) and the event team briefed on their roles.

Terms of reference

What is it?

Terms of reference (ToR) is the governance equivalent of roles and responsibilities, the difference being that it is applied to a body of people with a specific function instead of individuals. In many cases, this group is a steering committee, project board or change network. As well as defining the key responsibilities of the group, terms of reference establishes the group's operating parameters and relationship with other areas of the project. It is usually a short document or presentation.

Why do it?

Terms of reference defines the scope of the group and sets expectations about what the group actually does and its level of authority or position within the project.

When to do it

Design phase.

How to do it

The project governance structure is usually agreed and in place when the change manager comes on board. However, the terms of reference may not be explicit – especially in relation to authorisations or escalations from the change team – and after you have identified the required change governance you will need to establish the ToR for each of those groups.

Download template: *Example Terms of Reference Presentation*

Change leader profile

What is it?

Identifying change leaders, determining their roles and getting them on board is an early activity that sets up the conditions for the change success. These are the local sponsors of change – the line managers that people look to immediately when wondering whether or not to take a change seriously.

Why do it?

Identifying and aligning your change leaders to be as committed as your sponsor may be the most critical activity you can do to ensure successful change. A change leader has many of the same attributes and skills as a change manager, and has the tough task of making it work locally.

When to do it

Design phase.

How to do it

Step 1: Compile a list of candidates

There are varying levels of sponsorship in an organisation – while there is only one executive sponsor, there will be lots of change leaders (or 'local sponsors') who act as the sponsor's voice, speaking directly to employees. It is important to identify those people as well, as they will form the backbone to drive change through all the levels in a particular area.

Using your project sponsorship map with your sponsor, look at all the influencers or relationship 'hubs' and identify all the potential change leaders.

Step 2: Assess their suitability

Once you are aware of all the potential change leaders, assess each person against the following checklist. What does this person know about their role in the change, and how willing will they be to take on the following tasks to ensure success?

Change leader role checklist

- Build and secure local approval for the overall case for change, desired outcomes and change strategy.
- Identify and shape the initiatives required to fulfil the overall effort, including organisational, cultural and stakeholder initiatives.
- Input to the conditions for success and ensure their creation.
- Influence the design of essential change activities.
- Procure adequate resources for every phase of the change process and all major initiatives.
- Ensure successful alignment and integration of all change initiatives.
- Drive the change within individual lines of business or interface with the appropriate executives to do so.

- Direct and guide communications; communicate regularly about the change.
- Ensure and oversee a course correcting the project's outcomes, strategy and process.
- Build the capacity and skill of both managers and employees to succeed in future changes by ensuring that learning and development occurs throughout.
- Identify measurements and oversee the ongoing evaluation of benefits realisation.
- Ensure that the participation strategies selected are used effectively to mobilise support for the change.
- Mitigate key political pressures.
- Undergo changes in mindset and behaviour, and role model these changes for the organisation.

(Ackerman-Anderson and Anderson, 2002)

Step 3: Agree participation level/availability

Once the candidates have been identified and you have done an early assessment, plan to meet one to one with each person. Spend around 30 minutes describing what the change is about, why you are there speaking to the candidate about their role in leading change, and what will be required.

Think ahead as to what type of documentation you would like to bring to that meeting. It may include:

- project charter or initiation document
- change management strategy
- change plan
- change leader role description.

Agree the level of commitment and participation with each change leader and begin planning when and where this person will need to be involved. If possible, plan dates such as for kick-off workshops and steering group meetings and get these into their diaries.

Step 4: Evaluate effectiveness of change leaders regularly

Maintaining change leader commitment, and regularly revisiting roles and responsibilities, will contribute hugely to overall benefits realisation. Remember, a project should be designed by the business for the business, and change leaders will own this work once it transitions to 'business as usual'.

Review the change leaders in conjunction with your sponsorship map on a regular basis to ensure buy-in, understanding, commitment and alignment at critical stages of the project. If a change leader defaults on their responsibilities or leaves the organisation, you must recognise and address this immediately.

Change agent profile

What is it?

Change agents are the equivalent of employee representatives whose specific function is to champion the change in the business, and to act as the projects 'eyes and ears' by reporting back concerns and issues raised by employees. In large scale or decentralised change, change agents are essential to stakeholder management and can also be the group of people responsible for implementing the change in their department or business unit.

Why do it?

Effective change agents are essential to the success of any change implementation, which is why selection and development of change agents is often a CSF in the charter and project plan.

When to do it

Design or start of the develop phases.

How to do it

Step 1: Compile a list of candidates

You and your change sponsor should determine whether this will be an application process (job posting) or if potential candidates will be identified by the project board or steering committee. Once you have a list of possible candidates, you will need to assess their fitness for the role.

Step 2: Assess their suitability

Using the change agent profile (see Figure 7.1), assess each candidate against the criteria for experience and skills. Assessment against the other criteria – characteristics and activities – may be difficult but you can do this jointly with a representative from HR or through interviews with the candidates.

Download template: *Change Agent Profile and Assessment*

Step 3: Agree participation level/availability

Once the preferred candidates have been selected, their availability will need to be agreed with their line manager and the local change leader. You will need to be clear by this point how much time (i.e. hours per week) the change project will require. It is unlikely that this will be more than 1–2 days per week. You should also ensure that the prospective change agents are briefed regarding the activities of the role and development and that their personal KPIs or performance management targets will reflect their new responsibilities.

Change team roles and responsibilities

What is it?

Determining change team roles and responsibilities will help define what activities, skills, levels of effort and the number of resources required on the change team. You are essentially completing a small organisational design exercise, and the work will yield the best people/skill mix to execute the change plan.

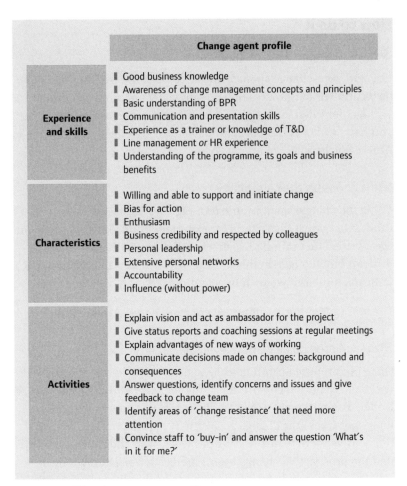

	Change agent profile
Experience and skills	∎ Good business knowledge ∎ Awareness of change management concepts and principles ∎ Basic understanding of BPR ∎ Communication and presentation skills ∎ Experience as a trainer or knowledge of T&D ∎ Line management *or* HR experience ∎ Understanding of the programme, its goals and business benefits
Characteristics	∎ Willing and able to support and initiate change ∎ Bias for action ∎ Enthusiasm ∎ Business credibility and respected by colleagues ∎ Personal leadership ∎ Extensive personal networks ∎ Accountability ∎ Influence (without power)
Activities	∎ Explain vision and act as ambassador for the project ∎ Give status reports and coaching sessions at regular meetings ∎ Explain advantages of new ways of working ∎ Communicate decisions made on changes: background and consequences ∎ Answer questions, identify concerns and issues and give feedback to change team ∎ Identify areas of 'change resistance' that need more attention ∎ Convince staff to 'buy-in' and answer the question 'What's in it for me?'

FIGURE 7.1 The change agent profile

Why do it?

Clear roles and responsibilities will help direct the change team resources to complete the work effectively. It will also allow the team members to understand interdependencies between each other and other project streams, and how their roles will contribute to the overall realised benefits of the change.

When to do it

Design phase.

How to do it

Step 1: Compile a list of activities, processes or milestones that are in the change plan

Drawing from the change plan, list all the activities, processes or milestones that will need to be completed over the course of the project.

Step 2: Identify the level of resource and effort needed for each activity (time and duration)

Complete a very rough estimate of the amount of time a particular activity will take, and the overall duration. For example, in a communications audit:

▌ the time would be three hours, and

▌ the duration would be four days.

This will help you see where you can begin to combine groups of activities to make up one full-time equivalent role, or where there will be peaks and troughs in the overall work that will need to be managed. If you have already completed a resource plan as part of your change plan, you can copy and paste that information here.

Step 3: Determine what kind of skills are needed to complete the activities

Typical skills and abilities of change teams are:

▌ understanding of project management

▌ understanding of process design and mapping

▌ capable of building relationships at all levels

▌ workshop design and facilitation skills

▌ knowledge of human dynamics and change management

■ research and analysis skills

■ excellent communication skills – both written and verbal

■ training design and delivery skills

■ HR process and job definition skills

■ understanding of culture and organisational behaviour.

Begin to cluster the skills next to the activities and resource levels, and watch for any trends that are emerging. For example, are there many activities that require communication skills, but only some that require project management? Are all the research and analysis activities loaded at the front end of the plan, with training at the back end?

Step 4: Consolidate the activities, effort required and skills into role descriptions

From this step, what will emerge is a headcount required for the change team and the kind of resources you will need to find. Here are some *rough* estimates from our experience, to help guide you (they are in addition to the change manager):

■ small-scale/scope change under 6 months – 1–2 full-time, with room to add on 0.5 full-time equivalent (FTE) as the implementation dates approach

■ medium-scale/scope change, 6–9 months – 2–4 full-time

■ medium- to large-scale/scope change, 9+ months – 3–4 full-time

■ large-scale/scope change, 9+ months – 5 or more full-time.

As an example, one of the largest change programme we have ever worked on was 18 months long, with medium to large scope and large scale, involving 100,000+ employees. There was a change team of over 20 FTE in place, with 8 streams of activity and deliverables.

As you construct the role descriptions, you may wish to add some generic change team responsibilities such as:

■ fulfilment of the deliverables of each major phase of the change plan, for one or more initiatives and/or products

❚ continuously gather new information about the change that may influence how it rolls out, and contributes to risks and issues

❚ being a role model of the values, behaviour and cultural changes required for a successful change.

Step 5: Agree change team roles and responsibilities with the project manager

You may need to work within budgetary and skill constraints, which will require some negotiation on what makes up the change team roles and responsibilities. Once you and the project manager have agreed on the final count and requirements (escalate to the change sponsor if needed), you will then begin to look for candidates, conduct interviews and fill the roles.

Step 6: On-board the change team

Once you have your people resources in place, you will need to on-board them and build them into a team. Refer to Chapter 14 for more information on this. You may want to spend time on activities such as reviewing the on-boarding pack, performing a team RACI exercise, and constructing a team charter and meeting schedule.

Programme team development plan

What is it?

Programme team development (this can also be applied to project, change or any team) enables a programme team to focus on the key elements that accelerate development into a high-performance team (HPT) and meet its objectives. All teams go through a development curve during their life cycle (forming, storming, norming and performing). The team has a choice of either going with the flow of this change and reacting to it or managing its way as quickly as possible through the unproductive times so that it is able to deliver as efficiently and effectively as possible.

The high-performance team (Katzenbach and Smith, 1994) framework was developed and applied by consultants operating in the mid- to late eighties and was the result of a large amount of statistical analysis observing how teams work and develop. The four orbits represent the areas within which a high-performance team operates: relationship, knowledge, ownership and discipline (see Figure 7.2). The intersecting lines signify areas of overlap between the areas. The whole effort and energy of the team focuses on delivering a common challenge, for example, the programme.

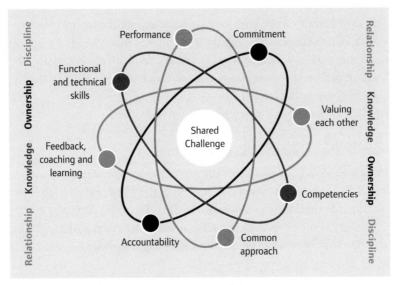

FIGURE 7.2 A high-performance team model

Why do it?

This provides structure for the learning and development activities the programme team need to concentrate on, and a checklist for the review and measurement of team performance. It creates ownership within the programme team for its own performance and a mutual trust that resolution of dependencies and issues will provide the best programme outcome.

When to do it

Design phase.

How to do it

Step 1: Determine where the team is starting from

In a meeting with your team, ask yourselves the following questions.

▌ Is our team newly formed, well-established or with new team members? (The team development cycle starts again when new members join a team, although if team norms are established, the development curve tends to be faster.)

▌ What stage do you think the team has reached:

  − forming: getting to know each other in different settings, building confidence

  − storming: members bargain with each other as they try to sort out what each of them individually and as a group want out of the process

  − norming: the group develops a way of working to achieve its objectives

  − performing: a fully mature group has now been created which can get on with its work.

▌ Does the team have a clear focus and plan yet?

▌ How close a team do you need to develop? Being a high-performing team may not be necessary.

You need to answer the basic demands of each stage in team development in order for the team to move on, meaning you can skip stages but some may take a shorter amount of time to pass through than others.

Step 2: Select the approach that will work best with the team

Learning styles or preferences of the team should be discussed and taken into account when building a development plan. For example, will the team respond best to theory or to practical application? Should we use the HPT model explicitly or not? Teams may be stronger in one segment than in others so work on the areas where you sense the team needs development. This is intuitive so trust your judgement. Also, get the team to think about and decide:

▌ how often the team will meet

▌ whether there are activities you can do as a team outside of the meetings/programme

▌ tools and techniques that can be used (e.g. Belbin team roles or MBTI) as a means of sharing strengths, weaknesses and preferences.

Plan for team members to start taking more initiative as the team develops so the leadership is shared among the members.

Step 3: Focus on development through addressing business needs

It is a common mistake to separate 'teambuilding' from how the team operates in the business environment. The activities need to blend work-related topics and team-building activity. The best way to build strong teams is to help them find their common focus. This can be done through a targeted discussion, production of a team charter or definition of team responsibility areas. For team development to be successful, the following criteria are essential:

▌ clearly defined and agreed goals within the team and with key stakeholders

▌ clearly defined roles and responsibilities

▌ common ways of working (e.g. operating procedures and internal processes)

▌ communication structure – both internal and external.

Step 4: Build and agree the team development plan

The team development plan will reflect the programme plan by defining the skills and capabilities necessary for delivery. Programme team development should cover core skills like leadership, communications, good meeting practice, facilitation and presentation skills, and also technical training in specific programme areas such as change management, programme management, systems overviews and process mapping. An example team development plan for a supply chain team (SCT) is shown opposite.

Objectives	To launch the team and build team working	To develop the team plan and accountabilities	To consolidate team processes and begin to build the SCT network	To build up SCT as a supporting network who share a common vision of ISCM	Does the team have the right skills and feel they are getting something out of it?	To see where we have got to as a team and learn a bit about the business
Tools	Performance challenge Ground rules Charter Shield exercise Openness exercise	PDR RACI Knowledge capture	Performance measures Share functional background Team temperature check	Team effectiveness Establish buddies 1:1 Share knowledge of ISCM model – apply to their SC	Agree SCT capability model and action plan to move forward	
Timing	Mtg 1	Mtg 2	Mtg 3	Mtg 4	Mtg 5	Mtg 6
Activities	■ Create performance challenge and charter ■ Establish ground rules ■ Agree mutual expectations of SCM, the facilitator and the team ■ Build relationships by sharing information ■ Agree the format and sequence of future team meetings	■ Develop PDR streams and key milestones ■ Agree team RACI ■ Set-up team knowledge capture process	■ PDR review ■ Team temperature check ■ Discussion of performance measures and establish a dashboard ■ Share the team's background: – Activities my dept does for SCM – Activities my dept does well for SCM – Activities my dept does badly for SCM – Opportunities for change	■ Team effectiveness assessment – agree the level and action plan to move forward ■ Create a SCT network of contacts and establish the concept of buddies and touching base outside meetings ■ 1:1 session to share successes and concerns for SCT ■ Set up process for 360 degree feedback	■ Identify what the roles are within the SCT and understand what the capabilities required are: – general SCT member – range management – stock management – facilitator	■ Review charter and RACI ■ Celebrate success ■ Visit to the customer
How the team feels	*I understand why we need to be a team and am beginning to get to know the team members*	*I understand what activities the team will undertake and what I am accountable for*	*I understand how the team operates. I know about the different backgrounds in the team and what they can offer to the team*	*I get help and support from being in a team and I understand our common goal*	*I understand my role in the team and where I have opportunities to grow*	*We have done lots of stuff as a team and we have a clear focus on what to do next*

It is good practice to review the progress of team development (i.e. against the HPT model) with a team temperature check and as a standing agenda item at regular meetings.

Download template: *Programme Team Development Plan*

Also recommended: 'The Really Fiendish Teambuilding Game' available from http://www. uncommonexpertise.co.uk

Change network development plan

What is it?

A change network is the group of identified change leaders and agents throughout the business who may be resourced part-time as part of the project. The change network development plan outlines the required change management skills for the change leader and agent roles and indicates training needs in the tools and techniques defined in the change plan. It is a mechanism to ensure that the capabilities exist in the change network to carry out activities necessary for the delivery of the change plan and deliverables.

Why do it?

A shortfall or mismatch of skills may impact the critical path of the project negatively, incurring time delays or additional costs. Unprepared change networks are impotent and this may create a perception that is damaging to the credibility of the change team and project.

When to do it

Develop phase.

How to do it

Step 1: Assess change network requirements

Review the draft change plan and extract a list of key activities and deliverables for the change network with their planned start and completion dates. In anticipation of each activity start date, add in change network training events which must be completed at least one to two days before the activity begins. As a rule of thumb, do not deliver training to change leaders and agents more than one week prior to the activity as without practical application, understanding and skills will degenerate.

Step 2: Assess the capability gap

For each change stream activity, you will need to assess how much involvement from the change network will be required. This will be any of the following:

▌ information – need to understand what is going on so that members can communicate with and answer questions from colleagues

▌ consultation – need to understand the activities, give input or comment to ensure the activity is effective with employees

▌ deployment – need to be able to conduct or run activities under the coordination of the change team (e.g. workshops, focus groups, interviews)

▌ network development – need to be able to explain, train and conduct the efforts of others (e.g. advocates or other agents).

You should conduct a briefing meeting with the entire change network to share with members the range of activities they will be involved in and the project expectations of their roles and responsibilities for those activities. As you discuss each activity, you should capture the level of awareness, ability and experience within the group and within key individuals, to assess training needs. For example:

▌ 0 = never heard of it or don't know what it is

▌ 1 = heard of it but never used it

▌ 2 = seen the activity or participated in one before

▌ 3 = have used the activity as a practitioner

▌ 4 = have used the activity and am able to train others.

This can simply be by a show of hands. Capture this information in a simple spreadsheet for your reference:

Activity	Capability/tool/ technique	Change agent involvement (I/C/D/N)	Baseline capability (scale of 0 to 4)
Change readiness assessment	CRA survey CRA workshops	C (consultation) D (deployment)	0 = 2 people 1 = 5 people 2 = 1 person
Stakeholder map	Stakeholder workshop	C (consultation)	1 = 3 people 2 = 4 people 4 = 1 person

Step 3: Draw up a schedule of change agent and change network training events

You may need to work within the confines of your resource agreement with the change agents' line managers or negotiate extra time for the training sessions. It is a good idea to try and book a regular half-day, like every Tuesday from 1–4.30pm or every other Wednesday for a set period, to minimise the impact on the business and to ensure the change network members are all available. If there is no training scheduled, the sessions can usefully be converted into meeting or Q&A time to resolve particular issues or concerns.

Once you have developed your schedule you should validate this with the change sponsor and the change network.

Step 4: Create capability development training materials

If you do not have access to an existing toolkit, you will need to create your own materials. As a starting point, you can adapt the 'step-by-step' guides in this book and use or share the templates downloaded from the website. For each event, you should plan on a face-to-face presentation or workshop-style event to include a worked example and, if appropriate, an opportunity to practise the activities in a risk-free environment.

Step 5: Conduct a feedback loop to assess learning

At the conclusion of each session, conduct a brief feedback session to make sure the participants are confident that they have the desired level of understanding and are confident in the role they must perform in relation to the specified activity.

Stakeholders and communication

Change prism lens	Step-by-step guides
Stakeholders and communication	Stakeholder analysis and map
	Stakeholder management plan
	Stakeholder review process
	Communications strategy
	Communications audit
	Communications plan and roadmap
	Downloadable templates
	Stakeholder Identification and Analysis
	Stakeholder Needs and Issues
	Stakeholder Commitment Matrix
	Stakeholder Map
	Stakeholder Review Meeting Output Capture
	Communications Strategy
	Communications Audit Questionnaire
	Communications Audit Report
	Communications Matrix
	Communications Roadmap

Stakeholder analysis and map

What is it?

STAKEHOLDERS ARE INDIVIDUALS OR GROUPS whose commitment is required for successful implementation of a change. Individual stakeholders can include sponsors and other senior leaders, opinion leaders, middle management, employees, customers, suppliers, partners, etc. Stakeholder groups can include leadership teams, departments, functions, the project's steering committee, etc.

A high-level stakeholder map is a visual tool to show where stakeholder groups sit relative to each other in terms of influence and commitment to the project. A stakeholder map provides a snapshot of the 'as-is' level of commitment compared with the level required for successful benefits realisation. A stakeholder analysis and map should be a confidential document.

Why do it?

A stakeholder analysis and map is an assessment of the current commitment of influential individuals and groups impacted by the project – a 'finger on the pulse' during the project stages. The positioning of stakeholder groups on the map provides an indication as to the level of stakeholder management required, which will inform project resource planning.

When to do it

Design phase (although a stakeholder analysis should be revised as critical aspects or stages of the project change).

How to do it

Step 1: Identification and briefing of workshop participants

Workshop participants should have a good knowledge of the overall business as well as their own business area. Usually this is reflected in terms of years of service and seniority in the organisation. If you have already identified your change network, this is an ideal group to perform this activity. The workshop participants should be given a briefing in the week preceding the workshop. The briefing should cover: workshop format and ground rules; a description of stakeholder analysis and management; project goals and objectives; workshop logistics such as workshop date, start and end times, and location.

Step 2: Plan the workshop and set the agenda

A facilitated discussion captures the perceived range of changes expected from the project implementation and other future threats and opportunities. This discussion focuses the participants on the activity, creating necessary thinking space away from their day-to-day duties.

Our experience has shown that using poster-size templates around the workshop room creates structure and focus for the stakeholder exercises and provides a visual pathway and direction for the activity. Other benefits of this structured approach include:

▌ participant attention focused on the outputs and delivery of the analysis

▌ 'real time' completion of the analysis

▌ an excellent snapshot of the work done and left to complete at any time

▌ easy electronic capture of the contributions post-workshop.

An example of a stakeholder analysis workshop agenda and plan is as follows:

Session name	Purpose/objectives
Introduction and objectives	Set context, scope and purpose for workshop
Stakeholder identification and prioritisation	Generate and capture list of all key stakeholders and discuss any relationships and dependencies relating to the project. Group and select most important stakeholders in terms of their criticality in making the project successful
Stakeholder assessment	Identify critical stakeholder characteristics that may impact the project. Complete identification and analysis template
Stakeholder needs and issues	Identify implications/needs and issues for each of the stakeholders
Stakeholder commitment	Identify current and desired levels of commitment for prioritised stakeholders
Stakeholder mapping	Prioritise again in terms of gaps and position on matrix (influence and commitment)

Step 3: Conduct the workshop

The stakeholder identification and prioritisation session should ensure that all the required stakeholder information is captured. An easy way to this is to provide a simple template for participants to use or follow. A copy of the template is shown below:

Stakeholder name or group	
Description	No. of people

An effective tool to capture this information is Post-it® notes, which are then stuck onto brown paper. The remaining sessions (shown in step 2) should focus on the completion of the workshop using the templates provided.

Download templates: *Stakeholder Identification and Analysis; Stakeholder Needs and Issues; Stakeholder Commitment Matrix; Stakeholder Map*

Stakeholder management plan

What is it?

Stakeholder management is the process of addressing stakeholders' needs and responsibilities through appropriate communication channels to deliver timely, relevant and useful messages that will positively influence behaviour. The stakeholder management cycle is shown in Figure 8.1. One hundred per cent of organisations rate good communications as a key success factor in implementing change and 34 per cent of organisations rate poor communication as the key barrier to implementing change successfully.

Why do it?

When stakeholder management is well implemented and monitored, it increases the chance of project success because problems can be anticipated and actions taken. It also enables the project team to make qualified decisions in regard to different stakeholders based on the analysis data. Motivation and understanding of the change in the business increases because people's needs are addressed and they feel a sense of responsibility for making the change work. Resistance can be reduced because specific stakeholder management strategies address specific problems.

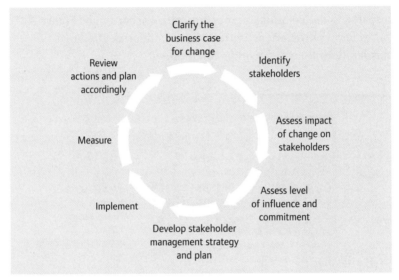

FIGURE 8.1 The stakeholder management cycle

When to do it

Develop phase.

How to do it

Step 1: Review stakeholder analysis and map

The difference between the current and future positioning of groups on the stakeholder map indicates the extent to which communications, change management interventions and training may be needed. Even where current and future positions are unchanged, a level of maintenance regarding communications and change management is required, equal to or greater to their treatment so far, to keep them operating at the required level.

Step 2: Define approach for stakeholder groups

Experience and best practice stakeholder management suggest approaches to stakeholder management are based on stakeholders' relative positioning. In other words, not all stakeholders are created equal – some are more important than others. It is important that distinctions are made regarding different approaches for stakeholder groups as each approach may require a level of resource to deliver and you must prioritise accordingly. Figure 8.2 below shows different activities you can undertake to move stakeholders along the road to commitment.

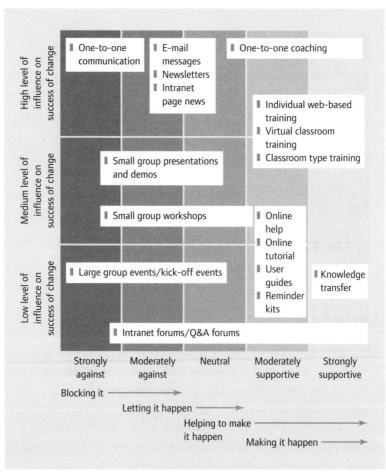

FIGURE 8.2 Stakeholder management activities

Moving from one level of commitment to the next requires a greater investment of time and resources the higher you go up the commitment scale. That means it is harder to move a 'moderate supporter' into a 'strong supporter' than it is to move a 'neutral' into a 'moderate supporter', even though it is only a single rating in both cases.

Step 3: Recommendations workshop for specific activities to close the gap

A workshop to validate approaches identified in step 2 and to discuss current and desired stakeholder communications and activities should be conducted. This can be done with the same group who performed the stakeholder analysis (e.g. change network) as a follow-up workshop (see Figure 8.3 as an example).

Step 4: Establish ownership and progress tracking

An owner for each stakeholder group should be identified to co-ordinate contacts and communications with that group. The owner will work with their stakeholders to understand their requirements in more detail and propose new or additional activities to increase their involvement and buy-in. The owner will also provide feedback and updates on the progress of the stakeholder group during stakeholder review meetings. Ensure as change manager that this activity links in with the roles and responsibilities of the change team.

Stakeholder review process

What is it?

The stakeholder review process is the mechanism to share and update the stakeholder analysis and management plans, review progress and define appropriate activities or involvement for the next stage or phase of the project. This should be carried out as a dedicated meeting with the stakeholder group owners and change team or project team. Review meetings should be included in the change plan as deliverables. Reviews should be conducted regularly or scheduled to coincide with a new project phase.

Stakeholder(s)/ group	Strongly against −2	Moderately against −1	Neutral 0	Moderately supportive +1	Strongly supportive/ advocates +2	Suggested approach to close gap
Staff groups – direct		As-is		To-be		Encourage staff to look at intranet or newsletter; regular updates at team briefs; group talks; classroom 1-to-1 training
Staff groups – indirect		As-is	To-be			Classroom/group training; regular updates at team briefs; encourage staff to look at intranet and newsletter
Unions	As-is	To-be				Maintain current communications levels and monthly meetings, etc.
Corporate communications			As-is	To-be		Maintain current communications levels and regular change team meetings
Heads of department				As-is	To-be	Identify quick wins; tradeshows/group demos popular; present to HoD meetings; more specific information
Directors			As-is	To-be		Maintain current levels of info/comms; more specific info tailored to individuals

FIGURE 8.3 Example of a stakeholder management approach

Why do it?

A stakeholder review coordinates the efforts and resources within the project and ensures everyone in contact with stakeholders understands what is going on with that group. Stakeholders will feel they are being dealt with in a joined-up and professional way and will minimise any incidences of duplication and frustration.

When to do it

Deliver phase.

How to do it

Step 1: Establish roles and responsibilities

As well as the stakeholder owner (change team/network member) each of the project work streams should identify a single point of contact (SPOC) for stakeholder management. This person will be responsible for identifying interactions with stakeholders, capturing issues and needs specific to their project/stream and scheduling future interactions. They will also be required to review their project plans regarding key communication and involvement milestones and activities, and feeding back risks or issues these may cause.

Step 2: Brief the stakeholder review team

After identifying roles and setting responsibilities, you will need to brief the review team members on the review process and agree a schedule for the review meetings. A typical stakeholder review process is shown in Figure 8.4.

Step 3: Stakeholder review meetings

Owners and SPOCs will participate and provide updates to the regular stakeholder review meetings. After each meeting, they will be responsible for revisions to stakeholder action plans, tracking activities and responses/outcomes, and liaising with stakeholder owners regarding needs and issues.

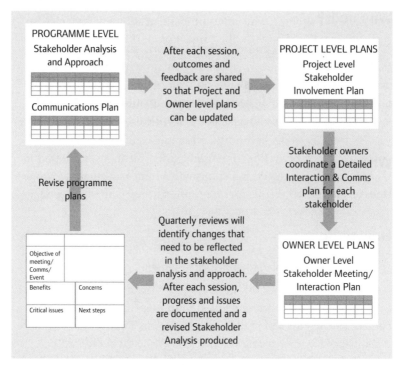

FIGURE 8.4 A stakeholder review process

Step 4: Share stakeholder review with communications and training teams

As stakeholders are shared across work streams, you should update all others on the project who will need the current information, such as the communications and training teams.

Download template: *Stakeholder Review Meeting Output Capture*

Communications strategy

What is it?

A communications strategy is the overall approach for setting up and executing change or project specific communication. It should be based on the first results of the assessment activities, the stakeholder analysis, and the results of the future state and scoping activities, and should support the objectives defined in the change management strategy. The communications strategy must also be linked to, and evolve with, the project plan. If it is not, the project cannot prepare people or deal with anticipated reactions.

A communications strategy covers all formal communication activities involving the business areas and employees affected by the project. It should include, for all identified stakeholder groups, the key messages, the communication means and channels, communication activities, timeframe and milestones, specified in a communications matrix. It also provides information about project roles and responsibilities for communications, which may be part of or complementary to the change team.

Why do it?

Communication is critical to prepare stakeholders – to inform, educate, motivate and call them to action. Communication is an area which can add value to a project by increasing or maintaining the speed at which change is implemented and the associated benefits realisation. Research shows that 70 per cent of change projects fail due to ineffective communication.

When to do it

Design phase.

How to do it

Step 1: Communications objectives and approach

Communications objectives should be enablers for and reflect the project and change objectives. Generally communications objectives include some or all of the following:

- ensure everyone affected by the project is aware of and understands the goals of the project
- create a desire and urgency for change among all stakeholder groups
- increase confidence of stakeholders and employees to embrace changes

▌ co-ordinate with the communication activities of other projects and business initiatives

▌ enable feedback from employees regarding concerns, issues and risks.

The communications approach should be based on what the project needs to achieve at each phase. The aim is to move people affected by the change to a stage of commitment or acceptance by providing timely and targeted information to build understanding. The commitment curve in Chapter 3 illustrates the journey of supporting the employee through the period of change.

If you are struggling with buy-in for a communications strategy at the project or sponsor level, you should try to relate examples of previous change or communication failure to emphasise the need for a sustained approach – for example:

> According to the stakeholders we spoke to, our organisation is effective at managing the employee to the 'I know what the change is' point, but then the cycle is broken and employees feel that they have been left in the dark until the project is completed – a perception clearly expressed in the results of the employee survey.

Step 2: Audience size and segmentation

There are a number of distinct audiences for communications and different things will be required for each of the audiences during the project phases. To identify different audience groups, you will need to review the stakeholder analysis and management plan. Depending on the number of different groups, you can further segment them based on geography or business unit, programme or organisational role, the commonality of stakeholder approach, or common needs and issues. You should be aware that the composition of your audience segments may change during the project, and these should be discussed as part of a stakeholder review meeting.

There may be a number of groups which need communications that require specialist knowledge or skills. These groups might include governance or compliance bodies, other programmes, trade unions and employee representatives, HR and public relations.

Step 3: Messages and channels

The holy grail of communications is getting the right messages to the right stakeholders when and in the format they need them. Communications messages will need to be developed for each audience group according to where they are in the stakeholder plan. Getting the messages right requires not only an understanding of the project and overall strategic plans but also an understanding of the concerns and issues of each audience group. Early phase messages to all levels of the target audience must introduce the project and its place within the wider business strategy. Later communications will need to discuss progress, future actions and how issues are being addressed. The messages will differ in degree of detail and emphasis depending on the specific audience segment for which it is designed. An important source of messages will be provided by feedback from the target audiences. Some generic messages will be appropriate for all audience groups and the table overleaf gives some examples of the generic messages you may need to give in each phase.

To determine which communications channels to use for each audience, you should refer to the communications audit findings and the stakeholder analysis. There are three main categories of communications channel:

1. face-to-face
   - mobilisation event
   - 'drop-in' surgeries
   - road shows
   - regular cascade briefings
   - workshops focus groups
   - model office and pilot groups
   - presentations
   - interview-based questionnaire
   - counselling

	Diagnosis	Design	Development	Delivery
Messages	▊ Description of the programme ▊ Overall scope ▊ Sponsorship ▊ Key stakeholders ▊ Why programme is needed ▊ Project vision ▊ Strategic context for the project ▊ Fit with broader company strategy ▊ Programme structure ▊ Fit with other initiatives ▊ Confirmation of key issues ▊ Development of solutions	▊ Sponsorship messages for each business area ▊ Key issues and how they are being addressed ▊ Begin to set expectations ▊ Explain the likely consequences of changes ▊ Clear objectives and roles ▊ Roles, responsibilities and outcomes	▊ Awareness workshops ▊ Progress and developments ▊ Timescales for implementation ▊ How changes will affect roles and structure ▊ Impact on individuals ▊ Required new ways of working ▊ Transition management awareness ▊ Provide training and tools to support teams in the business ▊ Explain what is in it for me ▊ Provide clear and robust HR/personnel communications	▊ Overall transition strategy ▊ Detailed transition plan ▊ Progress and developments ▊ How new solution works ▊ How to use the new system/process ▊ How to get more help and support ▊ How to deal with specific issues ▊ Systems or process training ▊ Confirmation of new roles for individuals (where appropriate) ▊ Transition tasks ▊ Cutover process ▊ Clarification of roles during cutover ▊ Agreement on cutover

2 paper-based

 – newsletters

 – bulletin boards

 – survey/questionnaire

 – article in the organisation's magazine

 – instruction booklet

- pamphlet
- job aids
- suggestion box

3 technology-based

- pre-recorded video
- e-mail/internal mail
- websites (intranet and internet)
- meetings or virtual conferences.

Step 4: Communications development process

As well as the objectives, approach, audience, message, timing and channels, you will need to define how this will all fit together and work in practice. What you should be aiming for in this section of the strategy is to outline your *modus operandi*. It should explain the process you will go through to develop project communications which will help other project team members understand how and when in the process they may be directly involved. A proven communications process is shown in Figure 8.5.

Step 5: Resources, roles and responsibilities

Once the communications strategy has been defined, you will need to determine the roles and resources necessary for required communications activities. You will also need to indicate responsibility for the success of change-specific communication, which sits at three levels.

Level 1: *Change sponsor*
The first level relates to the overall responsibility for ensuring that the comprehensive plan is supported, understood and implemented. This role lies with the change sponsor, who provides high-level guidance related to communications messages, with particular focus on strategic and organisational messages.

Level 2: *Change team*
The second level of responsibility is for the ongoing planning, development and implementation of specific communications activities. This role sits with the change team but must be supported by the project managers, team leaders and other members of the project team. As the project progresses, particularly

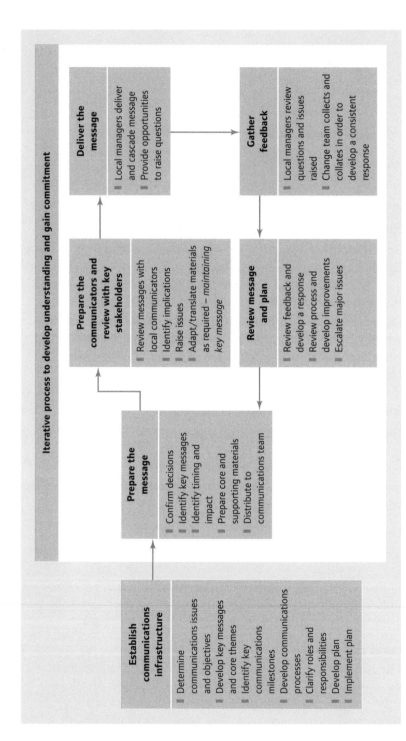

Iterative process to develop understanding and gain commitment

Establish communications infrastructure

- Determine communications issues and objectives
- Develop key messages and core themes
- Identify key communications milestones
- Develop communications processes
- Clarify roles and responsibilities
- Develop plan
- Implement plan

Prepare the message

- Confirm decisions
- Identify key messages
- Identify timing and impact
- Prepare core and supporting materials
- Distribute to communications team

Prepare the communicators and review with key stakeholders

- Review messages with local communicators
- Identify implications
- Raise issues
- Adapt/translate materials as required – *maintaining key message*

Deliver the message

- Local managers deliver and cascade message
- Provide opportunities to raise questions

Gather feedback

- Local managers review questions and issues raised
- Change team collects and collates in order to develop a consistent response

Review message and plan

- Review feedback and develop a response
- Review process and develop improvements
- Escalate major issues

FIGURE 8.5 A communications understanding and commitment process

as tactical and organisational messages become more important, more project team input will be required.

Level 3: *Change network*
The third, and perhaps most critical, level lies with identified change leaders and agents. They will have important responsibilities in sharing and gathering perceptions about the project. These are the people who will be dealing with staff impacted by the project on a daily basis. With the assistance of the project team, they must provide a constant flow of communication both to and from the employees/stakeholders.

Step 6: Assessment

In this section you will need to define what constitutes effective communication and what successful communications will look like. Based on that understanding, you should define how the communications effectiveness will be measured, how often and how this will be reported.

Step 7: Assumptions and summary

Once all the previous steps have been completed, you should include a list of your assumptions and dependencies and a management summary.

Download template: *Communications Strategy*

Communications audit

What is it?

A communications audit is a measure of the success of previous and existing communications. The scope of the audit will depend on the scope and scale of the project and covers:

▌ existing communications methods (e.g. intranet, e-mails, newsletters, management and team presentations, message boards) to tailor and target an effective project communications plan

▌ face-to-face communications – quantity, quality and reliability of information

▌ staff attitudes toward existing programme/project
communications.

The results of the communications audit will be used to identify
opportunities for improving project communication and ensuring
key audiences have sufficient knowledge about project activity.

Why do it?

A well-executed communications audit will produce a clear
understanding of how communications are really working and the
degree to which they are satisfying information needs. The results
from the audit will inform the programme about the effectiveness
of existing communication and indicate the best way to get key
messages across to different employee groups. It will enable project
staff to make informed decisions about future communications and
it can act as a benchmark for measuring the effectiveness of future
communications.

When to do it

Design phase.

How to do it

Step 1: Define the audit approach

The communications audit is comprised of a survey and a two to
three hour workshop which can be rerun as often as you need
depending on the range and number of employees you want to
include. The survey explores how existing channels of
communications work within different business areas and job
grades, and the current understanding of the project and
knowledge of project messages.

The workshop will take a forward look at preferred channels of
communication and different needs for project information. It
consists of a review of past communications issued from the

project and attendees are invited to express views on what they find most helpful or memorable.

Step 2: Conduct the survey

The survey can be run prior to the workshop or, more usually, with all the workshop participants assembled. In this instance, the workshop is split into two parts and you will need to reflect this in your introduction. There is a trade-off to be made here as you will have to consider participants' availability and you may need to spend some time on giving clarification or guidance to people who may be doing this activity for the first time.

Download template: *Communications Audit Questionnaire*

Step 3: Review of communications material

You will need to compile examples of communications materials that have been or are being used (e.g. broadcast, e-mails, newsletters, posters, memos, magazines, pod casts). These should be set up around the room for people to look through. At each station, there is a set of questions that are multiple choice or ratings, which each participant needs to respond to:

▌ Do you receive or have you seen this communication before?

▌ How did you receive or where did you find this information?

▌ How regularly do you get this item?

▌ How effective are the distribution channels for this item?

▌ Was this communication timely?

▌ What are the main messages or things you learned from this item?

▌ Is there a feedback mechanism?

▌ What is the general perception of this type of communication?

▌ What do you like and not like about this item?

▌ What suggestions could you make for improvement?

After all the items have been examined, conduct a facilitated discussion to draw out any themes or capture any final comments.

Step 4: Presentation of audit findings

This is a short document or presentation containing a combination of statistical analysis and commentary, recommendations and next steps, and is intended to inform the development of the communications plan.

Download template: *Communications Audit Report*

Communications plan and roadmap

What is it?

A communications plan and roadmap is a framework used to plan, co-ordinate and execute project communication activities. Change-specific communication is one of the most resource-intensive activities in the change management process. When done correctly, a substantial amount of time and thought goes into developing and disseminating the appropriate themes, messages and materials to the organisation's internal and external stakeholders. The communications plan must also address the issue of momentum – to mobilise staff and sustain energy and commitment. Communications planning is not a one-off activity, but a process that unfolds throughout a change project.

A communications roadmap creates a visual picture of the plan and maps activities across the six elements of communication: objectives; audiences; messages; communications channels; feedback mechanisms; and message timing. Figure 8.6 shows an example of a communications roadmap.

Why do it?

A communications plan and roadmap coordinates all elements of communications with stakeholders and ensures that relevant, accurate, and consistent information is provided to the right people in the organisation at the right times.

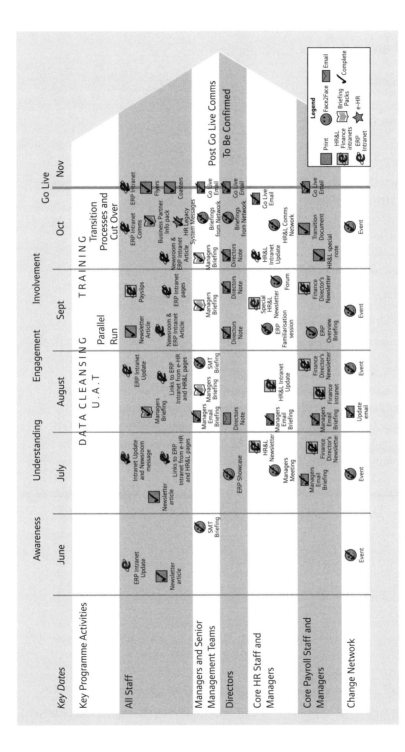

FIGURE 8.6 A communications roadmap

When to do it

Design phase.

How to do it

Step 1: Setting the communications scope

You will need to review the following documents (as a minimum) and extract information relating to the project scope, change objectives and stakeholders:

▌ project plan

▌ scope and scale of change document

▌ stakeholder map and stakeholder management plan

▌ communications audit

▌ communications strategy.

Using information you have identified, you will need to set up a communications matrix and populate it with the project phases, timelines and milestones. You should then add in the audience groupings, stakeholder approach and preferred communications channels. This template will form the basis for the communications planning workshop. Below is an example of a communications matrix.

Audience	Programme phase	Key milestones/ deliverables	Key messages	Approach /channel	Frequency	Communications activities

Download template: *Communications Matrix*

Step 2: Communications planning workshop

You will need to plan and conduct a workshop to capture details about the communications activities needed to implement the communications strategy. Through discussions with the project leadership, you will need to identify appropriate participants and provide them with an overview of the communications scope. In preparation for the planning element of the workshop, you should also describe the current communications vehicles used and provide definitions of audiences and stakeholders.

The planning focus should be on the specific needs of the different stakeholder groups. The workshop should include the following components.

- **Objectives:** the specific objectives to be accomplished as a result of the communications action.
- **Audience:** the specific group or individuals to whom the messages will be sent.
- **Key messages:** the specific messages given through the communication.
- **Channel:** the individual group, vehicle or medium through which the message will be sent to the audience.
- **Frequency:** the timing or date when the activity will take place.

Step 3: Populate communications plan matrix

You can choose to use the communications matrix template to guide and provide focus to the session. The benefit will be that you gather all the information directly into the matrix. However, if you feel this is not appropriate to your style, or may generate resistance or limit full discussion, you can populate the matrix after the event.

Step 4: Create the roadmap

Using the communications matrix information, you should now be able to generate your communications roadmap. It is usual to do this for each phase of the project, although some prefer to have a 'rolling' roadmap that is reviewed and updated every few weeks.

Download template: *Communications Roadmap*

Step 5: Regularly review communications plan

As well as reviewing the delivery and effectiveness of communications in the plan, regular meetings should also discuss any needs for situation-specific communication. The introduction or status of other change projects should be reviewed to identify possible overlap or opportunities for collaboration on communications.

9

Resilience and capacity

Change prism lens	Step-by-step guides
Resilience and capacity	Change impact assessment
	Organisation capacity review
	Resilience assessment
	Capacity mitigation and resilience plan
	Downloadable templates
	CIA Interview Questions
	CIA Workshop Agenda Example
	CIA Report
	Change Resiliency Questionnaire
	Organisation Capacity Review Questions
	Capacity Mitigation and Resilience Plan

Change impact assessment

What is it?

THE CHANGE IMPACT ASSESSMENT (CIA) is basically a gap analysis to understand where the greatest differences are between the future and current state (to-be and as-is) of the organisation and implications of the project on people, processes and technology. This is usually done by comparing current and future process maps. A CIA differentiates, by degrees of impact, which areas of the organisation will experience the most change or disruption. Conducting a CIA will:

■ provide opportunities to engage stakeholders and obtain buy-in from groups involved in the project – including business, technical and functional representatives

■ provide a high-level view across the organisation of impacted areas

■ contribute to the communications plan and identify requirements for tailored communications messages

■ identify areas of risk that will need to be managed and prioritisation of interventions.

The results of the CIA are documented in a brief report outlining the key findings by function and business unit. The report should also include recommendations for potential improvements and suggested actions or interventions. It is good practice to cross-reference a CIA with a change readiness assessment (CRA).

Why do it?

The CIA supports the development of targeted change activities, aimed at minimising and managing potential barriers to change. A CIA adds value to the project, and ultimately the business, by focusing attention on the problem/high-impact areas, so that resources can be deployed effectively and project timelines can be reduced. The tool can be used on an ongoing basis in subsequent project phases as a review and update of the impact to reflect any new issues that may affect implementation.

When to do it

Diagnose phase. If the project is technology-driven, the CIA should be aligned to the requirements and delivery dates of the conference room pilots (CRPs) – usually CRP3. The CIA should be revisited regularly to reflect any course changes in the project.

How to do it

Step 1: Define your approach

There are no hard and fast rules about the best way to conduct a CIA. The mechanism you choose will depend on the scope and scale of the project and the range of stakeholders that need to be consulted. Use the scope and scale document and stakeholder map to help you decide. The key activities are interviews, workshops and surveys. Interviews are good for small numbers as they are labour intensive and the output is qualitatively the best. Workshops are good for groups with similar job profiles or job grades, compromising only a little on the quality of output. Surveys are really only useful where there are large numbers of respondents consulted as the quality of output is low, but can be a quantitative supplement to interviews or workshops. A blended approach of interviews and workshops is considered best practice to get good coverage and depth.

Step 2: Select the participants

The participants of the change impact assessment are selected in partnership with the project leadership team based on the following criteria:

▌ knowledge and subject matter expertise

▌ grades – to ensure all levels of the business are consulted

▌ departments – to ensure the relevant parts of the business are involved

▌ availability – to avoid conflicts with other critical project and non-project activity

▌ change readiness assessment findings (if available)

▌ understanding or involvement in business process mapping (project phase 1).

The numbers of participants selected will depend on the approach taken – survey, interviews, workshops or a combination – and the resources available to conduct the assessment activities such as meeting rooms and time.

Step 3: Design the CIA questions

Generic, off-the-shelf, change impact questionnaires are available on the internet but a good starting point is to think about the potential change in terms of process, people and technology and to define what it is you want to know – your objectives – up front.

This will ensure that the questions you decide to use are relevant. Below is a real-life example of how this thought process was used to generate a CIA for a local council.

	Objective	Sample questions
Process	To understand how the future state differs from the current state	What are the key areas of difference between how things are done today and how you think they will be done in the future?
	To identify and quantify the areas of difference by process	Of these key differences, which have the greatest impact and why?
	To appreciate how the processes will differ in terms of number of steps, time taken and roles involved	Do you think the new processes will: ▌ be more or less complex ▌ take longer or less time ▌ be done by the same or different people?
	To gather volume data in order to prioritise impacted processes	What are the current transaction numbers for each process and how often are they done?
People	To understand how the future process will impact on roles and responsibilities (e.g. reallocation of activities or tasks)	Do you think the future process changes will result in: ▌ fewer tasks or jobs ▌ new tasks or jobs ▌ not more or less, but different to now?
	To appreciate how ways of working will be impacted	How do you think the differences identified will impact on: ▌ council culture ▌ organisation structures?
	To identify how the future process will affect culture (e.g. change from operational to advisory culture)	What differences do you think these changes will make to your way of working?

	Objective	Sample questions
Technology	To understand how the degree of future automation compares to current state	Is this process currently a manual process? Do you think this will change, and how?
	To identify perceived future skills and knowledge requirements	Will the same skills and experience be transferable to the new system – what new or different skills might be needed?
	To highlight training requirements for the roles within this new process	Will training be required? Will new skills need to be recruited?

The questions above were designed to be meaningful to the people participating in this particular assessment, and you will need to tailor your questions and language to your own organisation and project. It is also worth mentioning that the questions in the example assessment were in an order which this sponsor felt would be easier for the employees to follow. You should bear in mind that different degrees of detail may be required in the questions, depending on the method of asking (e.g. one-to-one interview, workshop or written survey).

For the best results, you should review your proposed questions with the project leads and check for any sensitivities or terminology issues with the business areas before conducting the assessment.

Download template: *CIA Interview Questions*

Step 4: Conducting CIA interviews and workshops

Interviews should be conducted face-to-face with selected people within the business and usually take one to two hours each. Workshops may take between a half and one day and the interviewer or workshop facilitator will ideally have copies of the future process maps for discussion. The participants will categorise each identified impacted area as: low; low–medium; medium–high; high. Using four categories will press participants to either a low or high bias – removing the tendency to take the default mid-point option.

Download template: *CIA Workshop Agenda Example*

Step 5: Analysis and report

The outputs from each of the interviews and workshops should be documented by process, function and business unit. The easiest and most consistent way of capturing this is with a pre-prepared template. The example below is a summary extract from a CIA conducted when shift workers in a manufacturing plant went from recording their hours using a manual clocking mechanism to an automated system networked to HR.

Function	Business unit	Process name	Impact (H, M-H, L-M, L)	No. of people (or % of organisation)	Output or recommen- dation
HR	Head office	Hours worked tracking	H	<1%	System user and report training
Operations	Manufacturing	Time recording	L	21%	Process briefing in teams
Payroll	Outsourcing partner	Salary data to payslip conversion	M	n/a	Parallel 'old and new' data formats supplied for three months

As well as the summary analysis, the report should contain information about when in the project the assessment was conducted, context and other influencing factors, assumptions and any themes highlighted by the assessment. In addition, the report should mention how this information will be used and an indication of when the CIA may be repeated.

Download template: *CIA Report*

Organisation capacity review

What is it?

An organisation capacity review is a way of uncovering if an organisation has unknowingly overloaded its employees. It is a way of gathering information about how pressurised the organisation is, and what that means to the people who work in it. In the form of a simple survey or interview, employees rate the level of stress or confusion they experience regularly in their day, and their perspective on whether this particular project has any hope of reaching fruition. It touches on employee cynicism ('the change is not going to last so I'll keep my head down and ignore it') and how adaptable the current environment is, 'Will the change integrate into how things are done, or drift away without notice?'

The organisation capacity review and resilience assessment as combined tools give you a view as to how quickly your organisation adapts to and bounces back from change.

Why do it?

Understanding the current capacity raises issues of commitment, and how likely it is that the change will be successful and achieve the desired benefits. It helps to quantify and provide evidence to sponsors so that if capacity is an issue, actions can be taken to resolve it. Capacity issues present a significant risk to benefits realisation, and identifying and acting upon this information could mean the difference between success and failure.

When to do it

Diagnose phase.

How to do it

Step 1: Define your approach

Assessing organisational capacity can be done in a number of ways. You can survey a group with a simple questionnaire, or conduct interviews/focus groups if you would like more robust qualitative data. If you are looking for a non-invasive approach (i.e. not speaking with employees), statistics on project completion, benefits realisation, change programme schedules and even employee morale, absenteeism and sickness, all point to an organisation's ability to managing multiple demands. Generally, there are pockets in an organisation where this is more of an issue, and you need to uncover where lack of capacity will affect your particular change project.

As this can be a totally 'employee perspective' data gathering exercise, it is possible for more disgruntled employees to skew the responses to suit their agenda. Therefore, a blend of direct questions and statistics to back up responses is useful, as is a comparison between areas.

Step 2: Identify the groups who will be most affected by change

Once you have determined your approach, the next step is to understand which groups will be most affected as a result of the project. This directly draws from work done in the change impact assessment so look for groups where there is medium to high impact. These will be the more risky areas where capacity will be needed to accommodate and adopt the change. This is where you should expect potential issues.

Step 3: Design the questionnaire

Decide on the kind of data you would like to focus on – the typical areas to explore at the employee level in organisational capacity are:

▊ day-to-day workload

▊ level of stress experienced

▊ skill at task prioritisation

▊ attitude toward previous changes

▊ attitude toward future changes.

You can ask questions about these topics using a five-point scale, such as:

5 = strongly agree

4 = agree

3 = neutral/don't know

2 = disagree

1 = strongly disagree.

You may also want to ask for specific examples, as this will make the point more effective when presenting results to senior leaders. Example questions are listed below (ODR, 1998).

1. In this department, we finish the projects we start instead of becoming sidetracked with other things.
2. On top of my regular workload, I am currently coping with a number of major changes besides this one.
3. From my perspective, the time lines and strategies for managing this change are realistic.
4. In this organisation I have felt pushed to adopt new ideas or plans without having time really to become committed to them.
5. I believe I have the time and energy needed to make this change and also keep up with my regular workload.
6. My manager will remove barriers and allocate the resources needed to accomplish the change (time, skills and funds).
7. My team is ready, willing and able to make the required changes that the business needs.
8. When this organisation completes a major project, we do a good job of evaluating how well it went and what we learned from it.
9. When I think of past changes, I can clearly recall the benefits both to the organisation and to myself.
10. In this department, we make decisions to change hastily, don't consider all the relevant information or fail to make decisions at all.

Download template: *Organisational Capacity Review Questions*

Step 4: Gather the information and analyse results

Depending on your method, you may want to set up a spreadsheet to capture the results, or add in additional columns to the CIA summary. Look for the particular danger areas where it looks like change has not been adopted in the past, and day-to-day workload and stress are high. You may want to rank or weight the responses depending on what is most critical to the success of the project.

Step 5: Presenting back and risk management

Present the results to the change sponsor, change team and project manager. If you have located areas or groups of people where capacity presents a significant risk to the success of the project, this will need to be addressed by sponsors and change leaders. This information, along with the resilience assessment, forms the basis of the capacity mitigation and resilience plan.

Resilience assessment

What is it?

A resilience assessment will help you understand how quickly the organisation and its people can bounce back from change, learn from difficult lessons and be ready to take on more.

There are a number of researchers and authors writing about resilience, with similar ideas about what the characteristics of a resilient person are – whether at home or at work. Common traits are: positive or optimistic, flexible, organised, self-confident, see humour in situations and learn from experience.

The organisational capacity review and resilience assessment tools in combination give you a view as to how quickly your organisation adapts and bounces back from change. Increasing resilience is like building change muscle, so that when capacity challenges come up in the future, you are ready, willing and able to manage change.

Why do it?

Lack of resilience in an organisation can stop any project from being successful and, if left long enough, will result in long-term declining performance. Providing insight, education and activities to increase resiliency improves the overall chance that the change will be absorbed and the benefits realised.

When to do it

Design phase.

How to do it

Step 1: Define your approach

Assessing resilience can be done either individually or by group. The simplest way to gather the information is a survey, online or otherwise, or you can conduct one-to-one interviews or focus groups. As resilience is not likely to be an issue in every area, focus on those that are most relevant to the project.

Step 2: Identify the groups who will be most affected by change

Once you have your approach, the next step is to understand which groups will be most affected as a result of the project. This directly draws from work done in the change impact assessment, so look for groups where there is medium to high impact. These will be areas of higher risk – where people will need to bounce back quickly and be ready to take on more. This is where you should be most aware of potential resilience issues.

Step 3: Design the questionnaire

Decide on the kind of data you would like to focus on – the typical areas to explore at the employee level in resilience are:

- ability to absorb change
- flexibility
- organisation
- confidence
- ability to learn and reapply learning.

You can ask questions about these topics using a five-point scale, such as that overleaf (Siebert, 2005).

Rate yourself from 1 to 5 on the following: (1 = very little, 5 = very strong)

1 2 3 4 5

☐☐☐☐☐ In a crisis or chaotic situation, I calm myself and focus on taking useful actions.

☐☐☐☐☐ I'm usually optimistic. I see difficulties as temporary and expect to overcome them.

☐☐☐☐☐ I can tolerate high levels of ambiguity and uncertainty about situations.

☐☐☐☐☐ I adapt quickly to new developments. I'm good at bouncing back from difficulties.

☐☐☐☐☐ I'm playful. I find the humour in rough situations, and can laugh at myself.

☐☐☐☐☐ I'm able to recover emotionally from losses and setbacks. I have friends I can talk with. I can express my feelings to others and ask for help. Feelings of anger, loss and discouragement don't last long.

☐☐☐☐☐ I feel self-confident, appreciate myself, and have a healthy concept of who I am.

☐☐☐☐☐ I'm curious. I ask questions. I want to know how things work. I like to try new ways of doing things.

☐☐☐☐☐ I learn valuable lessons from my experiences and from the experiences of others.

☐☐☐☐☐ I'm good at solving problems. I can use analytical logic, be creative or use practical common sense.

☐☐☐☐☐ I'm good at making things work well. I'm often asked to lead groups and projects.

☐☐☐☐☐ I'm very flexible. I feel comfortable with my paradoxical complexity. I'm optimistic and pessimistic, trusting and cautious, unselfish and selfish, and so forth.

☐☐☐☐☐ I'm always myself, but I've noticed that I'm different in different situations.

1	2	3	4	5	
☐	☐	☐	☐	☐	I prefer to work without a written job description. I'm more effective when I'm free to do what I think is best in each situation.
☐	☐	☐	☐	☐	I 'read' people well and trust my intuition.
☐	☐	☐	☐	☐	I'm a good listener. I have good empathy skills.
☐	☐	☐	☐	☐	I'm non-judgmental about others and adapt to people's different personality styles.
☐	☐	☐	☐	☐	I'm very durable. I hold up well during tough times. I have an independent spirit underneath my cooperative way of working with others.
☐	☐	☐	☐	☐	I've been made stronger and better by difficult experiences.
☐	☐	☐	☐	☐	I've converted misfortune into good luck and found benefits in bad experiences.

Source: From *The Resiliency Advantage* by Al Siebert, PhD.
Reprinted with permission. © Copyright 2005, Al Siebert, PhD.

Resiliency quiz scoring

Low score: A self-rating score under 50 indicates that life is probably a struggle for you and you know it. You may not handle pressure well. You don't learn anything useful from bad experiences. You feel hurt when people criticise you. You may sometimes feel helpless and without hope.

If these statements fit you, ask yourself, 'Would I like to learn how to handle my difficulties better?' If your answer is 'yes' then a good way to start is to meet with others who are working to develop their resiliency skills. Let them coach, encourage and guide you. Another way, if you work for a large employer, is to get resiliency coaching from a counsellor with the employee assistance programme (if one is available). The fact that you feel motivated to become more resilient is a positive sign.

Lower middle scores: If you scored in the 50–69 range, you appear to be fairly adequate, but you may be under-rating yourself. A much larger percentage of people under-rate themselves than over-rate themselves on the quiz. Some people have a habit of being modest and automatically give themselves a 3 on every item for a total score of 60. If your score is in the 50–69 range, you need to find out how valid your self-rating is. See the suggestion below.

Upper middle scores: If you agreed with many of the statements and scored in the 70–89 range, that is very good. It means you can gain a lot from reading and learning about resiliency and will become even more self-confident and resilient than before. You are a self-motivated learner and can become better and better at bouncing back from adversities.

High score: If you rated yourself high on most of the statements, you have a score over 90. This means you know you're already good at bouncing back from life's setbacks and will hold up under non-stop pressure. For you, the quiz validates many things you are doing right. And, because you like learning new ways to be even better, it will show you how to take your already good skills to a very high level – something like reaching an advanced black-belt level in the martial arts.

A question for you to consider is how much you feel willing to tell your resiliency stories to others and make yourself available to people who are trying to learn how to cope better with their adversities. People gain inspiration from real-life role models. You could be one.

Note: A validity check for your scoring is to ask two people who know you well to rate you on the items and see what scores they come up with. Have a discussion with them about each of the items where there is a discrepancy and listen to what they say.[1]

Download template: *Change Resiliency Questionnaire*

Step 4: Gather the information and analyse results

Depending on your method, you may want to set up a spreadsheet to capture the results – you may wish to combine them with the

---

1 © Copyright 2005, Al Siebert, PhD, from Chapter 2 in *The Resiliency Advantage: Master Change, Thrive Under Pressure, and Bounce Back from Setbacks*, by Al Siebert, PhD. Reprinted with permission.

CIA and capacity assessment results. Look for the particular danger areas where there is low flexibility, optimism and ability to take on change. You may want to rank or weight the responses depending on what is most critical to the success of the project.

Step 5: Presenting back and risk management

Present back the results to the change team, change sponsor and project manager. If you have located areas or groups of people where resilience presents a significant risk to the success of the project, this will need to be addressed by the sponsor and change leaders. This work, along with the results from assessing organisational capacity, forms the basis of the capacity mitigation and resilience plan.

Capacity mitigation and resilience plan

What is it?

A capacity mitigation and resilience plan is a tangible, executable plan that aims to reduce capacity issues and increase resiliency. From the organisational capacity assessment and resilience assessments you will have an analysis that will indicate if either of these factors poses a risk to the successful implementation of the project in a particular area. The mitigation plan can include activities from the strategic to the individual level. Typical plans at the strategic level may include project prioritisation workshops, mapping projects and operations to strategy, and launching revised quarterly plans to improve capacity and resilience.

Plans at the individual level will ideally link to professional development and performance management, and should include conversations between the employee and manager about workload, stress, resilience and priorities.

Why do it?

The capacity mitigation and resilience plan gives you an insight as to how quickly your organisation manages workload, adapts and bounces back from change.

These are very real challenges for leadership and present a significant risk to benefits realisation.

When to do it

Develop and deliver phases.

How to do it

Step 1: Gain agreement from the change sponsor and change leader that a capacity mitigation and resilience plan is required

Once you have completed your analysis of the capacity and resilience of the most affected areas, warning signs may begin to appear for certain departments or groups. These signs must be discussed with the change sponsor, change leader and project manager, to gain agreement that they pose a serious risk to benefits realisation and, at the very least, require a short-term plan to safeguard the success of the project.

The plan cycle is shown in Figure 9.1.

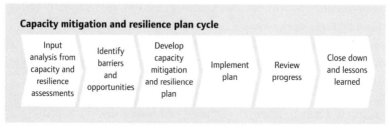

Capacity mitigation and resilience plan cycle

Input analysis from capacity and resilience assessments → Identify barriers and opportunities → Develop capacity mitigation and resilience plan → Implement plan → Review progress → Close down and lessons learned

FIGURE 9.1 A capacity mitigation and resilience plan cycle

Step 2: Meet with the change leaders of the high-risk areas and build the plan

Once you have the endorsement of the change sponsor and change leaders, set up one-to-one meetings with the business leaders of the high-risk areas. Discuss the results of the organisational capacity assessment and resilience assessments, and agree that there is a potential problem and risk to the project success. Propose a simple workshop with the management team to address the issues and formulate an action plan. Figure 9.2 shows an example of different departments that require activities to address both capacity and resilience, or just capacity or resilience.

Step 3: Run leadership sessions on capacity and resilience to develop departmental plans

These may be new concepts to the leadership or management, so begin with education about what this means and why it is important to monitor. Include a presentation to them on the results of the organisational capacity assessment and resilience assessments, and begin action planning how to resolve issues. As the example template shows (see Figure 9.2), not every area will need the same plan – some will need to focus on capacity, some on resilience, some on both.

The ideal session output is an action plan with agreed dates for progress updates. Also gain agreement to run workshops for employees to develop individual plans, that link back to professional development and performance management.

Step 4: Conduct employee workshops to develop individual plans

While the leadership and management are working on the more strategic approach to resolving capacity and resilience issues, much can be done at the individual level. Again, begin with education about what this means, why it is important to monitor and what leadership has agreed to address. Challenge each person to develop an individual action plan to improve their capacity and resilience, and to include it in their professional development plans. Agree dates they will discuss their plans with their managers and provide progress updates.

Step 5: Repeat the organisational capacity assessment and resilience assessments

Now you have a baseline, repeat the assessments regularly to track overall improvements or setbacks. Present the results, whether positive or negative, back to the leadership, management and employees for discussion and further action planning.

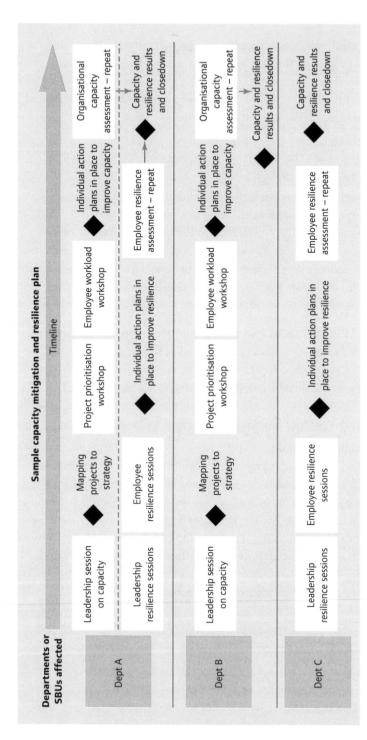

FIGURE 9.2 An example capacity mitigation and resilience plan

Step 6: Closedown and lessons learned

Although the plan is a project deliverable, the execution and management of organisational capacity and developing resilience will continue long after the project finishes. It has relevance to all projects, day-to-day working and the overall performance of an organisation. If the work continues post-project, then an owner will need to be found in the department to monitor and progress the plans. Ideally, this is the change leader or someone who is part of the senior leadership team.

Download template: *Capacity Mitigation and Resilience Plan*

Organisation alignment

10

Change prism lens	Step-by-step guides
Organisation alignment	Organisation design principles
	Strategic (macro) organisation design
	Operational (detailed) organisation design
	Role profiles
	Transition plan
	Downloadable templates
	Organisation Design Principles
	Role Profile
	Transition Roadmap
	Transition Plan Document

Organisation design principles

What is it?

ORGANISATION DESIGN (OD) is the planning and development of the structure, processes, systems, governance and capabilities of the organisation that enable it to achieve and sustain its strategy and vision. It is a complex discipline requiring specialist knowledge and skills. The objectives of organisation design in a project context are:

▌ to achieve an effective integration of the change and co-ordinate the old and the new in the business

▌ to encourage and facilitate the flow of information

▌ to improve organisational productivity.

Organisation design is a six-step process (see Figure 10.1) and organisation design principles are the key deliverable of the first step: organisation assessment and strategy.

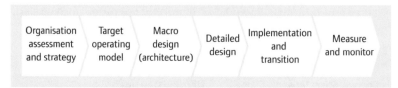

FIGURE 10.1 Organisation design six-step process

Why do it?

Organisation design principles for the project set the parameters and the success criteria for a new way of operating. The principles are the equivalent of a pre-nuptial agreement – to focus decisions and agree what the scope of change will be so that when the pressure and emotional temperature rises, we can refer to them for guidance.

When to do it

Diagnose and design phases.

How to do it

Step 1: Organisation review

The first step is to build a good understanding of what the organisation 'as-is' looks like. A strategic review comprises a number of tools and assessments, some of which you can access through the business strategy and project blueprint documents. You may need to supplement these with process maps and change-specific analyses (e.g. CRA, CIA and stakeholder analysis). This assessment should highlight the change drivers on which the OD principles will be based.

Step 2: Define focus areas

Your next task will be to determine the characteristics of the future organisation. This should be done through a series of meetings with the project leadership teams, sponsor, change leaders and key decision makers in the business. If you have already completed some of this work in the organisation future look and feel (in the culture and behaviours lens), and the guiding principles (in the strategy and future state lens), use that in this section. Once agreed, the focus areas should be captured into the design principles template. Figure 10.2 shows an example from a local government organisation implementing a CRM programme.

Download template: *Organisation Design Principles*

Step 3: Future operating principles

Collectively, the business and project teams need to identify elements that break down the focus areas into specifics. It is the 'as-is', 'to-be', change drivers and guiding principles all in one place. Once identified, the team must take this one step further and try to imagine how this would look and feel when the change has been achieved. This is the final column in the template shown in Figure 10.3.

Step 4: Validation and acceptance

Remember this is your foundation, the 'stake in the ground' which you will come back to when the going gets rough and people get uncomfortable with the level of organisational change. Once you have the OD principles captured it is critical to get them validated with the decision makers and sponsors.

Strategic (macro) organisation design

What is it?

Strategic organisation design is the process of developing and selecting high-level options for how the organisation will be structured and for the restructuring of operations. If the project scope and scale have identified this will be in scope, then you will need to consider using these tools. This strategic level of OD is dependent on the target operating model (TOM) being defined, which should be part of the overall business strategy.

FIGURE 10.2 Organisation design principles example

Strategic OD is comprised of the following key activities:

- definition of critical success factors (CSFs)

- structure types: identification, assessment and selection

- high-level governance structure

- organisation architecture

- accountabilities and capabilities.

The way we are now …	The way we want to be …	How we will get there …
Complex queries resolution process Variety of processes doing the same thing Multiple contact points for complex queries (e.g. funding) Limited support for front line Standard service proposition	Customer-centric	Answer customer first time if possible All processes aligned to customer delivery CRM system in place Front office staff (call centre and others) valued and supported Differentiated customer relationships
Single expertise for call handlers Traditional office based working Slow and limited MI on which to base decisions Change skills limited to a few Decision-making processes convoluted	Flexible	Multiple areas of expertise for call handlers New working environments (e.g. remote working, full-time or part-time opportunity) Flexible shift pattern and shift bidding/swapping Real time MI allows constant business improvement Change skills in all parts of organisation
Information not available for decision making People reluctant to hand over parts of process Differing levels of clarity about accountability for decisions Decisions taken high up the hierarchy	Empowered	Up-to-date information and clear guidelines allow decisions to be made in the right place Better control over use of own time and feedback on performance Decisions at the appropriate level with clear accountability No blame culture – we learn from our mistakes
Piecemeal career development and competencies Customer contact development focused on grade not competency Expert staff handle admin. and minor queries	Professional	Expert roles recognised and supported Clear competency development programme for staff Customer contact valued as a specialism Delivery experts staff focus on delivery Systems automate routine tasks
Knowledge and best practice sharing limited Organisation structure silos Internal trading and cross-charging Duplication Third parties not integrated	Cooperative	Knowledge and best practice shared Used to cross-unit working Council services first choice for council staff Integration Longer-term collaboration with partners

FIGURE 10.3 Future operating principles

Why do it?

Defining the strategic OD provides a framework for assessment and selection of a new organisation structure and how the organisation will meet its performance objectives. The analysis also provides essential information for an organisation-specific business case to be developed so that an informed investment decision can be made.

When to do it

Design phase.

How to do it

Step 1: Develop CSFs (strategic design criteria)

Using the design principles, review the issues identified that the new organisation needs to address. Sometimes these can be superficial or generic and so you may need to gather more detail or a different range of perceptions. You can achieve this through a number of means, such as focus groups, a review by stakeholders or a brief analysis of business processes.

A strategic design criteria example is shown in Figure 10.4.

Step 2: Identify organisation structure options

> An organisation is a rule-driven, social system whose members align their behaviour with an underlying goal, and whose formal structure exists to achieve that goal.
>
> Capgemini Consulting

Benchmarking and research shows there are 10 basic types or models of organisation structure (see Figure 10.5). The appropriateness of each of the types can be linked to two dimensions: leadership style and environment. Based on your knowledge of the organisation, you should be able to shortlist three or four options for further assessment.

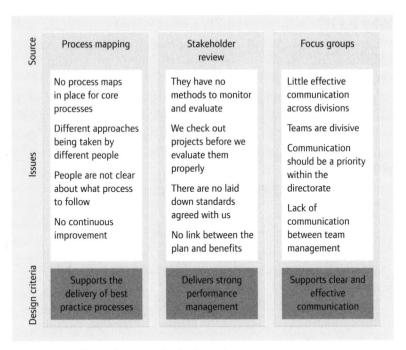

FIGURE 10.4 Example strategic design criteria

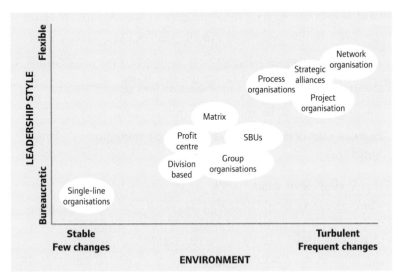

FIGURE 10.5 Types of organisation structure

Step 3: Assess structures against design criteria

When you have identified the three or four possible options, you need to conduct an assessment against the design criteria you identified in step 1. It is a good idea to consider weighting these criteria as not all will be of equal importance (see Figure 10.6). It is essential to involve high-influence stakeholders in the assessment, so that they understand and agree to the criteria being applied, the relative weighting and the scoring.

Step 4: Define capability areas and accountabilities

Research and benchmarking can give you valuable insight into the major capabilities or 'organisational buckets' required for a department or business unit to perform its function. You should 'test' the incoming work and information flows between the groupings, using future process maps and high-level scenarios, to ensure there are no barriers or that process steps can be completed by the appropriate capability area. Figure 10.7 shows an example of high-level capability areas.

The future state structure (organisation architecture) should be shared and validated with the management team(s) through OD workshops. In the workshops you should aim to:

▌ capture implications, issues and assumptions for the future structure

▌ determine role numbers and grade mix for capability areas

▌ identify critical skills and roles for priority fulfilment

▌ capture a list of risks and issues regarding transition to the new structure.

Step 5: High-level governance

The final stage in strategic organisation design is the management hierarchy – i.e. spans of control needed for the business to function. Span of control ratios (manager:employees) are dependent on the factors overleaf:

Options analysis

Key design criteria and weighting	Weighting	Process	Product	Customer	Matrix structure	Project structure	Network
Supports clear internal communication	10	30	30	30	70	50	0
Supports clear external communication	10	70	50	100	100	70	30
Supports innovation	7	70	21	35	49	35	49
Creates strong relationship mgmt	10	70	30	100	100	30	30
Supports staff development and recognises achievement	10	30	30	30	70	70	50
Supports performance mgmt and continual improvement	7	35	21	35	35	35	21
Supports project mgmt	7	49	35	49	49	70	49
Maximises use of IT to support business processes	7	21	21	21	35	49	21
Creates output focus	10	100	50	70	70	70	50
Creates flexible structure to cope with priorities	7	21	21	21	35	49	49
Maximises resources	10	70	0	30	30	70	70
Supports flexible working	3	9	15	21	21	30	21
Reduces duplication/bureaucracy	7	49	0	0	35	35	35
Supports efficient knowlege management	10	30	30	30	70	70	0
Ensures role clarity	7	70	35	49	21	49	35
Reduces silo working	3	0	0	0	21	9	21
Total possible weighted score	1580	724	389	621	811	791	531
% of possible weighting		46	25	39	51	50	34

FIGURE 10.6 Detailed assessment against weighted design criteria

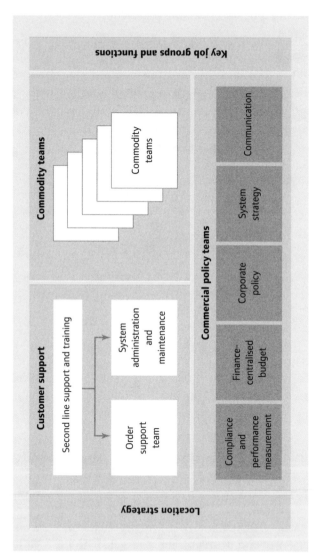

FIGURE 10.7 Example of an organisation architecture for a public sector purchasing group

▌ ability

▌ culture

▌ scope and level of work

▌ amount and type of interaction required.

In general the modern approach is to move from command-and-control structures to ones that are more empowered, so in theory we should be looking to increase the manager:team ratios and flatten hierarchical structures. However, if the managers also have a coaching/mentoring role for their staff then this will limit the spread. Research by the Saratoga Institute in 2001 explored the relationship between management ratios and corporate performance. It found that increasing spans of control were inversely proportional to revenue growth.

Our experience has culminated in a useful 'ready-reckoner' for management ratios:

▌ level 1 (1)

▌ level 2 (1:5–7)

▌ level 3 (1:7–10)

▌ level 4 (1:12–15).

By applying these ratios to the number of employees in the impacted parts of the business, you should be able to estimate how many managers at each of the top four grades are required in the new structure.

Operational (detailed) organisation design

What is it?

The operational (detailed) organisation design is very much the 'bottom up' element of organisation design. With the high-level organisation structure signed off, the detail of the new organisation must be completed, down to individual job descriptions. An effective design should ensure that the new structure is aligned to the current context of the company's vision, strategy, processes and capabilities, reflects the changes the project is introducing, and is able to respond to the external drivers such as competition, customer demand and technology trends.

Organisation redesign involves much more than 'changing the structure'. Every organisation design is unique and cannot be 'pasted' into another situation. Each arrangement will differ, based on differing reactions to environmental forces, unique internal processes, structures and capabilities.

Detailed design typically works hand in hand with process redesign activities (or with the implementation of a new technology system, with the development of modules). Throughout this project stage a more detailed business case is developed to ensure that the microdesign is feasible – especially if headcount reduction, with its associated cost is a factor.

Why do it?

The detailed design defines the organisation infrastructure and workflow changes defined by the project. Detailed design provides opportunities for value creation, for example outsourcing the tasks in a particular area, combining functions/departments and balancing staffing levels with automation.

When to do it

Develop phase.

How to do it

Step 1: Key activities

With the organisation architecture defined you will also need to understand the new processes for each affected area. The future process maps will provide you with the necessary detail as to the key activities within the business area. Having identified the main activities, you should review them with the appropriate change leader and together agree the main groupings or teams. Figure 10.8 is an example for a council finance department.

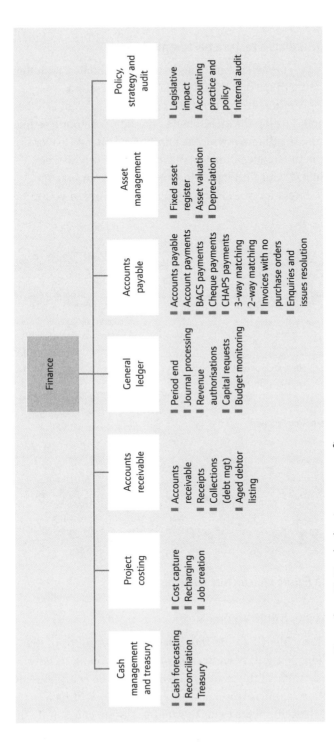

FIGURE 10.8 Example activities by business area – finance

Step 2: Future architecture paradigm

Once the future processes/activities have been validated with the business, you will need to map them to the organisation architecture. Use the design principles as a guide to what is to be achieved and develop the architecture paradigm together (see Figure 10.9), or at least validate it with the appropriate change leader (in this example the finance director). Benchmarking can also be helpful, but use your findings as indicators of current practice – what may be right for one organisation may not work in yours.

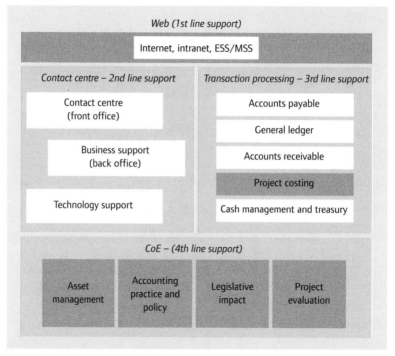

FIGURE 10.9 Future architecture paradigm

Step 3: Assess future volumes

Once you have identified the activities and work groups of the future design, you will need to assess how much work or how many transactions of the same type will need to be completed. If the overall project involves a new IT system, they will have forecasted these numbers to make sure the system can handle the data/activity (i.e. load testing). IT folk call these data 'volumetrics'. If these data are not available to you, you will need to go back to the business area and get the information from the change leader.

Step 4: Future resource assessment

When you know what and how much is to be done (including daily rates or targets), you can start to identify how many resources are required for each activity/team (see Figure 10.10). Your first attempt should be from a 'top-down' perspective. What is the minimum number of people required for the process or activity to get done? Again, you can look at benchmark data, but be sure that you are comparing like with like, such as similar systems and levels of automation, same industry and size of business, degree of outsourcing, etc.

Once you have these numbers defined (and they may be imposed on you as headcount targets!), you will need to discuss and validate them with the business to make sure there is enough resource to absorb *ad hoc* activities, contingency, workflow fluctuations, provisions for sickness, absence and flexibility of work patterns. We recommend that you conduct a series of workshops with the impacted business areas to collect the information. Sharing information at this stage makes the design process transparent and, if managed carefully, can build trust.

Remember, for an organisation to operate effectively after a major change, the solution must be sustainable. So you should anticipate for future growth and additional capacity for developing new capabilities.

Step 5: Develop high-level organisation map

At this stage, you combine the spans of control identified in the macro-design to the work groupings and validated resource numbers to produce a high-level organisation map. This is the time when the organisation begins to take the recognisable form you see laid out as an organisation chart. Staying with the finance example, this should look something like Figure 10.11.

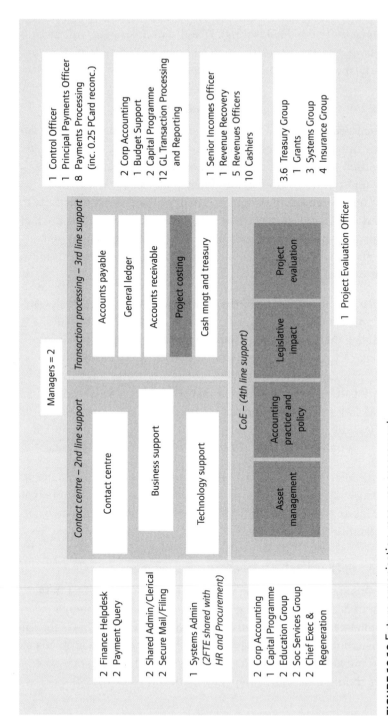

FIGURE 10.10 Future organisation resource assessment

Accounting services team

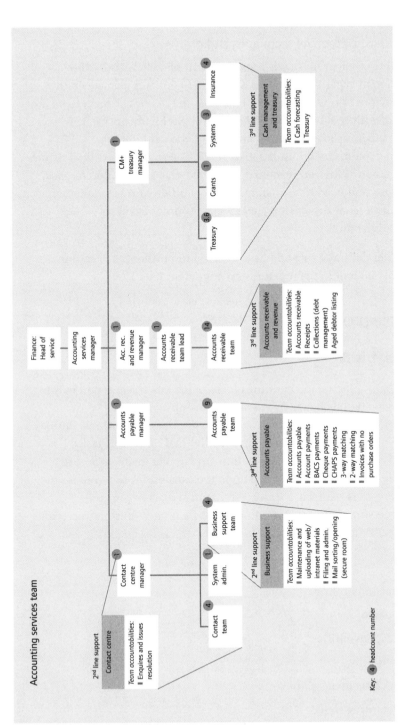

FIGURE 10.11 High-level organisation map

Step 6: Determine team roles and profiles

Within each grouping or team, you will need to identify the different types of role necessary to carry out and manage all the activities and workflow. For example, in the contact team there are four resources identified (mid-level left in Figure 10.11). However, the business may require a mixture of contact handling, supervision and administration roles. The roles are likely to require common skills and responsibilities, but also some different ones. These will need to be distinguished as different role profiles: contact team supervisor, contact agent, junior agent or administrator.

(What defines a role and how to develop profiles is covered in a separate tool in the organisation alignment lens.)

Role profiles

What is it?

Role profiles are the building blocks of job descriptions and may be created based on similar characteristics such as tasks, responsibilities, specialism or client/supplier relationships. Profiles are overall groupings made up of individual roles – the tasks, activities and process steps within a particular business area or team. Role profiles are based upon the capabilities or resources in the organisation that require a common skillset or process ownership. Role profiles introduced by a project must respect wider organisation constraints such as grade structures and job levels.

Role profiles should contain information on:

▮ accountabilities

▮ span of control

▮ responsibilities

▮ activities

▮ process ownership

▮ reporting lines.

Why do it?

Role profiling ensures that all activities and process steps are resourced, so that bottlenecks or breaks in the workflow can be avoided. Profiles also provide necessary information about new jobs or new capabilities required in the future organisation and form the basis of job descriptions which are both a legal requirement and necessary for recruitment. Role profiles are essential to enable job to role mapping in IT systems implementations.

When to do it

Develop and deliver phases.

How to do it

Step 1: Scope of process delivery

You must be clear on what the focus or scope of the processes within the future organisation and specific business areas are. For example:

- **process ownership:** delivery and accountability for an end-to-end process
- **geographic focus:** specific process steps are dependent on location (e.g. for costs or labour)
- **subprocess:** processes split into subprocesses so hand-offs to other teams would be necessary for the process to be completed
- **product group/business unit:** organised according to the internal customers
- **external customer:** processes organised according to groups of external customers or suppliers (e.g. processing of all customer queries in a combined front office).

Step 2: Group activities

You must then define the process steps and activities within the ownership or accountability of the business area being redesigned. Once these steps have been defined, they should be grouped either by common characteristics, the skills required or by existing or future capabilities. This is shown in Figure 10.12, which outlines the relationship between processes, groups and roles.

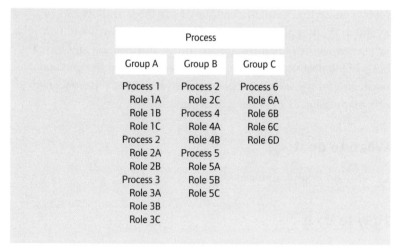

	Process	
Group A	Group B	Group C
Process 1	Process 2	Process 6
Role 1A	Role 2C	Role 6A
Role 1B	Process 4	Role 6B
Role 1C	Role 4A	Role 6C
Process 2	Role 4B	Role 6D
Role 2A	Role 4B	
Role 2B	Process 5	
Process 3	Role 5A	
Role 3A	Role 5B	
Role 3B	Role 5C	
Role 3C		

FIGURE 10.12 Defining group activities

Step 3: Develop preliminary role profiles

For each of the groupings you identify in step 2, you will then need to populate a role profile similar to that in Figure 10.13.

Role profile
Function: Role name:
Tasks and activities:
Key links and reporting line (if known):

Figure 10.13 Role profile template

Download template: *Role Profile*

Step 4: Validate profiles

When you have defined the role profiles, it is a good idea to test them, both individually and as a team to make sure that the work can be completed as expected. We recommend that you use several types of test to do this, including the following.

▍ **'Day in the life'** – where you shadow an employee actually doing the role to see how the work gets done and if there are any issues or barriers. (This tool is available in the culture and behaviours lens.)

▍ **Scenario testing** – where you run end-to-end processes to validate the workflow.

▍ **Efficiency evaluation** – where you measure the speed or productivity of a particular process such as the number of invoices processed in an hour/day and document cycle times.

▍ **Focused interviews** – where you ask employees doing similar roles (inside or external to the organisation) whether in practice it makes sense for this task to be (a) done at all or (b) by this role profile.

When you are satisfied that the role profiles support the workflow and that the team/business area can deliver the processes/ accountabilities you can finalise the role profiles.

Step 5: Finalise role profiles

After any adjustments required by the validation, the role profiles can be finalised. The next stage is for the role profiles to be converted into job descriptions (see Figure 10.14). Usually at this point, the role profiles are handed over to HR who then work with the business to break down the activities and responsibilities in to competencies and skills and identify KPIs.

Unless you have a background in HR, you should challenge expectations that the change team should complete this task. Downstream activities, such as job evaluation, will depend on HR understanding the job so that the appropriate grade and salary can be awarded to the post. Also, recruitment depends on job descriptions and there are compliance and employment law considerations which you may not be aware of.

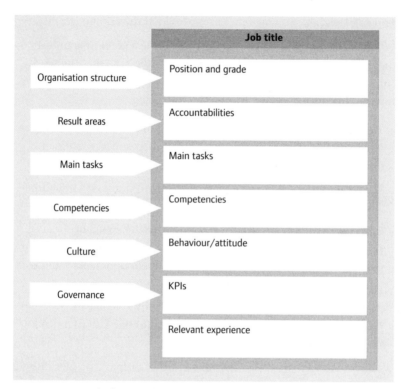

FIGURE 10.14 Job description components

Transition plan[1]

What is it?

Transition plans outline the activities and interim requirements to implement the future organisation design. A transition plan defines the approach to the changeover, the processes and policies for managing the changeover, and series of steps or activities to implement the new organisation. If the move to the future organisation is to be phased, interim structures and processes may need to be identified and temporary resources (both in the business

1 The transition roadmap and plan may be in or out of scope of the change project and the change team, as it may be a separate project in its own right. If that is the case, this should be agreed at the diagnose phase of the project and planned to be handed over to an agreed and identified project manager as a deliverable of the change stream.

and to manage the change process) provided during the transition period. Key activities in transition planning are:

▌ capability assessment (of incumbent staff)

▌ internal appointments

▌ external recruitment

▌ training and development

▌ performance indicators.

Why do it?

Transition planning focuses on the continuity of business operations ('business as usual') during the transition period. It also assesses capabilities so that training needs can be assessed and role transitions planned and implemented. Transition planning considers the degree of change that an individual will undergo and plans to support individuals are anticipated and provided. It helps to ensure successful implementation so that the future organisation architecture will be effective.

When to do it

Deliver phase.

How to do it

Step 1: Define the approach

You should review the CIA and CRA to understand the implications of the change on each of the impacted business areas. You will need to share this information with HR and seek its views on the approach to implementing the new organisation structure – should this be a series of steps phased over time or a step change directly to the future structure? Early engagement and consultation with HR is vital as it will be pivotal during the implementation of the new structure.

Regardless of phasing, the general process for delivering the future structure will be something along the lines of that shown in Figure 10.15.

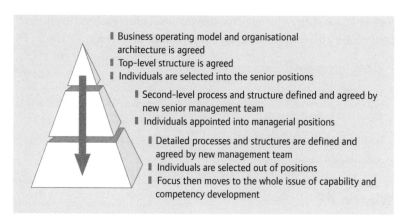

FIGURE 10.15 Transition approach

Step 2: Establish a transition project team

In your role as change manager your main task in this area is to set up a transition team. You may be expected to stay on in an advisory or team member capacity, but the accountability should sit within the business area/unit and HR.

Transition will require some specialist HR expertise and also high-level sponsorship to make decisions on issues such as the transition approach, authorisation of redundancies/early retirement programmes, key business roles, location and accommodation requirements and transition communications.

The team will be responsible for developing the transition plan and implementation, and its remit should include:

▌ mobilise resources

▌ address and plan for capability and service gaps

▌ plan for transition requirements (interim)

▌ fulfil posts in the new organisation design

▌ exit/redeployment of resources (where needed)

▌ demonstrate and reinforce culture and values.

Step 3: Key role identification

From the organisation design work, the team will need to identify and prioritise business critical roles that will provide the necessary governance for operations but also have responsibilities for shaping and building their teams. Job descriptions and the process for job applications/matching must be defined and timelines agreed with HR.

If moving to the future organisation involves changes to terms and conditions or redundancies you must ensure that HR have the capability and capacity to manage it. You must also understand that the pace of transition cannot go faster than legislation or trade union agreements.

Step 4: Define policies and processes for transition

In the light of the changes required for implementation of the future organisation, it is a good idea to review the policies and procedures in place to see if they are fit for this purpose. Some HR policies may not exist or be outdated because they have not been in regular use (e.g. redundancy). Figure 10.16 is an example of a transition process.

It is essential that the policies are ready for use before any communications about the transition process or new organisation design are made. In the absence of detail about specific positions or jobs, the process itself can be communicated much earlier so that stakeholders and employees are not alienated.

Step 5: Conduct capability gap analysis

The team should review the change impact assessment and the list of future roles identified through detailed organisation design and role profiling to determine the future capability requirements of the organisation. This will need to be compared to an 'as-is' assessment of capabilities (i.e. existing resources). A good place to find 'as-is' information is current job descriptions. The transition team should be seeking to answer the following strategic business questions:

▌ What skills do we need in the future organisation?

▌ Which gaps can training close and which do we need to recruit?

▌ How do we resource the interim and permanent organisations?

▌ Do we need any temporary and/or project resource to make the change?

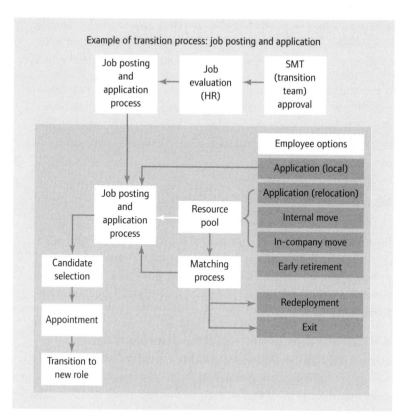

FIGURE 10.16 Example transition process

Step 6: Develop an activity plan

Using the findings and recommendations from the capability gap analysis, key role definition, and policy/process review, the team will need to identify activities, tasks and dependencies to get from the 'as-is' to the 'to-be' organisation.

A transition plan for the business can be a version of the change roadmap (see Figure 5.1), which is a useful framework to structure planning discussions and activities and capture the implementation steps for a new organisation. This will need to be project managed, tracked and monitored to ensure all the necessary actions are taken at the right time.

Download templates: *Transition Roadmap; Transition Plan Document*

Culture and behaviours

Change prism lens	Step-by-step guides
Culture and behaviours	Future organisation look and feel
	Culture assessment
	Culture audit
	Culture action plan
	Downloadable templates
	Culture Web
	Culture Alignment Framework
	Day In The Life Of Diagnostic
	Culture Audit
	Polarity Maps
	Culture Action Plan

Future organisation look and feel

What is it?

THE FUTURE ORGANISATION LOOK AND FEEL describes how activities, behaviours and interactions will be carried out once the change is in place. It is a microcosm of organisational culture, and paints a picture that everyone can carry around in their head of 'how things are done around here', at a very real level. It is the behavioural 'to-be', and differs from organisational design principles in that those emphasise *what* you do – culture is *how* you do it.

Why do it?

Defining the future look and feel will crystallise what it will be like once the change is in place. What will it bring? What will be different? It is the time to dream about what you are trying to achieve, and what that would be like on a day-to-day basis when it comes to fruition. This will allow you to drill down into what will be the journey between 'as-is' and 'to-be', and include specific activities in the culture action plan.

When to do it

Design phase.

How to do it

Step 1: Define your approach

The guide for formulating the future look and feel could follow on from the culture web or culture alignment framework tools that are included in the culture assessment. Defining future look and feel can be done a number of ways (individual interviews, focus groups or workshops) and for this exercise you need to decide on a preferred culture framework to guide the effort.

Step 2: Identify who should be involved

Once you have your approach, the next step is to decide who should be involved. It should always be a cross-section of those who are part of the change network, as well as those who are your change leaders and employees in the most affected areas.

Step 3: Design the workshop

The main objective is for participants to walk away from the 'future look and feel' workshop with a clear picture of what it will be like once the change is in place. This is from an individual perspective, so many different perspectives may need to be covered during the workshop. Perspectives to consider are: employee, manager, customer, support staff and leadership.

You should draw on the work done in identifying the guiding principles of the change, and the overall intent, business case, strategy and organisation design principles. This will give you the broad view of what you are trying to achieve in the future.

You may want to follow this design and agenda for the workshop.

1. Purpose and objectives of workshop.

2. What is the change? Draw from change driver/business case/strategy work.

3. Who will be affected? Draw from stakeholder work.

4. Future look and feel from 'your' perspective (this could be done in break-out groups of functional/role/hierarchical areas):

   (a) Give all groups the same starting guidelines, which are drawn from the change drivers or business case. These are the broad statements of what the change will bring and what it is trying to achieve.

   (b) Using a framework like the Culture Alignment Framework, have the break-out groups ask the question, 'What does this mean to me, my day, my behaviours, my activities, my role?' in each of the culture areas.

   (c) Document the outputs.

5. Groups present back all perspectives on future look and feel.

6. Gain agreement that the perspectives are in alignment, adjust any that are not.

7. Identify how to communicate the future look and feel (this can be done by filming a video 'day in the life of' style, by documenting a commitment to the future, by building a 3-D image that represents the vision etc.).

Step 4: Sharing the future and risk management

Share the overall outcome of the future look and feel with the change sponsor, change team and project manager. Once you have agreed and finalised the future look and feel, compare it with the culture assessment and audit to see if there are any gaps between the current culture and the future vision. Those gaps will need to be addressed as activities in the culture action plan.

Overleaf is an example of a future look and feel from the leadership of a medium-sized public sector organisation. The leadership team interpreted their future cultural vision to make a more relevant story which staff in the organisation can more closely identify with. You as a change manager facilitate this work, so it is up to you to press to the level of detail that is relevant for your project and business context.

	We will	We will not
We focus on our clients	▌ Actively listen to clients, providing them with relevant information on the progress of their case and what they can expect to happen and when ▌ Take ownership of a case and deliver outcomes for clients ▌ Keep our promises to clients	▌ Be selective with the truth ▌ Hand the client to other caseworkers and make them go through their whole explanation again ▌ Avoid taking action we have committed to do
We are professional	▌ Treat our clients as we would expect to be treated ourselves ▌ Take responsibility for learning so we have the right level of technical knowledge and skills to do our jobs effectively and efficiently ▌ Take pride in the quality and accuracy of our work ▌ Actively help our colleagues ▌ Set and maintain standards ▌ Ensure everything we do achieves an outcome	▌ Have people working for us who do not provide an adequate service to the client ▌ Give less than 100% effort and commitment to achieving positive outcomes for the client ▌ Waste time or resources on non-productive activities
We are open and honest	▌ Tell it how it is; no secrets, no hidden agendas ▌ Give clients and colleagues opportunities to feedback ▌ Regularly invite colleagues to discussions with board members ▌ Be visible and outward facing ▌ Apologise when we get it wrong	▌ Play a numbers game ▌ Fudge the issue ▌ Ignore client's and colleague feedback ▌ Hide behind grade or status
We are fair but firm	▌ Recognise and reward achievements ▌ Be fair with all our clients, but firm where appropriate, and forceful when necessary ▌ Set targets that are client driven, challenging but achievable ▌ Ensure our people have access and support for personal development to ensure excellent delivery	▌ Tolerate poor behaviour and work effort ▌ Shirk from the full use of the enforcement powers we have ▌ Set unachievable, non-client-focused targets ▌ Tolerate poor performance or conduct

Culture assessment

What is it?

A culture assessment allows you to gather information about how the current culture operates in real terms. Culture is often defined as 'the way we do things around here', and encompasses behaviours, symbols, rewards and measurement, systems and processes. It is the behavioural 'as-is'.

Why do it?

When you introduce a specific change, and it comes up against an established culture, culture wins. Culture can stall or swallow an initiative with which it does not align so efforts must be made to either revise the change to fit the culture or alter the culture to better accommodate the change – we call this 'making room in the culture for the change'. Knowing and understanding the culture enables the change manager to target specific aspects and identify which interventions to use. It is in the best interest of the organisation to understand the current culture and the project's potential fit, as that has a direct correlation to the success.

Cautionary note: If you are new to the study or diagnosis of culture, everyone needs to start somewhere so do try out some of the tools and techniques. Culture is an extremely challenging area to work in, as it is alternatively conceptual and practical, invisible and tangible, something you can describe precisely and something completely woolly. If you find yourself getting lost or confused, do not abandon the work or try to dismiss it as unimportant. Look for help to make your way through the confusion from a more experienced practitioner or an organisational culture expert.

When to do it

Diagnose phase.

How to do it

Step 1: Determine the level of culture assessment needed for the specific change

When you did work on scope and scale of the change, what was the level? If it is high, you will require more effort using a number of tools to understand the current culture and check for alignment to the change. If it is low, save yourself the effort and do a simple assessment. If it is somewhere in between, what you may wish to do is select one or two of the tools, and once those have yielded results, decide if you need more analysis.

Step 2: Define your approach: how and with whom?

Who participates in the culture assessment should be directly linked with the groups identified in your CRA and CIA. You should also include other stakeholders, determining how influential they are setting the tone of the current culture (leadership, team managers, human resources etc.). If your assessment determines that the culture requires some changes, it's best to have included those with the power to do so from the very beginning.

How you go about assessing culture really rests on one question – What do you require as an output of your culture assessment? Do you want it to be quantitative or qualitative? A small indicator of the current culture or a full-blown diagnosis? A view of one particular group, or the entire organisation?

For large organisation transformation programmes, such as moving from a product-oriented to service-oriented environment, or a centralised structure to decentralised, you will need to use an assortment of the following:

▌ culture web

▌ culture alignment framework

▌ day in the life of (DILO) diagnostic.

For smaller scale changes, select one or two of the tools, and if you require more analysis you can decide to broaden the assessment.

Culture web

Gerry Johnson and Kevan Scholes defined this (Johnson and Scholes, 1993), looking at the following five areas that influence and interact with an organisation's espoused paradigm: what the organisation is about; what it does; its mission; its values. These five areas are:

1. control systems
2. organisational structures
3. power structures
4. symbols
5. rituals and routines.

This tool yields qualitative results, in a comprehensive cultural framework. It can yield quantitative results if you use questionnaires instead of interviews, focus groups or observations.

Download template: *Culture Web*

Culture alignment framework

The alignment framework looks at four particular culture levers:

- symbols
- behaviours
- business context
- rewards and measurement.

This tool yields qualitative results, in a simplified cultural framework. As with the culture web, it can yield quantitative results if you use questionnaires instead of interviews, focus groups or observations.

Download template: *Culture Alignment Framework*

DILO diagnostic

This is a tool that is more individually specific and based on observation. The change manager or other team member spends a full day 'shadowing' an employee. You observe and record the employee's activities, asking occasional questions for clarification and better understanding. In addition, the employee can keep their own diary notes.

This tool yields qualitative results, based on a simplified cultural framework.

Download template: *Day In The Life Of Diagnostic*

Step 3: Design and customise your tools

Once you have selected your tool, design your approach, questions and visuals to probe around areas in the organisation most affected by the change. Keep your questions precise and specific, and cover all areas of culture. All of the culture diagnosis tools can be documented as a series of questions for use in one-to-one interviews, focus groups or an observation checklist. Workshops are another alternative – for example you could run a workshop using the culture web as the basic structure, asking participants to articulate what occurs in the current culture. Example questions are included in the downloadable templates.

Make sure in whatever format you choose, your questions probe for specific examples and drive for tangible responses about the 'how?', not the 'what?'. This will make presenting your results back to senior leaders more effective, and will help you recommend an action plan. The need for structure here cannot be overemphasised. Culture as a concept resists structure, so be very clear in your own head what you are trying to achieve as you construct the tools to do so.

Step 4: Gather the information and analyse results

This is the key part of the 'culture assessment' process and must be done thoroughly and with a critical eye. This is the step that separates those who dabble in culture from those who become culture gurus. You can have great tools and great questions, but all that can go out the door when you are in a room with a sceptical interviewee. Be prepared to talk about what you are doing and why, and explain how their responses will be used. This is good practice with any data gathering and, in that moment, will test every fibre of your understanding of culture. If the interviewee picks up that you are becoming confused or overwhelmed, or cannot really explain why you are there, you may as well shut down the interview. Keep yourself focused and structured, allow the conversation to go where it needs to, and pull it back to the tangible areas of culture you are assessing.

Depending on your tools and approach, you may want to set up a table to capture the results of your analysis. Alternatively, you may want to mimic the models and how those are presented visually, looking for trends and obvious areas of focus, in a presentation slide format.

Step 5: Sharing results and risk management

Share the results of your culture assessment with the change sponsor, change team and project manager. If you have located areas or groups of people where culture presents a significant risk to the success of the project, this will need to be addressed by sponsors and change leaders.

Culture audit

What is it?

A culture audit looks at all the documents, existing projects, data, statistics, websites, posters, etc. that set the behavioural tone in an organisation ('how we do things around here'), and checks for alignment to the change project. It is a 360-degree scan of the organisation, and is your due diligence that you have considered where the change could impact indirectly or inadvertently.

Why do it?

A culture audit reveals all the specific areas where there is behavioural alignment and potential conflict between the as-is and the to-be. If these areas are not revealed proactively, there is little chance that the introduced change will be sustained once the ownership transfers from the project to 'business as usual'. At the very least, someone will have to do some serious mop-up after the fact, and the culture audit greatly reduces the chance of that happening. A culture audit also brings to light the decentralised nature of culture, allowing the change manager to identify where those specific areas of culture ownership are located.

When to do it

Design phase.

How to do it

Step 1: Identify all the materials

Create a list of all the existing local and organisational documents, websites, posters, reports, data, etc. that would be included in a culture audit. These could include specific examples under the following broad headings:

1. Training and development materials
   - Leadership development programme objectives
   - Employee orientation programme objectives
   - Training offered by area/level
2. Employee recruitment and retention
   - Employee promise
   - Employee surveys
   - Role descriptions
   - Dress code policies
3. Targets and measures
   - Retention, turnover data
   - Productivity measures
   - Knowledge management measures
   - Sales targets
   - Performance management measures, scorecards
4. Strategic planning
   - Organisation vision, mission, values
   - Project charters
   - Transformation programme objectives
   - Service level agreements between customers or between working areas

5 Marketing and public relations

- Customer promise
- Brochures, posters etc.

6 Internal communications

- Newsletters
- Quarterly communications from leadership
- Annual reports
- Intranet sites

Step 2: Analyse the materials for potential conflict or support

In each area, analyse the material for potential areas of conflicting behaviour between the current culture and the future look and feel of the change you are introducing. Keep an eye out for areas of close alignment, as this will help bring sustainability to the change. Allowing the future look and feel to attach itself to the existing culture demonstrates that there is an overall direction, and reassures employees where they, with others, are heading.

Step 3: Determine any changes or activities required

Once you have categorised all the potential areas of conflict or support, list them for consideration into the culture action plan. The following table is a culture audit example – moving to a service-oriented organisation.

Area	Alignment	Conflict

▌Training and development materials:
  – Leadership development programme objectives
  – Employee orientation programme objectives
  – Training offered by area/level
	▌Leadership development objectives align and leaders are challenged to develop service-oriented metrics	▌Employee orientation makes mention of product-orientation, not service-orientation
		▌Little or no training on service offered at mid-manager level

Download template: *Culture Audit*

Culture action plan

What is it?

A culture action plan is a structured way to introduce change into the existing culture, without embarking on complete cultural change. This is used when there are limited activities to complete, which will not stretch beyond the duration of the change project.

The culture action plan takes into account the behavioural 'to-be' (future organisation look and feel), the current culture 'as-is' (culture assessment), and what documents, data, websites, programmes, etc. exist in the organisation (culture audit). The action plan brings all the existing analysis together, and turns it into tangible activities that will align either the change to the culture, or the culture to the change.

Why do it?

The culture action plan allows you to make adjustments to the current culture, to allow a particular change to take place. It keeps activities limited to specific areas of business, with specific ownership, and within a limited period of time. It also allows you to track activities, check for any potential overlap and manage multiple fronts of activity simultaneously.

When to do it

Develop phases.

How to do it

Step 1: Gain agreement that a culture action plan is required

Once you have completed your analysis of the current culture in the most affected areas, warning signs may begin to appear for certain departments or groups that could endanger the realisation of the future look and feel. These signs must be discussed and agreed with the change sponsor and project manager in that they pose a serious risk to the benefits realisation.

Step 2: Analysing culture 'as-is' and 'to-be'

Based on the culture assessment and culture audit, what will need to change to support the future look and feel the project is trying to create?

In comparing the 'as-is' and the 'to-be':

▌ What cultural strengths have been highlighted as enabling your change project?

▌ What factors are hindering your project or are misaligned with one another?

▌ What factors will you encourage and reinforce?

▌ Which factors do you need to change?

▌ What new beliefs and behaviours do you need to promote?

▌ What are the documents, statistics or websites that are in support or conflict with the change?

Step 3: Develop a first draft action plan

This could contain activities such as:

▌ change the office layout

▌ hold employee sessions on 'mindset shift'

▌ hold leadership sessions on 'mindset shift' and role modelling behaviour

▌ remove old posters/signs that refer to previous behaviours

▌ align 'to-be' behaviours with process mapping (roles and responsibilities)

▌ align 'to-be' behaviours with performance and rewards

▌ align 'to-be' behaviours with training requirements

▌ align 'to-be' behaviours with recruitment criteria and induction processes

▌ align organisation future look and feel with the organisation intranet site

▌ align change drivers to performance measures, management information systems and statistics

▌ align 'to-be' to affected HR policies and processes.

The 'mindset shift' is an exercise that is best done in a workshop setting, and instructions and examples can be accessed via the template *Polarity Maps*.

Download template: *Polarity Maps*

The change manager is responsible for monitoring the overall plan and ensuring continual alignment as the activities are completed – this may be by the change network or the change leaders. To help with this, you may want to develop an overall roadmap of what is occurring in each area of the organisation. You can use existing plan and roadmap templates from the organisation alignment lens.

Step 4: Agree and implement an action plan

Once you have a first draft, it is time to decentralise ownership to the areas that hold accountability. You can hold individual meetings or a workshop with change leaders or the change network, whichever way will assign responsibility in an agreed timeframe. Figure 11.1 is an example of one owner's action plan.

Owner	Alan Jones	Contract ID	Respect for Leadership			Change Contract

1. Objectives/Performance Challenge

e.g. To make Leadership team and processes more visible and transparent to staff. To increase staff confidence by taking, and labelling, key decisions attracting staff. To create a culture where we can admit when we are wrong or do not know and live the value of being open, fair and honest.

2. Team members

e.g. J Smith (Training); AN Other; HR representative; TU representative

3. Activities/Actions

	R	A	C	I
e.g. Review deputisation reports to identify numbers, names and duration of assignments	HR Rep	HR BP		
e.g. Review policies and guidelines to clarify and confirm maximum periods for temporary assignments				
e.g. Conduct training needs assessment for temporary promoted managers re: people management skills/ requirements	J. Smith	Training DP		

4. Requirements & Dependencies

e.g. HR Resource re: reports	0.5 days

5. Measures

e.g. Increase in response to Question x	*2007 Staff attitude survey*

6. Timelines & Milestones

e.g. Proposal/paper for Board approval	*End Feb 07*

7. Sign off

Activities completed	signature
Timelines and Milestones delivered	signature
Measures realised	signature
Performance Challenge met	signature

FIGURE 11.1 Culture action plan template

Employee motivation and skills

Change prism lens	Step-by-step guides
Employee motivation and skills	Change readiness assessment
	Resistance assessment and approach
	Training strategy and plan
	Training needs analysis
	Training course design
	Training effectiveness measures
	Downloadable templates
	Preparatory CRA Workshop Output
	CRA Ratings Analysis Spreadsheet
	CRA Dashboard and Example RAG Criteria
	CRA Review Workshop Agenda
	CRA Action Plan
	Identifying and Managing Resistance
	Polarity Maps
	Training Rollout Schedule
	Training Strategy and Plan
	Training Needs Analysis (Spreadsheet)
	Training Course Design Planner
	Training Evaluation and Measures (Worked Example)

Change readiness assessment

What is it?

CHANGE READINESS ASSESSMENT (CRA) is a methodology used to determine the readiness of an organisation, or parts of it, to introduce change. It uses a set of eight criteria which have been found to be key indicators of successful change implementations. Conducting a change readiness assessment will:

▌ identify the organisational impact of the change

▌ obtain an index and benchmark of key stakeholders and operational areas regarding their 'readiness' for change

▌ identify enablers and barriers to change

▌ set priorities for the way that resources are used for change management activities and interventions.

A CRA is typically carried out using a combination of workshops and questionnaires supplemented, if appropriate, by focus groups and one-to-one interviews. It should be refreshed regularly to track how far agreed actions have closed any identified gaps.

Why do it?

As well as ensuring that limited resources are used effectively and at the right time, the CRA supports leadership thinking about what success will look like in terms of behaviours and actions, and project teams with an indicator of readiness for implementation. Like the CIA, the CRA drives the development of targeted change activities, aimed at minimising and managing potential barriers to change. It is good practice to cross-reference the CRA assessment with the CIA to identify the 'hotspots', which are any areas of high impact but low readiness.

When to do it

The diagnose/design phases. Subsequent reviews of the level of change readiness can be conducted:

▌ at key project milestones – sign-off, end of a phase, critical points to measure progress

▌ when a project is perceived to be getting into difficulties.

How to do it

Step 1: Define your approach

The CRA is usually delivered in three stages: preparatory CRA
workshop; survey; review workshop.

Step 2: Select your participants

Workshop participants should be those who can give an informed
and representative opinion about the current level of
understanding and perceptions in different areas of the business. It
is important that participants are willing and able to offer open and
honest opinions about current attitudes and issues. Participants
should include, but not be limited to, the following: change
leaders; subject matter experts; change networks and other
stakeholders. An effective workshop will normally not have more
than 25–30 attendees. If necessary, a prioritisation exercise should
be conducted.

Step 3: Preparatory CRA workshop

The workshop should last approximately half a day and should be
structured around brainstorming and discussions on three topics
that will be documented and used to inform the CRA
questionnaire:

1. understanding and clarification on the objectives and nature of
   the project
2. identification of up to eight critical success factors (CSFs) in
   language that makes sense to employees
3. a high-level review of potential barriers to change based on
   previous experiences of change.

It will make your life much easier if you can align or match the
CSFs chosen to the eight lenses of the framework. Even if the
terminology changes, try to maintain the groupings/subject matter
as this will enable you to use the templates virtually unchanged. If
this is not possible, you will need to redraw and reorganise the
criteria for assessment.

Download template: *Preparatory CRA Workshop Output*

Step 4: Design the CRA questionnaire

The CSFs and identified barriers from the preparatory CRA workshop should be reflected in the content of the questionnaire. The questionnaire must be prepared early to allow time for people to receive, complete and return the forms. You must also take into account the channels to use (e-surveys, web-based or paper-based surveys) that (1) are likely to give you the greatest percentage return and (2) reach all the representative groups. An example selection of questions across the eight lenses below was used by an organisation – in practice we grouped the questions differently and the CSF names were changed to be more meaningful to the employees:

Critical success factors	Issue	Score 1 2 3 4 5
Strategy and future state	I understand the business reasons for implementing the project.	☐ ☐ ☐ ☐ ☐
	I understand the impact of the project on the organisation.	☐ ☐ ☐ ☐ ☐
	I understand how the programme fits in with other business initiatives.	☐ ☐ ☐ ☐ ☐
Planning and management	I have confidence in the project plan in place and have been informed about progress.	☐ ☐ ☐ ☐ ☐
	Project planning takes into account local projects and other business priorities.	☐ ☐ ☐ ☐ ☐
	I am confident that an effective process for identifying and resolving problems and issues during the project is in place.	☐ ☐ ☐ ☐ ☐
Leadership and capability	Project sponsors demonstrate commitment to the project through their actions.	☐ ☐ ☐ ☐ ☐

Critical success factors	Issue	Score 1 2 3 4 5
	Change leaders and the change network help create energy and enthusiasm around the change.	☐ ☐ ☐ ☐ ☐
	I am confident that the right resources, based on knowledge, skills and attitude are allocated to the project.	☐ ☐ ☐ ☐ ☐
Stakeholders and communication	I have a clear understanding of 'What's in it for me?'	☐ ☐ ☐ ☐ ☐
	I am confident that strategies are in place to build understanding, commitment and buy-in from each group affected by the project.	☐ ☐ ☐ ☐ ☐
	I know where to find information or who to contact if I need information on the project.	☐ ☐ ☐ ☐ ☐
	I receive information at the right time and in the right way and am supported to giving feedback to the project.	☐ ☐ ☐ ☐ ☐
Organisation alignment	Some people will have to change what they do to get the most out of the new working practices or processes.	☐ ☐ ☐ ☐ ☐
	There is a clear link between organisation objectives, functional objectives and individual objectives.	☐ ☐ ☐ ☐ ☐
	Work targets will be adjusted to reflect the new ways of working.	☐ ☐ ☐ ☐ ☐
Resilience and capacity	I believe this project is necessary and will be successful.	☐ ☐ ☐ ☐ ☐

▶

Critical success factors	Issue	Score
		1 2 3 4 5
	Sponsors will remove barriers and allocate the resources needed to accomplish the change (time, best people and funds).	☐ ☐ ☐ ☐ ☐
	My team is ready, willing and able to make the required changes that the business needs.	☐ ☐ ☐ ☐ ☐
Culture and behaviours	I am clear what the future behaviours are.	☐ ☐ ☐ ☐ ☐
	Existing behaviours are being taken into account by the project; some resistance to the change is anticipated and will be addressed.	☐ ☐ ☐ ☐ ☐
Employee motivation and skills	I am confident that participation in the project is viewed as a development opportunity rather than a risk.	☐ ☐ ☐ ☐ ☐
	I am confident that the concerns of people affected by the project will be addressed.	☐ ☐ ☐ ☐ ☐
	I am confident that the skills I will need to learn will be identified and that a relevant training programme will be delivered at the right time to give people the right skills.	☐ ☐ ☐ ☐ ☐

Recipients are asked to assign a score for each factor, using a point scale, such as:

5 = I strongly agree

4 = I agree

3 = I am neutral about this factor

2 = I disagree

1 = I strongly disagree.

Once the questions are drafted they should be agreed with the programme leadership team and the business leaders.

Do not get carried away and be indiscriminate about sending surveys to all and sundry. Remember – you will have to process and analyse what comes back.

It is worth considering at this point, whether you want to identify results from certain groups (departments or job grades) in which case you will need to insert some demographic questions to enable later analysis. Be careful not to over-segment as it may deter people from responding if they think their answers can be traced back to them.

Step 5: Preliminary analysis of results

If you (and the respondents) have access to PCs and the internet, electronic survey software and providers exist that will analyse the results for you. However, if you are processing paper copies manually, it is best to use a spreadsheet which will allow you to sort and manipulate your data. An example of such a spreadsheet is as follows:

CSF	Question	Rated 1	Rated 2	Rated 3	Rated 4	Rated 5	Average rating

The average rating is calculated as:

$$\frac{(1 \times \text{no. ratings}) + (2 \times \text{no. ratings}) + (3 \times \text{no. of ratings}) + (4 \times \text{no. of ratings}) + (5 \times \text{no. of ratings})}{\text{Total number of responses (inc. don't knows or blanks)}}$$

A readiness indication scale is then applied to the average rating score for each question. This will tell you which questions and areas/CSFs are in poor readiness and require action planning:

Average rating between	0.00–2.74	High readiness
Average rating between	2.75–3.74	Some concerns/issues
Average rating between	3.75–5.00	Low readiness

Download template: *CRA Ratings Analysis Spreadsheet*

Step 6: Presentation of findings

The most common and visual way of reviewing and prioritising the CRA findings is to use a dashboard. Each critical success factor is rated against the 'What does successful look like?' criteria identified in the preparatory workshop to give a red, amber or green (RAG) status. Red indicates low readiness, amber indicates some issues requiring solutions and green indicates no significant issues. Assuming that the critical success factors are aligned with the eight lenses, this will look something like Figure 12.1.

FIGURE 12.1 Change readiness dashboard

To drill down into more detail, you can use the analysis spreadsheet (step 5), with the 'average rating' column colour-coded to show the RAG status for each question. This is particularly useful to focus attention on specific issues and in response to challenges or attempts to dismiss findings by stakeholders.

Download template: *CRA Dashboard and Example RAG Criteria*

Step 7: Review workshop

The third component of the assessment is the review workshop. The purpose of this workshop is to inform stakeholders and key project team members of the assessment findings and collectively to formulate action plans to address specific areas of concern.

The workshop will be structured around:

▌a walkthrough of results from the change readiness questionnaire

▌a discussion to identify ways to address barriers to change highlighted by the results

▌an exercise to develop recommended action plans for each of the eight critical success factors.

Pre-defined templates/exercises to document the outputs from brainstorming and discussions are very useful as they focus the attention of the participants on the outputs required and also provide structure to the discussions. It will also make your life or that of your facilitator much easier. However, this is a matter of style and you may choose not to do this. An example of an action plan template is shown in Figure 12.2.

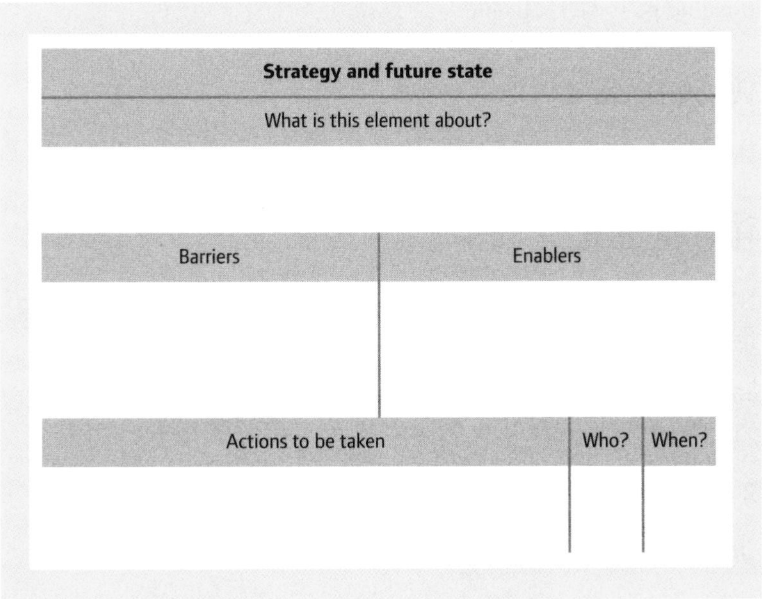

FIGURE 12.2 CRA workshop output and action plan

Download templates: *CRA Review Workshop Agenda; CRA Action Plan*

Resistance assessment and approach

What is it?

A resistance assessment and approach is part of managing stakeholders through the change. This aligns closely to motivation, in that it helps you to identify pockets of resistance, and equips you with the skills and tools to manage it.

Why do it?

Resistance to change crops up in many aspects of the project, in any number of groups. Identifying resistance and managing it actively will smooth the path for the change, and allow activities to occur without costly delays. It also sets up the conditions required for the change to be successful, and ultimately for the benefits of the change to be realised.

When to do it

Design phase (repeated in develop and deliver phases).

How to do it

Step 1: Up-skill your change team in identifying and managing resistance

Conduct a simple knowledge session on identifying and managing resistance. The purpose is to equip the change team with basic skills so that they can unblock resistance when they see it occurring.

Download template: *Identifying and Managing Resistance*

Step 2: Identify groups where resistance has already occurred or where it is likely to occur

Use your stakeholder analysis, sponsorship map, CIA and CRA to identify areas of potential resistance or where resistance has already occurred. This is best done in a group with the change team, so a full picture is provided. It is important to remember that change leaders and the change network are meant to role model accepting the change, so those are your priority groups for dealing with any areas of resistance.

Step 3: Develop an approach to manage resistance

Your resistance management approach should be planned and organised. Ideally, it is short, sharp and could easily embed into other scheduled activities. Examples of activities to include in the resistance management plan are:

- group education sessions about managing personal change and resilience
- one-to-one meetings with key resistors to air concerns and develop trust or acceptance of the project and the team
- workshop sessions using polarity maps for 'mindset shift'.

Timing is important. Manage resistance in your change leaders and change network first, and then with targets/employees as the change implementation approaches. Attacking resistance too early means the change may not have become meaningful enough, and it is a less valuable conceptual discussion rather than a strong, realistic one.

Download template: *Polarity Maps*

Step 4: Execute the plan and monitor for additional, unexpected resistance

Once you have begun to uncover and manage resistance, check if it is making any difference. You should see roadblocks being removed, timelines being met, decisions being made, people reading communications, attending training and generally showing signs of acceptance. If more resistance surfaces, go back to the concerns raised and manage them. This is likely to have been done many times over the course of the project, and more frequently as it becomes 'real' to people and no longer something that may occur in a hazy future.

As a change manager, achieving commitment is ideal, but moving someone from resistance to acceptance is good enough!

Step 5: Report or escalate any persisting resistance to the change sponsor

If all else fails, it is up to the change sponsor to determine how best to deal with persistent resistance. Coach your sponsor on how to manage resistance and have a frank discussion about the consequences of inaction. Monitor the resistance and report back again if needed.

Training strategy and plan

What is it?

Training[1] plays an important role in developing desired attitude, knowledge, skills and performance. The training strategy outlines the objectives, approach and requirements for the delivery of training and aims to ensure that employees affected by change are able to perform their jobs/roles effectively in the new organisation. The training strategy should be developed in cooperation with, and agreed to by, the key stakeholders and include:

▌ training model and approach

▌ governance

▌ summary of training needs analysis

▌ overview of training/learning solution

▌ high-level training plan

▌ rollout schedule

▌ transition arrangements (if required)

▌ training delivery considerations

▌ training evaluation.

Why do it?

Development of a training strategy ensures that resources and requirements for training delivery are identified early in the

1 Training is defined by the CIPD as 'an activity which is instructor-led and content-based'.

programme. It also provides guidance on how training will be developed and delivered so that dependencies can be identified and also communicated to reassure staff impacted by the project. These benefits may be manifested as higher levels of motivation amongst staff, lower turnover and higher productivity.

When to do it

Design/develop phases.

How to do it

Step 1: Strategy selection

We recommend that you conduct a meeting with the project leadership to discuss the options and agree the training approach. There are several options available to you such as: analysis of scenarios or case studies; model offices or simulations; classroom-based learning; self-directed learning; outdoor training; and experiential learning (aka 'on the job' learning). You will need to make a decision about which approach to adopt based on your knowledge of the organisation, culture, the training parameters you need to keep within and learning style preferences from the training needs analysis.

As well as deciding the training approach, you will need to define how the training will be delivered. The course can be a single intervention that is run as a stand-alone event and that everyone will attend (it can be one big event or several identical events run in parallel). The course could be delivered as stand-alone events, but phased over time, with different groups receiving training at different times. There is also a modular approach which delivers training content in chunks with gaps between different topics or modules.

When you have decided on the type of training and delivery, you will need to decide the delivery channel and how the training will actually be administered: instructor-led training; peer-to-peer training; web-based training; or blended learning.

An important factor in developing the training approach is whether the organisation will be transitioning through any interim stages before the future organisation is achieved. If changes are being introduced piecemeal, you may need to deliver the training in discrete packages to meet specific requirements or even provide an interim-state training strategy and plan to deliver the training required.

Step 2: Establish training governance

While the project life cycle is active, the project team has ownership for developing and delivering the training. However, once the project has been wrapped up and changes become 'business-as-usual' the ownership for training transfers to the business. This means that training for new staff, refresher training and the review and updates of training material will be conducted by the organisation's training department.

You will find it easier to hand over this responsibility if the training department is familiar with the approach and delivery so you should set up meetings to share the strategy and involve them in development discussions early. Your training department can also give you essential information regarding capacity and capability for the type of training you have identified. It can also help you decide whether the training can be delivered by internal resources or needs external expertise or manpower.

Before finalising this part of the strategy, you should also have a discussion with your training or HR department to ensure that the behaviours and skills you will be training either fit with existing competency frameworks or that the necessary changes will be made to those frameworks (this will also form part of your culture action plan).

Step 3: Summary of training needs

In this section, you will need to review the training needs analysis and draw out the common themes and preferences, learning styles, service, experience profiles, gaps and prerequisite training. You should indicate:

▌ numbers of groups and the criteria for grouping

▌ numbers of staff in each group

▌ the key tasks/processes each group is impacted by

▌ the capabilities to be developed for each group.

Step 4: Overview of solution

Your next step is to define and propose a high-level solution. Basically this is an outline of the intended course structure, duration and format. You will need to be clear at this stage what is in scope and out of scope regarding the course content. When you are designing a solution, there are a number of issues that you will need to explore and resolve, including:

▌ How much time is reasonable for employees to be released from daily operations? (This is especially challenging for field-based employees.)

▌ What is necessary or core ('must haves') to the training and what are the 'nice to haves'?

▌ How much background, 'big picture' or business knowledge are the participants likely to have and what should the course provide?

▌ What are the training objectives?

▌ Is this a 'stand-alone' session or a series of courses over a period of time?

Step 5: High-level plan

The high-level plan is a project plan or roadmap showing the order and timing of the key training activities and deliverables. Consider the following aspects in your plan:

▌ produce a training strategy

▌ develop learning objectives

▌ conduct training needs analysis

▌ design a training course framework

▌ design review meetings

▌ preparation and research (including copyright and licensing, diversity, legislation and codes of practice)

▌ communication

- budget management
- identify trainers
- design and develop materials
- test materials and update
- train the trainers
- identify IT requirements and support
- training administration and scheduling
- define measures of success
- evaluation and feedback.

An example of a plan is shown in Figure 12.3.

Step 6: Training rollout/deployment

The deployment or rollout schedule is a time plan showing which group and course will be run at what time and in what sequence. It is also good practice to include key activities, dependencies and programme milestones. The most common way to represent the rollout schedule is in the form of a Gantt chart (see Figure 12.4).

Presenting the deployment in a visual form like this means this chart can double up as a communication tool and changes and updates can be easily incorporated and are transparent to other project stream members and stakeholders.

Download template: *Training Rollout Schedule*

Step 7: Training administration

Depending on the chosen approach to training (step 1), there will be a significant role in making the arrangements so that the training can take place. As well as communications with the learners/employees on when?, where?, directions, start and end times, there are also logistical considerations to be addressed:

- training scheduling and administration
- travel arrangements and accommodation
- travel time

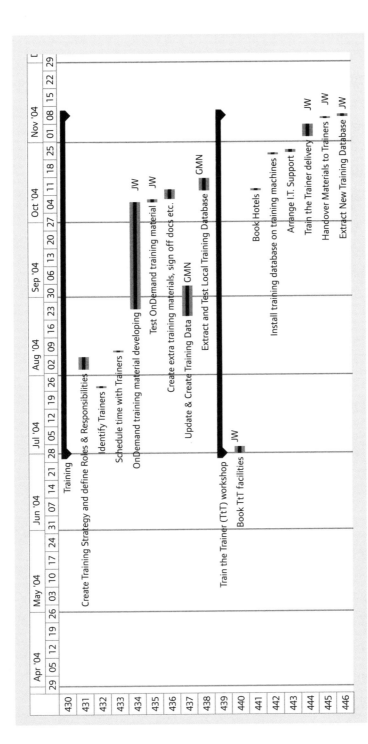

FIGURE 12.3 Example of training plan held in MS Project

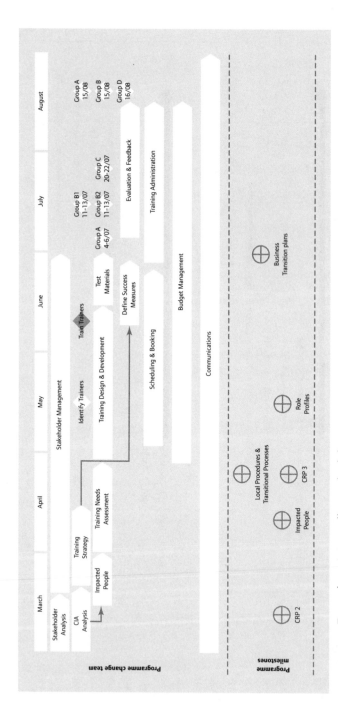

FIGURE 12.4 Example training rollout schedule

▌ meals and expenses

▌ lost training time (e.g. sick days, holidays)

▌ availability of training rooms

▌ costs – training room, trainers (e.g. if outsourced)

▌ training infrastructure (e.g. computers, networks, training environments, information)

▌ availability of trainers

▌ training requirements of trainers.

For e-learning based delivery, additional considerations include:

▌ IT support available on site

▌ context sensitive help

▌ links to other support and information mechanisms (e.g. policy information)

▌ network capacity and load on the network when accessing the e-learning application.

Step 8: Training evaluation and support

At each stage of training delivery, you should assess whether the training has been effective. Has it met learners' needs and expectations and provided them with the skills and knowledge to conduct their daily tasks? You (and the project team) will need to identify success measures based on the training/learning objectives. You will need to decide how to gather data from the learners. You can do this in several ways or by using a combination of approaches:

▌ student feedback – a quantitative and qualitative survey

▌ student examination – a written or oral test

▌ trainer reports regarding student performance

▌ system-generated student evaluations (for e-learning solutions).

Once training is delivered, it is important that employees have access to workplace support to help embed and reinforce their learning experience. Workplace support could take the form of:

▌ Q&A sessions, 'surgeries' or floor-walker support

▌ access to a helpdesk (usually by telephone or e-mail)

▌ desk aids or quick reference guides

▌ procedure manuals

▌ simulations/demonstrations that teach users the new ways of working.

Download template: *Training Strategy and Plan*

Training needs analysis

What is it?

Training needs analysis (TNA) is the systematic gathering of data to find out where there are gaps in the skills, knowledge and behaviours of employees. It involves the gathering of data about existing employees' capabilities and future organisation demands for skills, and the implications for changes in capability and roles. In its most basic form it is a gap analysis of current and required skills. Assessments are role-based (rather than process-based) and cover:

▌ audience size and locations

▌ future skills, knowledge and behaviours

▌ current levels of skills and competencies

▌ levels of pre-requisite/foundational learning required for users to get to the defined level of skills.

Key activities in training needs analysis are workshops and interviews conducted with business stakeholders.

Why do it?

A training needs analysis scopes out the breadth and depth of training required by role, giving clarity to the training strategy and informing the training plan. A TNA also gives an indication of the resources required to deliver the training.

When to do it

Design phase.

How to do it

Step 1: Identify impacted people requiring training

Using the job profiles and the change impact assessment, you will need to identify all those jobs/roles whose ways of working will be affected by the project implementation. These data can be generated effectively through a workshop or focused interviews with key stakeholders. During these activities, you should discuss the following questions:

▌ What problem needs to be solved?

▌ What training is needed and how should it happen?

▌ How must employee performance change to overcome the deficiency?

You should aim to collect, or at least verify, the following data:

Name	Department	Present job	Future job/role	Level of impact (H, M, L)

Step 2: Conduct learner analysis

Once you know who your target audience is you need to understand a little more about them so that you can tailor the training course design to be relevant and effective. You can find the information you need either by asking the corporate training team for the information or by conducting a short survey directly with the target audience. Either way, you need to be asking the right questions:

▌ What do they already know about the project or system?

▌ What standard/compulsory training have they received?

▮ What type of training was this (e.g. classroom, web-based, self-directed)?

▮ How would they rate themselves in the specific skills/competencies?

▮ How do they like or prefer to receive training, or learning style if known?

▮ General demographics – service, location, specific constraints or requirements.

Step 3: Context analysis

You will need to understand your training delivery parameters. These include availability of trainee time, project deliverables/timelines, costs, equipment, facilities and location. Another very important factor you should consider is the organisation's training culture: what are expectations likely to be; what has worked before; who needs to participate in or endorse the training; are there issues with training attendance levels?

Step 4: Job/task analysis

The last stage of the training needs analysis is to define the different tasks and activities performed by each of the different roles within the trainee group. This will inform your decisions on which individuals or roles can be trained together and how many separate groups will need training. This has implications on the number of different courses you may need to design and materials development.

The four tables over the next two pages provide an example of a training needs analysis conducted for the customer services department of a pharmaceutical company:

Customer response centre

Job role	#	Computer literacy	Tasks/modules	Learning style
Senior manager	1	Good	Navigation; querying; calendar; contacts; time off territory; activities; service request reports; reports; accounts; enquiry handling (tier 2)	Trainer led
Senior agent	2	Medium to good	Navigation; querying; calendar; contacts; time off territory; activities; service request reports; manage orders; accounts; manage standard answers; managing categories; FPOC enquiry handling	Trainer led
Agent	13	Medium to good	As above	Trainer led
Commercial/ switchboard	3	Medium to good	Navigation; querying; calendar; contacts	Online training (web)

Medical Information team

Job role	#	Computer literacy	Tasks/modules	Learning style
Manager	1	Medium	Navigation; activities; querying; contacts; accounts; service request reports; reports	Trainer led
Medical info officer	1	Good	As above and answer queries; medical information letters; manage solutions	Trainer led

Orders to cash

Job role	#	Computer literacy	Tasks/modules	Learning style
Financial manager (new in role)	1	Good	Navigation; activities; querying; sales reports; accounts; manage orders	PC using system-based training
Financial analyst	3	Medium	As above and FPOC enquiry handling	As above

Teleweb team

Job role	#	Computer literacy	Tasks/modules	Learning style
Manager	1	Good	Navigation; activities; querying; service request reports; reports; contacts; accounts; mobilise web/telephone campaigns; calendar; target lists; objectives	Trainer led and online training
E-detailing agent	8	Good	As above and answer queries; e-detailing permissions; schedule and conduct e-detail	As above

You now have a significant amount of information to inform the training strategy and plan. We recommend that you capture the data you have collected in a single document, such as a spreadsheet.

Download template: *Training Needs Analysis Spreadsheet*

Be aware! If the programme is delivering a new IT system, there will be a separate training team to identify and deliver systems/end-user training. You will need to work together to unify your strategy and approach, and ensure consistency between skills and behaviours.

Training course design

What is it?

Training course design is the process of developing a course and designing materials to educate, encourage and equip employees to deliver the business change. A training course can take the form of classroom-based learning, e-learning applications, outdoor events, web-enabled learning, coaching, team briefings or a 'blend' of these. Functional (technical) skills, process and role-specific dimensions should be covered in the content, opportunities for discussion for clarification and interpretation, and periods of reflection to internalise the learning.

Training course design should reflect Gagne's 'Nine Events of Instruction': gain attention; share learning objectives; recall prior knowledge; present material; provide guidance; elicit performance; provide feedback; assess performance; retention and transfer (Gagne, 1965).

Why do it?

Training course design ensures that the course is leveraged as the most powerful (and last) opportunity to communicate and share the change management objectives and messages.

When to do it

Develop/deliver phases.

How to do it

Step 1: Design course content and agenda

The first thing you will need to do is define the topics or sessions that will make up the training course. We recommend that you start by setting the context of the change before launching into the specific actions, tasks or system elements of the training. The context or background to the training should cover the following:

- introductions (trainers and participants – can incorporate 'icebreakers')
- house-keeping (toilets, fire exits, training rules – e.g. use of phones, breaks and refreshments)
- training overview (structure, course length, style of sessions, assessment, feedback etc.)
- training objectives (trainer *and* participant objectives and/or expectations)
- detailed programme (for specific day)
- business concepts and background for change (global and regional perspective)
- fit with local priorities and initiatives (affiliate specific).

The majority (70 per cent or more) of the sessions should be focused on changes to skills, knowledge and behaviours. You should try to construct the topics so that they tell a story: successful stories start with simple and few facts and build up through the course of the narrative into the full and complex situation. You will have to consider any narrative dependencies – topics that are dependent on participants having other information are scheduled after those 'pre-requisite' topics in the running order.

You may be in the position where several groups/roles are attending the same course, but where some topics are common, others may not be. It is sensible then to try and group the topics in a way to minimise interruptions and people dropping in and out of sessions. We have found that working through a rigorous planning exercise is the most effective way to build a course outline. An example from a national government agency is shown opposite:

No:	Session name	Sub-session	Nature	Intent/purpose	Methodology	Timing
0	Set up and preparation		n/a	Get everything ready	n/a	Previous evening /early morning
1	Objectives and outline agenda		Plenary	Overview of activities, structure and agree expectations	Review agenda outline, time contract and ways of working. Capture participant expectations on flip chart	10 mins
2	Sponsor overview	Where are we going and why? What do we need to do to get there?	Plenary	Validate intent, and position work done as an 'evolution not revolution'	Basic diagram (e.g. analogy of planning a journey) linking aim, purpose, values and behaviours. Share FI findings re: memorability of 'old' purpose – emphasising the intent of being good but too many words getting in the way. Share new purpose 'I will statements' – how they were developed and the commitment/ process by leadership	50 mins
3	Culture change programme		Wallwalk/ tradeshow	Moving from planning and preparation to implementation	Share the cultural vision statement and roadmap (based on Tmap issues) explaining the steps so far and the involvement of staff in shaping it	30 mins
	Break					15 mins
4	Agency leadership model	'What the journey looks like'	Group discussion /exercise	Making the behaviours meaningful to individuals	Share model template (with purpose and values completed) and run 'fridge magnet' exercise to match 'I wills' to values. Encourage debate and discussion	60 mins
5		Gaining commit-ment and buy-in	Facilitated discussion	Identify USPs and selling points for the model	Facilitated discussion about the characteristics and feelings we want the leadership (model) to convey	15 mins

No:	Session name	Sub-session	Nature	Intent/purpose	Methodology	Timing
6	Function of leaders		Plenary	Recognise own contribution re: behaviours and also what role is vs. others	Share 'hearts and minds' concept and apply to dichotomy of the leadership model (left brain/side = logical/analytical; right brain/side = emotional/feeling)	15 mins
	Lunch					30 mins
7	Decision-making matrix		Trade-show	Roll out the agency decision-making matrix	Brown paper tradeshow	20 mins
8	Delivering the communi-cation cascade	Meaningful communi-cation	Trade-show	Share communication models tools to increase buy-in	Brown paper tradeshow	20 mins
9			Practice	Revisit purpose of teamtime and revise meeting format	Split into two groups. Using the two models each team to decide the 'what' and the 'how' of teamtime. Exam questions are: (1) what role/level of engagement for DPs/G7s; and (2) where else can we apply this approach to other key communications/processes?	30 mins
10		Promoting a positive outlook	Group discus-sion	Answer the question 'Why is this time different?' and potential to influence future outcomes	Share examples of positive role models in and outside agency – brainstorm what makes them positive. What is their impact and what can we learn from them?	20 mins
11		Identifying and managing resistance	Trade-show	Provide techniques to respond to resistance	Brown paper tradeshow	20 mins
12			Practice	Prepare for possible challenges in workplace	Groups of four. Two case studies (one per pair): 5 mins preparation, 5 mins role play, 5 mins discussion	30 mins

No:	Session name	Sub-session	Nature	Intent/purpose	Methodology	Timing
	Break					15 mins
13	Culture change programme – your role and next steps	Next steps	Plenary	Increase commitment and buy-in	5 mins to consider exam question and write on a postcard what they will personally commit to doing differently re leadership and communication. Each to stand and read out before posting self-addressed postcard into the box	20 mins
14	Summary and wrap-up		Plenary	Ensure expectations and objectives are met	Review objectives and expectations captured in session 2, agree next steps where necessary and drive advocacy	20 mins

Once the topics and content have been identified and the running order established, you can add details such as the type or style of each session and even the activities that will happen in each session. At this stage you should also try and estimate how much time can be allocated for each session (defined in the solution outline section of the training strategy tool). Your activity planner can now double as your draft agenda.

Be sure to make provision for comfort or refreshment breaks and bear in mind the capacity of your learners – in other words, how much they can absorb in one day!

Step 2: Develop training materials

Having developed your outline agenda and the different sessions, you will need to prepare the materials you need to run the sessions. These can be presentation slides, practical exercises, templates or questions for discussions, clippings for collages, posters and tradeshows, working documents such as brown papers, manuals and handouts.

You should always give the materials you develop a 'dry run' to see how much time each topic/session takes. Working within the constraints imposed means the content and/or running order may need to be adjusted. The timings provide a useful frame for the trainer to operate within and sticking to timings will be essential if all course elements are to be covered effectively. The key here is to be honest about how long something will take – you will only cheat yourself and the participants if you cannot stick to them.

Step 3: Test with target groups and trainers

When the training course design is complete (end of step 2) you should conduct a pilot of the training course, preferably with the trainers who will be delivering the course as your audience. This pilot will act as a review (or integration test) of the course and all its elements. By doing this you can:

▌ familiarise the trainers with the course structure

▌ check your timings are accurate

▌ ensure the running order makes sense

▌ collect input from colleagues acting as participants

▌ make sure nothing has been missed out

▌ ensure the training objectives are met.

Also test the training administration arrangements are satisfactory.

Step 4: Finalise materials

The last stage in development is to adjust the course design, timings and/or materials based on the feedback from the pilot.

Step 5: Sign off

Finally, you will need to get the training course approved by the project leadership and/or change sponsor.

Download template: *Training Course Design Planner*

Training effectiveness measures

What is it?

Training effectiveness measures are quantitative and qualitative criteria that confirm that learning has been translated into better capabilities to perform the job and has brought about a sustained improvement or change. The criteria or measures must reflect issues important to the managers in the organisation:

▌ Can you apply what you learned to the needs of your job, your team/department, and the priorities of the business?

▌ Can you integrate what you learned into further learning opportunities available to you, and the developing requirements of your job, your team/department?

▌ What was the most important or valuable learning for you? Why? How did you learn this?

Why do it?

Measuring training effectiveness establishes whether the training provided has met requirements, expectations and that the necessary learning has taken place.

When to do it

Deliver phase.

How to do it

Step 1: Define the approach

You will need to consider the view of the project and of managers at all levels in the organisation about suitable metrics for assessing and reporting on the value of training. Performance in the business will depend on the capabilities developed by the learners. To gather this information, you should conduct a focus group or series of short interviews with management representatives. The key question to explore with them is: What measurable results (both short-term and long-term) from the training would you like to see for your area of responsibility?

Some possible measures you can use to develop the discussion are as below.

Quantitative	Qualitative
Reduced production and process costs	Improvement in demonstrated competencies
Reduced cycle times	Improvements in employee attitude survey ratings/feedback
Increased sales, market share, numbers of new customers etc.	Reduced problems – e.g. fewer accidents as a result of health and safety training, and grievances following employee relations training
Increased service quality, stakeholder satisfaction, etc.	Student testing/examination
ROI (return on investment)	Student perception/feedback

Step 2: Define the data collection method

When you have decided what to measure, you need to think about how you will gather data. The main ways are as follows.

▌ Questionnaires from the training team – these need to be very carefully thought through and piloted to check for question purpose and clarity, and the ease of, and time taken for, completion. They are useful in large projects, where interviews and focus groups might be too time consuming.

▌ Interviews and focus groups – allow for discussion and real exploration about learning, but take time and can not cover many people quickly.

▌ Feedback from performance reviews – a much under-used source of evidence for the value of learning. A few organisations do include a box to cover training, but hardly any take the chance to link the results to projects, plans and metrics.

- One-to-one discussions between managers and their staff – different behaviour/attitude demonstrated on return from a learning event, evidence of impact on the job and on the bottom line of the business.

- Self-reporting by learners – encourages people to think about what and how they have learned and are continuing to develop, to retain ownership of and responsibility for their development and growth.

Step 3: Inform and educate the trainers

You will need to ensure that all trainers and facilitators understand the measures and know how to relate the metrics to the training course and the business. You may wish to use the end result of training effectiveness measures as part of the lessons learned on the project.

Download template: *Training Evaluation and Measures (Worked Example)*

3 part

The change manager in action

Setting up for success

IN CHAPTERS 1 TO 4, we looked at the evolution of change management, its classification, analysis and the project management of change. In this and the following two chapters we will be looking more closely at the responsibilities of the change manager. The change manager's role has been described in Chapter 2, but here we try and share with you what this means in terms of your 'day job'. In other words, looking at the expectations of the change stream lead in projects and trying to answer the question 'What does a change manager do?'

In this chapter we look at the initial stage (diagnose) of a project when the change manager's focus is on understanding the business need and drivers for the change. Setting up for success includes some preparatory work before actual diagnosis can begin and building your awareness of the organisation context for the change. This context will be valuable as you decide on the order and timing of change management activities including what benefits the change is expected to bring, and the roles people will play in making the change come to life.

Myth: *If you know what to do, you'll be successful.*

Mythbuster: *Knowing what needs to be done is not the same as knowing how, and when, to do it.*

Understanding the relationship between project and business

There is a natural tension between change projects and the business. In an organisational landscape where there is always so much going on – strategy being set, new initiatives and projects introducing improvements, the challenge of running the business as usual whilst absorbing change, and decommissioning old stuff that doesn't work anymore – this is not surprising.

Projects that seek to introduce change don't float in a special bubble on a certain floor or in some ivory tower away from the day-to-day business. Projects should be designed by the business for the benefit of the business. While this may seem obvious and even simplistic, there are many project teams currently working away in organisations that seem oblivious to the idea that what is being created will ultimately be owned by someone else. It is easy for a project team to get tunnel-vision when working on one thing all day. Look at the strategic business case if you need to remind yourself of who owns the benefits.

> remind yourself of who owns the benefits

The reality of the business is that there are many competing priorities – a typical operations manager or director may need to link with day-to-day management of their area, with marketing, sales, finance and human resources, as well as projects – and how successfully change will be absorbed into that mix requires a deft hand and constant monitoring.

Organisational maturity

As you begin to build up a picture of your organisation and the context for the change, you will seek out documentation, reports, presentations and results. Some you may find, others you would expect to find but can't. What are the key performance indicators (KPIs)? What drives the business and how does it know it's doing well?

Organisations follow a fairly predictable evolutionary route, which results in reaching a certain level of organisational maturity (Humphrey, 1989)[1]. Organisations cannot skip levels of maturity, they can only transform one step at a time. It is important to know the current maturity of your company before embarking on any change or transformation, so that the scope and benefits are realistic. The level of maturity can be determined very informally (during meetings, while gathering data) or formally (using a questionnaire, one-to-one interviews or focus groups).

How mature is your organisation?

Level	How people describe the level	Question to determine level
Level 1: *Ad hoc*, inconsistent	'Fire fighting is a way of life'	What are the current KPIs in the organisation?
Level 2: Managed	'Success depends on management support'	What measures and processes are in place to maintain and manage KPIs?
Level 3: Consistent, repeatable, standardised	'Processes and technology to support are in place and results are shared'	What measures are in place to judge the success of KPIs?
Level 4: Comprehensive, quantitatively managed	'Data are consistently evaluated and trends are analysed'	How is the success of KPIs communicated to those who are responsible for influencing the measure?
Level 5: Optimised, continuously improved	'Processes are continuously and systematically improved'	What structures are in place to evolve and improve KPIs?

Very few organisations have mastered level 5. Most established organisations are at level 3 and want to improve to level 4. Because

1 Humphrey introduced the capability maturity model as a tool for objectively assessing the ability of government contractors' *processes* to perform a contracted software project. Though it comes from the area of software development, it can be applied as a general model to many areas of an organisation, such as systems engineering, project management and people management.

different areas of an organisation may mature at different times, it is not unusual for a level 2–3 improvement project to be underway in technology support, while a level 3–4 project is underway in finance.

By gaining an understanding of the KPIs in place, the change manager can cross-check that the vision being communicated and the proposed benefits are achievable with the existing level of maturity.

Factors driving change – pain and vision

In any company, there are a number of things that anyone will be working on to be proactive or reactive to the changing environment. As organisations become mature, their preferred approach to driving change becomes clear. As discussed in Chapter 3, many changes begin as ideas. What makes some ideas seem mandatory and some 'nice to have'? How is the change described? There are a number of factors, and most have to do with the way an organisation makes decisions about priorities, the culture and what it values, and the personality and preferences of the person at the top of the organisation.

There are two schools of thought on what motivates or drives change in organisations – are the change ideas pain-based or vision-based?

Pain-based

Change that is based on 'fixing something that's broken' is called 'pain-based change'. 'Pain management' is the conscious process of identifying and communicating targeted information to generate sufficient pain such that people who need to change are willing to change' (ODR, 1998).

If the prevailing culture in your organisation is to look constantly for gaps and then systematically close them, Figure 13.1 may be helpful. The quadrants show that there are problems and there are opportunities, both now and in the future, and correspondingly, what the pain that will drive change is.

is it a small scratch or a gaping wound?

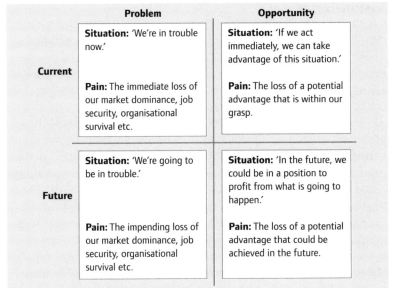

	Problem	Opportunity
Current	**Situation:** 'We're in trouble now.' **Pain:** The immediate loss of our market dominance, job security, organisational survival etc.	**Situation:** 'If we act immediately, we can take advantage of this situation.' **Pain:** The loss of a potential advantage that is within our grasp.
Future	**Situation:** 'We're going to be in trouble.' **Pain:** The impending loss of our market dominance, job security, organisational survival etc.	**Situation:** 'In the future, we could be in a position to profit from what is going to happen.' **Pain:** The loss of a potential advantage that could be achieved in the future.

Source: ODR (1998) *Fundamentals of Change Management*, Atlanta: ODR. Reprinted with permission.

FIGURE 13.1 Pain-based change matrix

Once you can describe the pain that drives the change, it is time to ask more questions about the priority of the pain – is it a small scratch or a gaping wound? In prioritising short-term (current problem) and long-term (future opportunity) projects, what are the costs of fixing something painful versus not fixing it? What are the benefits? And when will they be realised?

Most organisations prioritise the top-left corner to fix current problems. When you are working with the strategy and future state lens, it is helpful to raise this as a point of debate, particularly if there is a bundle of projects or programme that seems focused on the current problems without the balance of future (and longer-term) opportunities.

Employees will sense this 'current problem' approach as you help them make sense of and commit to the change, and it could unintentionally create a short-term view of the organisation's future. This will play out in your communications strategy and key messages to stakeholders. If this is acceptable, then it should be acknowledged as such and not left to be interpreted as something that has been inadvertently overlooked.

Vision-based

Another view is that change is based on creating a compelling vision of the future. 'Providing a vision of a better state or condition motivates someone to leave the status quo and begin the change process' (ODR, 1998).

This approach ignores the present and uses a technique similar to appreciative inquiry to probe into what's possible: What are the current strengths? How should we leverage those to get better? If your organisation responds to a change driver that is a vision of how things *could* be, then capture the words and describe the change in that way. For help with articulating the vision from different perspectives, there are tools to help you in three of the lenses – strategy and future state, culture and behaviours and organisation alignment.

If you choose a solely vision-based change, employees will sense this and the sceptics will need to see how the vision will make their lives better immediately. Often having either pain or vision is not enough.

HINTS+TIPS

Having done this exercise many times, we have subscribed to hybrid, bi-directional thinking: 'as-is' cannot exist without a 'to-be', and vice versa. You must have a foot firmly planted in each state, constantly scanning back and forth to deepen the understanding of both states, and managing the rift between with a good change plan. We recommend that you first define the 'to-be' as you and your colleagues' thinking is less likely to be constrained. You can fully explore the possible and will be less likely to dismiss ideas if you are not referencing the present situation and applying preconceived filters to the 'workability' of opportunities.

Whether you start from 'as-is' (i.e. a place of pain or list of gaps to close) or start from 'to-be' (i.e. a compelling vision of what's possible), both need to be taken into account when you firm up what that journey and change plan looks like. If you start with 'to-be', define what that means in real terms and measures, then look back to where you are now and see the difference. If you start with 'as-is', you will need to envision and commit to a 'to-be' so you know when you have reached your goal.

Change depends on urgency

Once you know the drivers of change, establishing a sense of urgency is essential in making change happen. Whichever school of thought you subscribe to, pain or vision, you cannot drive change without urgency. If there is no urgency, running the business as usual will take up all the available energy in the organisation and your change will never take shape, let alone be implemented.

Kotter (1996) believes that urgency can be either pain-based or vision-based, but always has to be steeped in reality and needs to give a good kick to complacency. Kotter has many ideas to establish urgency, and our favourites are:

▌ create a crisis by allowing a financial loss, exposing managers to major weaknesses *vis-à-vis* competitors, or allowing errors to blow up instead of being corrected at the last minute

▌ set revenue, income, productivity, customer satisfaction, and cycle-time targets so high that they can't be reached by conducting business as usual

▌ insist that people talk regularly to unsatisfied customers, unhappy suppliers and disgruntled shareholders

▌ use consultants and other means to force more relevant data and honest discussion into management meetings

▌ bombard people with information on future opportunities, on the wonderful rewards for capitalising on those opportunities, and on the organisation's current inability to pursue those opportunities.

The drivers and urgency need to be in place, in a way that makes sense and is clearly articulated, before an organisation's journey along the commitment curve can begin.

Setting the parameters

While drivers and urgency address some of the emotional aspects of change management, we strongly advise that you keep a clear and analytical head about what the change is there to achieve.

Large international bank help-desk consolidation

This project was to consolidate a number of local help desks into one central hub at a large bank, and lasted for three years. The project hummed along for the three years, moving desks, replacing systems and centralising resources. Once achieved, the project celebrated its success and disbanded. After six months of turmoil, staff quitting and unhappy customers, a rescue project was initiated to realise the expected benefits of lower costs by standardising new processes and ways of working. Almost 18 months had passed since the original project disbanded by the time those savings actually hit the business's balance sheet and customer satisfaction increased.

> you must have a clear definition of the desired business results

There are lots of reasons to drive change, but many projects do not have clear parameters of what they are there ultimately to deliver. Before deciding the level of effort you as a change manager need apply, you must have a clear definition of the desired business results early in the process.

Establishing a vision

If there is already a project vision ('to-be') for the future state of the organisation, the best place to look for this work is in the high-level business case or in the strategic objectives documented by the organisation. If this work has not been done before you join the project, you may have to take a role in facilitating the development of a clear project vision of the future. If this is the case, you should avail yourself of a copy of the strategic (or SWOT)[2] analysis which identifies the strengths, weaknesses, opportunities and threats that the organisation is facing, which can be used, by means of a workshop, to define what the future can or will look like.

---

2 A SWOT analysis template is shown in Appendix 1.

If the project vision is already defined, you need to understand how the decision making was accomplished. Check that the process followed reflects how your organisation works at an operational level. If it does, then that will smooth the path for you as a change manager in helping people understand what behaviours are required to make the change stick. The model below (Senge *et al.*, 1994) shows there are several different ways of decision making to establish a vision.

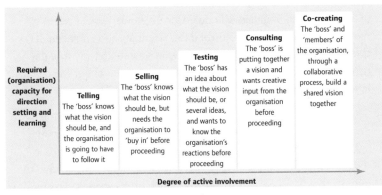

Source: From THE FIFTH DISCIPLINE by Peter M. Senge, copyright © 1990, 2006 by Peter M. Senge. Used by permission of Doubleday, a division of Random House, Inc.

FIGURE 13.2 Methods of decision making

If your organisation normally makes decisions in a 'consulting' manner, and the project vision was constructed in a 'telling' manner, then as a change manager you will need to put the vision through a consulting process so that it fits with the culture of the organisation. If not, it will be rejected, despite the sense of urgency or the drivers associated with it. If you need help articulating and documenting the vision, draw upon the tools in the strategy and future state lens.

The vision needs to be road-tested as what can occasionally happen with a vision, especially if it is set collaboratively, is the phenomenon known as groupthink. Groupthink is exhibited in collaborative settings by members who try to minimise conflict and reach consensus without critically testing, analysing or evaluating ideas.

Groupthink often occurs without people being aware or knowing it has occurred, and it happens for all kinds of very understandable reasons: a desire to avoid being seen as foolish; or a desire to avoid embarrassing or angering other members of the group. Groupthink may result in hasty, irrational decisions, where individual doubts are set aside for fear of upsetting the group's balance. While achieving a cohesive team is a desirable goal, it does not come without its own risks.

The space shuttle Challenger disaster in 1986

The Challenger exploded shortly after lift off on 28 January, 1986. The launch had been originally scheduled for 22 January, but a series of problems pushed back the launch date. Scientists and engineers throughout NASA were eager to get the mission underway. The day before the launch an engineer brought up a concern about the o-rings in the booster rockets.

Several conference calls were held to discuss the problem and the decision to go ahead with the launch was agreed upon. The group involved in making the Challenger decision exhibited several of the symptoms of groupthink. They ignored warnings that contradicted the group's goal. The goal was to get the launch off as soon as possible. Group members also suffered from a feeling of invulnerability, and therefore failed to examine completely the risks of their decision. Another factor that had suppressed the few engineers who were 'going against the grain' and 'sounding the alarm' was that pressure was on NASA not to delay the launch and Congress was seeking to earmark large funding to NASA given the large amount of publicity linked to the Teacher in Space programme. These misjudgements led to the tragic loss of several astronauts, and a huge black mark on the space shuttle's near perfect safety record.

Once you have a (1) road-tested, (2) realistic, (3) detailed and (4) executive sponsor agreed project vision of what the change is going to bring, the next step is to determine how you will know it has been achieved and when the results are expected.

Understanding the results and timing

Most changes in business, especially those formulated at senior levels in large organisations, seek to reduce cost, improve service and streamline efficiencies. But when do those things actually show up in the operations of the business and its people? What things need to change and by how much for those objectives to be met? It is critical that as change manager you understand the impact of realising the objectives on the areas of the organisation likely to be affected by the change. Conducting a change impact assessment will inform your understanding and also highlight areas that you will need to focus attention and effort on when you are planning activities and resources. Guiding principles for change will be written by this stage, and the change strategy will be starting to take shape. Tools to help you with this are included in Chapters 5 to 12.

How will those that are charged with making the change happen know that those changes have occurred? What are the measures that are in place that will move up or down to show whether you have achieved your goal? And what can you monitor along the way that will indicate if you are going to be successful?

Figure 13.3 illustrates the interdependencies between introducing change and realising the benefits. Your success and reputation may be viewed by the project and/or the organisation according to how

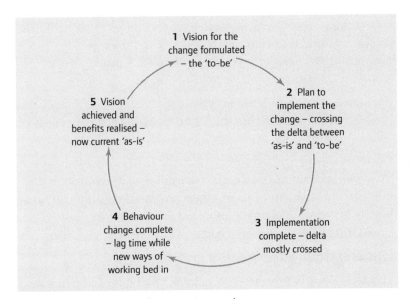

FIGURE 13.3 Change implementation cycle

much benefit your change delivers and when, so a shared and common understanding of what you are there to achieve will save you a massive amount of frustration in the future.

Change management depends on your clearly defining what you want to change and how you will measure the change along the way. This is all clearly tied to a business case for change, and if there is not one around on the day you arrive on a project, then find out who needs to build one or jump in yourself and start one.

Measuring future success

Increasingly, change management emphasis is on benefits tracking and measurement. Benefits identification and delivery is a specialised set of skills and there are people who work full-time identifying, measuring and tracking what exactly the organisation is getting from their project investment. From a project-wide perspective, this activity falls into the remit of the project manager, or the project management team, and should be part of the high-level business case. Depending on the scope of your role, it may be enough to equip yourself with knowledge about the expected benefits, knowing which people and processes are affected, and finding indicators along the way which will give evidence it is or isn't working. The change manager's role is up for debate (and like us, you may find it in your remit), but at a minimum we recommend you ensure that the 'people-related' benefits are not overlooked, misunderstood or double-counted.

> benefits identification and delivery is a specialised set of skills

There are some simple questions you can ask to find out what the indicators and benefits of your project are. What they are will relate directly to organisational maturity, and the availability and accessibility of data needed to measure any change in benefit:

▌ How is the strategy implementation being measured by the senior leaders? What is considered long term, short term and quick win?

▌ What are the measures that are expected to change as a result of this project?

- Who measures those, and how often? (Who owns the benefit is a key pitfall – always establish clear responsibility of who will be responsible for driving the change that results in the benefit, and who will measure the benefit.)
- What are those measures now, and what do you expect to see change?
- Over the duration of the project, how will you report to senior leaders and other stakeholders quantitatively and qualitatively to demonstrate progress?
- What are the phases along the project going to produce in short-term benefits, and how do those link to the ultimate project goals and sustainability by the business?

Measuring along the way

While working on a project which aimed to improve the lives of children who had serious needs (such as health, family, education, development), it was essential to change how social workers recorded information and shared it with others. To do that, social workers needed good practice, processes and IT to support the quality and mobility of the information. We decided to align the change deliverables to measures. As the deliverables were issued, we monitored them to see how they affected employees and regularly sampled to see if there was a change in the ultimate measure, the improvement in the lives of children.

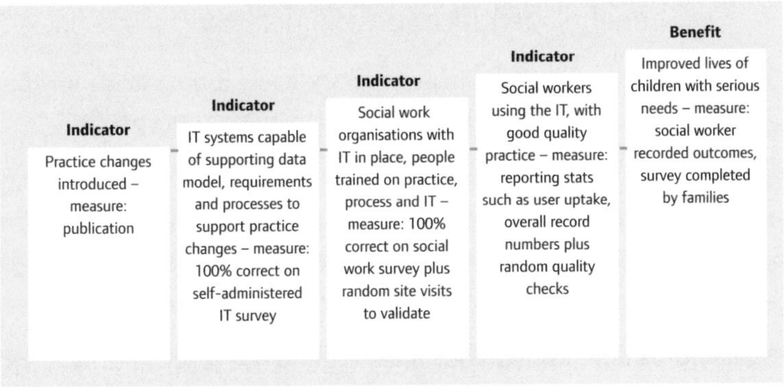

FIGURE 13.4 Change indicators and benefits

Setting the baseline

Once you have identified the vision and the measures associated with the vision, and before any more change work starts rolling, you need to set the baseline. This will need to be done in further detail in the diagnose phase, but a rough and ready measure as a 'stake in the ground' should be taken as early as possible.

Choose a day to take a 'snapshot in time' for all the measures that (1) you have defined as your future success criteria or KPIs and (2) may be useful indicators or proxy measures for new KPIs yet to be introduced. It doesn't matter if the measures are six months old at that time (e.g. resulting from an employee perception survey that went out earlier in the year) or are just measured that day. It is more important that you document the current performance and list your assumptions associated with specific measures.

Setting the baseline, as described above, sounds easy: it isn't. The measures could exist in many areas around the organisation, they will be owned by different people, and will be in various states of quality and accuracy. Be prepared to have a dialogue with each of the owners early so they know the snapshot day that the measure is required, and share a rough plan of how often they will be required to report on the measure over the course of the project.

> **HINTS+TIPS**
>
> This dialogue offers an ideal opportunity for you to gain some insight into owners' input, buy-in or understanding of the vision, and their views on reporting, progress and expectations.

Once you have a baseline measure, look back at the vision for the change – does that still hold true? Are the measures specific, reasonable and achievable? Are measures appropriate to the level of organisation maturity?

Change management roles and governance

Once you have wrapped your head around the scope and scale of the change, the drivers, urgency and measures, the next question often is 'Who is going to do all this?' Mapping change roles is a good place to start. Understanding how people relate to one another in an organisation is as important as understanding what they do on a daily basis.

Often, it is easy to confuse a role in project change management with a role in making change stick (business-as-usual). These are *not* the same thing.

Sometimes labels used to describe roles are used interchangeably (sponsor or change leader, agents or champions), so don't get too hung up on what you label a role. What is important is a common understanding of the role and its responsibilities, and how you title it is up to you. Once you choose a label, make sure you stick with it for the duration of the project, unless there is a sound project or business reason not to.

Change manager

This is the person who is responsible for identifying, leading and owning the people-related activities to deliver the change. The change manager may have an existing reporting relationship with the executive sponsor, or be assigned to the sponsor at the start of a project. Whatever the circumstances, the change manager and the sponsor will need to work closely together to effect change.

The change manager will work closely with the project manager, or may hold both roles on a project. If the change manager is part of a larger project team, aligning activities and understanding dependencies will be essential, especially if new processes or technology are introduced. If the change and the project manager are the same person, it may make life easier as less communication is needed, but your day will certainly be more hectic!

A change manager may be 100 per cent dedicated to the project and a member of the project leadership team. On smaller or less complex projects, change managers' remits may include completing the tasks themselves, or on bigger projects include management of a team or change network resources.

Alternatively, change management responsibility may be dispersed into a variety of roles from project managers and/or HR resources, whose main job is not change management and who may be allocating only 10–15 per cent of their time to change management activities. Your level of involvement, availability and the resources at your disposal will determine how much change management you undertake.

Sponsor

The sponsor is the single most important role in driving successful change. The sponsor is the *one* person within the business who has the power to stop and start a project. Sometimes called the executive sponsor, initiating sponsor or authorising sponsor, in a large organisation this person is usually a senior executive or equivalent, who has the power to direct others to allocate resources to a change (financial, technical and human). This person has the accountability for the change within their remit and will set the tone within the project.

It is important to identify early on who the sponsor is as this person plays a critical role in establishing and safeguarding the change vision, making decisions, influencing others, and will be recognisable and high-profile. This person may head up a steering group, take a lead role in workshops, and will be the person that others look to when deciding if this change is something to be taken seriously. This may not always be the most appropriate person for the change: be aware if this is the case, log the risk and move on.

> it is important to identify early on who the sponsor is

Even if you are in a completely flat organisation, such as a collective, cooperative or self-managing, there will always be a single executive sponsor, but they may not have any positional power external to the project.

HINTS+TIPS

* There can only ever be *one* top sponsor. Can we say this enough? Sponsorship by committee may exist on paper, but when it comes down to it, there must be *one* accountable

budget, *one* accountable leader, *one* accountable executive
who has the power and authority to oversee starting or stopping
a change.

⭐ If you can't find just *one* person, keep asking the question 'Who
does that person report to/take day-to-day direction from?'
until you have reached the top of the food chain.

⭐ It's important to understand at the same time the scope and
scale of the change, as the sponsor will be the person who can
make decisions and legitimise activities that fall within their span
of control. If the scale is large, then the sponsor will be the
person who has that scale in their span of control. Trust us –
keep asking the questions until you find the sponsor.

Change sponsor

In small projects this role is unnecessary and performed by the
sponsor. In large-scale change projects, there may be a designated
change sponsor who is different from the executive sponsor. The
change sponsor will be the 'first-point-of-contact' for the change
manager, and will provide operational advice decisions and means
of escalation during the project. This person will need to have the
trust and ear of the executive sponsor, the power and authority to
make decisions, and be given full reign to approve activities owned
by the change stream.

For a change manager, having a designated change sponsor can be a
very good thing – getting time on this person's agenda will be much
easier than getting any executive sponsor time, and you can use
your change sponsor as a sounding board for recommendations and
issues, and to act as your advocate for decisions at executive and
board levels.

For help with the role of the change sponsor, refer to the change
sponsor selection tool.

Change leaders

Change leaders are the 'local sponsors' of change, the line managers
that people look to when considering whether or not to take a

change seriously. Identifying and developing your change leaders to be as committed as your sponsor may be the most critical activity you can do to ensure successful change – they are the critical mass that will drive change through the organisation. The CEO may say it's important, but if your immediate line manager says to ignore it then chances are you will.

A change leader shares many of the same attributes and skills as a change manager. Below are examples of what may be required from change leaders (Ackerman-Anderson and Anderson, 2002).

- Build and secure local approval for the overall case for change, desired outcomes, and change strategy.
- Identify and shape the individual initiatives required to fulfil the overall effort, including organisational/technical and cultural/human initiatives.
- Input to the conditions for success and ensure their creation.
- Influence the design of essential change activities.
- Procure adequate resources for every phase of the change process and all major initiatives.
- Ensure successful alignment and integration of all change initiatives.
- Drive the change within individual lines of business or interface with the appropriate executives to do so.
- Direct and guide communications; communicate regularly about the change.
- Ensure and oversee the course correcting the project's outcomes, strategy and process.
- Build the capacity and skill of both managers and employees to succeed in future changes by ensuring that learning and development occur throughout.
- Identify measurements and oversee ongoing evaluation of benefits realisation.
- Ensure that the participation strategies selected are used effectively to mobilise support for the change.
- Mitigate key political pressures.

▌ Undergo changes in mindset and behaviour, and role model these changes for the organisation.

Change leaders also have the tough task of getting change accepted locally. That means standing firm in the face of direct employee opposition, publicly and privately supporting the change, recognising and praising success, and dishing out the consequences for poor behaviour.

For more information on defining the role of a change leader, refer to the tool in the leadership and capability lens.

Change agent

The change agent is the local conduit for the change. Reporting to the change leader, they are the point of contact for their colleagues providing clarity on the change. They are also invaluable in providing information back to the project on the issues and concerns raised by their colleagues. In large-scale change, there may be many change agents working together, forming a change network or being 'change champions' and completing activities on the change plan. The job of the agent is to interpret the vision of the sponsor for different groups (usually their own group, where they have intimate knowledge), and communicating it effectively while preserving the overall essence of the message.

▌ the change agent is the local conduit for the change

The change agent works alongside the change leaders to build commitment in the organisation, keep momentum going when things gets tough, and in driving local benefits realisation. The agent will need to have the skills of identifying, understanding and overcoming resistance, as they will experience it on a daily basis. Figure 13.5 shows the change agent's remit.

It's very easy as a change agent to get caught up in the emotions of change – you liaise between those who have the vision (exuding emotions like excitement, optimism, ambition) and those who have the reaction (may be angry, confused, sceptical or cynical). It is very important that agents maintain a neutral status and have no personal bias or agenda concerning the change. This can be very challenging as they may be asked to implement a change they disagree with, or be tempted to cut corners in order to make it easier for the people in turmoil.

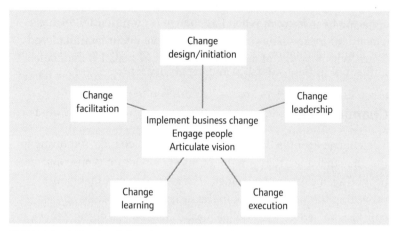

FIGURE 13.5 Remit of the change agent role

Targets or constituents

These are the large groups of people who will do something different as a result of the change initiative, project or programme. These are the people concerned in the from/to statements (Chapter 2). Part or all of their job may change, the technology they use may change, or relationships in the organisation will change. They will sell new products, use new processes or adapt to a different location.

Change agents, sponsors and change leaders all may be targets for change. In fact, looking at those groups initially, helping them understand they are targets themselves and need to commit to the change, will make large target populations much more open to the project. Targets exist at all levels, and while the change may be the right thing to do, it often seems better when everyone else except for you has to do it.

Consultants/contractors

These are 'hired guns' and are usually change managers or change team members. This can be the best option when the change being introduced is controversial, confidential, lengthy or you don't have the skills in-house. Hire a consultant when there is controversy, as sometimes it is more effective for an outsider to give tough, contentious messages. When the change is confidential, hiring a consultant makes sense as the activities can occur behind closed doors, with less risk of details leaking out in casual water-cooler conversation. If the change is lengthy, the resource toll may be too much for employees to take on in addition to their day jobs, so a consultant is an extra pair of hands. Your organisation simply may not have the change skill in-house, so experts are needed.

Advocates

These are people who want the change and are supportive. They may sit outside the formal and informal relationships driving the change, but have influence at all levels. They are best used to help win over highly resistant senior executives, change leaders, agents and targets.

All the roles above exist in any change, and how many exist depends on the scope, scale and nature of the change. Having a clear understanding of the roles, the numbers of roles and the personalities involved in making change happen will influence what change management activities you will select. Building relationships with key influencers, such as sponsors, will help you deal with what the change will bring and where to look for support. The programme sponsorship map, change governance structure and terms of reference tools will help you identify roles, and set clear responsibilities.

Getting agreement to begin the change

Once you have the parameters defined for the vision, high-level measures (identified and baselined) and roles mapped out, it is time to start serious project documentation. Although you will be spending much of your time running workshops, gathering requirements, expectations and data analysis, you will need to formulate and document a change strategy, a change plan and at least contribute to a benefits case. Having a clear understanding of the project and where it sits within the business, setting operating parameters and having an insight into the constraints and limitations of your organisation is often called transformation set-up.

> determine the expectations of what the change
> stream is to achieve

Setting and managing expectations and getting agreement on what the change stream will deliver is also a key activity at this time. Establishing the change governance structure and process should be high on your agenda (and part of the change strategy document), as should be producing a change charter, which should be signed off before you move into the design phase.

Your diligence in conducting assessments, producing project documentation such as the change strategy and charter, and getting agreement, will determine the expectations of what the change stream is to achieve within the boundaries and reality of the organisation.

Planning and preparing for change

IN THIS CHAPTER, THE EMPHASIS is on defining how the change manager is going to meet the objectives and work within the parameters and limitations described in the previous chapter. Once the preparations for change are complete, you will move into the planning activities – 'bridging' the gap between where the organisation is today and where it wants to be. In terms of the 4Ds, planning takes place during the design and develop phases and the focus is on how and by what means we are going to make change happen.

The planning and development lens of the change prism (Chapter 4) identifies key planning activities which, when combined, will occupy the majority of your time and which we will cover in this chapter. These activities are:

- the mobilisation of change team resources defined in the change charter
- determining milestones, deliverables and products re: the change plan
- risk management and reporting
- transition planning.

Myth: *No change management is better than some change management.*

Mythbuster: *Ideally we would all be able to do all the things we would like but in reality we have conflicting demands on our limited time. The key is to do a few things and see them through, not take on lots of things we 'ought to do' and then let them drop before they're completed.*

Change team resources

The change team is charged with implementing the change and it is critical that you get the right mix of people in the team and create the conditions for success. You will find tools in Part 2 to help you with change team roles and responsibilities. Building, managing or being part of a team is always an investment. Effective teams do not just happen, they need a lot of work, preparation and follow up. If you are bringing together people from different backgrounds and experience you need to allow time for them to develop as a team.

> effective teams do not just happen

Team member selection

You may have the luxury of handpicking your own team or having an established team in place which moves with you from project to project. However, in many cases, business leaders will identify potential candidates for change team roles and you will be limited to making your selection from among them. In selecting your team you need to include people with a variety of skills, such as knowledge of particular tools or techniques (e.g. a change impact assessment or stakeholder management) and/or subject matter experts (e.g. in employee communications or business processes).

You are more likely to satisfy all your requirements by not prescribing which roles specific characteristics, experience and skills should fit into, but rather creating the roles retrospectively within the team. An added benefit of this approach is that team members can participate in and have ownership of how the team is organised.

> A team is not a bunch of people with job titles, but a congregation of individuals, each of whom has a role which is understood by other members. Members of a team seek out certain roles and they perform most effectively in the ones that are most natural to them.
>
> Belbin, 1993

The skill mix within the team is important but the team must also be ready, willing and able to challenge the status quo and offer solutions that impact across the organisation. So, in addition to skills and experience, a successful change team must:

▌ have the confidence of both the management and the staff affected by the change

▌ understand and represent the different areas affected by the change

▌ demonstrate commitment to the change.

Resource allocation to the team and performance reporting is an important consideration that you must address. There are generally three options (in order of preference):

1. dedicated to one project, reporting directly to the change manager

2. dedicated to one project but reporting to a line manager or another/project manager

3. working on several projects at once with a department head and change manager jointly monitoring performance.

How the team members' time is allocated will have a massive impact on the operation and cohesiveness of the change team.

Change team development

All teams go through an evolutionary life cycle and there is a large body of literature on the development of teams. The best known is the Tuckman (1965) model which describes four[1] distinct stages as a team comes together and starts to operate. These stages of team development are commonly referred to as forming, storming, norming and performing. The team has a choice of either going with the flow of this change and reacting to it or actively managing its way through the unproductive times so that it is able to deliver as quickly as possible. This process can be subconscious, although an understanding of the stages can help teams reach effectiveness more quickly and less painfully. As the change manager you will need to

1 Tuckman refined and developed the model in 1977 (in conjunction with Mary Ann Jensen) with the addition of a fifth stage – adjourning.

consider how close a team you need to develop and being a high-performance team may not be necessary. This will depend on the complexity and duration of the project and organisation of change team roles and responsibilities. More information about team development can be found in Chapter 7, Leadership and capability.

In any new team or team new to a project, there a number of key activities you will need to undertake to get your change team functioning and effective. These are as follows.

Understand the project challenge

All team members should understand your projects' objectives and be committed to them. As soon as the team members are identified (and released from their previous roles) a team kick-off workshop or briefing should be held to ensure the project context, goals and focus for the change team are established and understood. This kind of event will also give the team members an opportunity to meet and get to know each other, which is particularly valuable if the team is to be 'virtual' or dispersed, for example co-located with client groups.

Agree common ways of working

Your team members may be chosen for their specialist experience or skills in a particular function but they will bring to the team their own style of working and problem solving. Understanding and leveraging individual styles and preferences will help the team become effective, but there also needs to be common and agreed ways of doing things (e.g. status reporting, meeting management, escalations, team communications) if the team is to be productive and seen to be professional.

Determine and allocate roles and responsibilities

In addition to the roles required to deliver the change stream products and deliverables, there are also some team administration tasks and activities which need allocating. A useful tool to capture who is doing what is RACI charting. RACI defines four roles and levels of participation: responsible (who does it), accountable (who owns it), consulted (who has input to make) and informed (who it is communicated to). The rule of thumb for executive sponsorship applies in team roles as well – you have to have one named person who is overall accountable for the activity.

In the example shown in Figure 14.1, the RACI was recharted every three months to cycle tasks around the team and give everyone development and team leadership opportunities. For more on RACI, refer to Appendix 5.

Activity \ Name	IB	JS	LM	RM	FS
Maintain team work planner	R	C	C	C	A
Weekly status reporting and Team ABCD	C	I	I	R	A
Knowledge manager (documentation and change control)	I	A/R	I	I	I
Benefits case	R	R	–	–	A
Fun and cake minister	C	C	A	R	C
Updating of shoebox visuals	A/R	I	I	I	I
Learning co-ordinator	I	R	A	C	I
Daily team facilitation, next steps and follow-up	R	R	R	R	A

FIGURE 14.1 Example of a change team RACI chart

Begin to develop relationships

As well as project activities, you will need to schedule in some 'team time' for relationships to be established and to grow. Regardless of whether the team is virtual, dispersed or co-located, you will need to think about how often the team will meet and for what purpose. You should also be thinking about how to blend work-related topics and team-building activity and whether there are activities you can do as a team outside of the meetings to continue development of working relationships. Finally, you should factor in how the team can start taking more initiative or leadership as it matures. The high-performance team (HPT) framework, and other techniques such as Belbin team roles and Myers-Briggs (MBTI), can also promote openness, sharing and understanding. The journey has been done before, it is largely predictable and you can help the team through it. Communicating quick wins also helps consolidate the trust and enthusiasm of team members.

> blend work-related topics and team-building activity

Review competency and skills needs

In small projects, very basic training or a detailed briefing may be all that is required at the outset. In more major undertakings, time invested in developing your team will help ensure you make the right decisions. Reviewing capability needs and training requirements can and should be factored into the 'team time' you schedule. If the knowledge is not there in the team, you need to work out jointly how to acquire it, and team members should be willing to teach and learn from each other. What we have found useful, as activities become 'live', is to hold team briefings on each topic and as the activity is closed out, the team shares experiences and learning. If you have the resources available, doubling up on key activities is a really good way to build specific competencies and overall change capability.

Monitor progress

The team can use either the Tuckman or the HPT framework to assess where it thinks it is in its development, but a more personal way is to allow the team to measure itself by creating its own assessment criteria or team temperature check. One of the drivers behind using these tools is to encourage openness and also because it is vital to identify and resolve conflict within the team as early as possible. In a new team (forming stage) we would advise that this is kept relatively simple and criteria are objective and impartial, such as:

- accountability
- commitment
- valuing others
- feedback and learning
- competencies
- technical skills
- common approach
- measurement.

An example of a team temperature questionnaire, which includes questions on each of these criteria can be found in Appendix 6. When a team get to the storming and norming stages, emotions and personal issues will need to be addressed, but we recommend this is done separately, for example through an off-site team exercise.

Programme/project team development

In addition to development for your own team, as the 'people' expert you will inevitably be called upon by the programme or project teams to plan, facilitate and deliver many of the same activities for them. You will find a tool to help you with this called the 'programme team development plan'. The change manager is also the person most often called upon to provide on-boarding for incoming team members throughout the project and coaching for colleagues and executives in the programme. It is up to you to agree the level of involvement and acceptable demands on your time that this will take. Whatever you decide, these activities will require preparation and hands-on delivery time and you must ensure that this is resourced properly in your change plan.

Products, deliverables and milestones

Basically, products and deliverables are what it is we as a change team are actually going to produce as an output of the activities in the change plan. As with planning generally, the discipline and effort you need to put in can be quite challenging, but the more specific you can be will be beneficial for you, your team and your project manager, and facilitate project updates and communications. The change management dashboard will help you with progress reporting of products and deliverables.

Products and deliverables can be tangible (e.g. a report, presentation or action plan) or intangible (e.g. a change in employee attitude or stakeholder commitment), but this does not mean that they are not measurable. As change manager you are accountable for delivering to project expectations and taking the time to describe exactly what your end point will look like for (1) an activity and (2) each project phase. This will help everyone be clear about what you are working towards and what they can expect from you when the work is done. In some projects, we've had the experience of having to create written descriptions of every activity and expected end point or outcome.

CASE STUDY

Project 'over-management' in local government

One memorable instance was working with a local government client with whom my employer had strained and prolonged contractual negotiations. In the first three weeks, a colleague and I wrote over 20 detailed product descriptions (PDs) which we had to fit around planning, doing the planned activities, building the change team and delivering project kick-off events. Each PD was then reviewed by the business and we made the required amendments. Sometimes four or five iterations were necessary before the sponsor would sign the PDs off. Interestingly, due to the time this took and tight project timelines, several products were completed before the PDs had been approved! As the programme progressed, the approval process for deliverables was so bureaucratic that the project stream I was managing had completed all the activities and had dispersed before most of the approvals were signed off. The learning here is that it is good to be rigorous about project management, but not at the expense of progress or the risk of unforeseen time and costs of rework if the deliverables were not signed off.

If you can also define quality criteria for each of your deliverables then from a commercial standpoint you protect yourself from scope creep or having goalposts changed. From an integrity standpoint, you protect yourself from accusations and blame for not delivering. Knowing and defining your change products and deliverables will also give you a foundation upon which to develop a change benefits case. It is in your personal and professional interest to be able to substantiate benefits and improvements so that you can clearly demonstrate that your team are creating value for the project and organisation.

> clearly demonstrate that your team are creating value

Risks and issues management

A risk is an unplanned event or situation that may occur but has not yet occurred *and* if it does occur, would have an impact on the project/programme's ability to achieve its objectives: cost, benefits, timescale and quality. A risk becomes an issue when it reaches its due date, and what you anticipated might happen actually happens.

The management of risk will be an ongoing activity throughout the project life cycle and will involve all members of the project team. You will need to be aware and understand the potential impact and consequences of all risks raised from other streams and communicate them to your team members. These risks may turn into additional and unplanned work for the change team.

As the change manager, you will be accountable for identifying issues and risks raised by the activities of the change team and the behaviour or reactions of employees, including sponsors. The change team is responsible for ensuring that these change-specific risks are identified, recorded and regularly reviewed by the project leadership or board. This series of activities and events is known as the risk management cycle.

A list of the most common change management risks can be found in the summary, themes and tips.

The task of managing risk is focused on taking action to keep the project (and organisation's) exposure to an acceptable level, in a cost-effective way. That means that sometimes risks are tolerated – either because nothing can be done to mitigate them (or done at a reasonable cost), or that the likelihood and impact of the risks are deemed to be at an acceptable level. You can see where this is leading … you will need to evaluate all risks in respect of their impact and probability. The table below shows an example of the definitions and ratings used for assessing impact and likelihood.

Impact – description	Rating	Likelihood – description	Rating
▌Programme/project/function/ activity performance not materially affected.	1	Unlikely to occur	1
▌Slight inconvenience or difficulty in performance of programme/ project/function/activity. ▌Recovery from such consequences would be handled quickly without the need to divert resources from core activity areas.	2	Lower than average chance of occurrence in most circumstances	2
▌Performance of the programme/ project/function/activity would be compromised to the extent that revised planning would be required to overcome difficulties experienced.	3	Even chance of occurrence (i.e. 50/50)	3
▌Performance of the programme/ project/functions/activity would be severely affected to the extent that significant revised planning would be required to overcome difficulties experienced. ▌Recovering from consequences would be highly complicated and time consuming.	4	Higher than average chance of occurrence in most circumstances	4
▌Performance of the programme/ project/functions/activity would be affected to the extent that it could not deliver to meet its obligations.	5	Expected to occur in most circumstances	5

Having identified and evaluated the risks, possible actions or countermeasures to deal with them need to be considered and appropriate action taken. Different types of actions could include:

- prevention – do things differently to remove the threat or problem from occurring
- reduction – try to control the risk in some way by reducing the likelihood or limiting the impact
- transference – pass the impact to a third party (e.g. through an insurance policy or penalty clause)
- contingency – where actions are planned to come into force if and when the risk occurs.

The risks are captured and documented in a risk log or risk register, and their analysis, impact/likelihood scores, countermeasures and status are regularly reviewed by the project or programme manager and board.

Risk management requires you to plan and mobilise the required resources to carry out the actions you have selected to deal with the risks. Once agreed, you will need to monitor and report on the actions to ensure that the activities are having the desired effect on the risk. The format and process you will need to follow will be defined by your PMO, although in smaller projects this may be less rigorous. Guidance on this should be provided by your project manager.

Transition planning

Change management is not the process of defining a business solution, but rather the tools and techniques required to realise this business solution through people and filter it into the workplace.

> change does not just miraculously 'happen'

In no place or time is this more apparent than when the planning is done and the solution is defined. What happens then? Change does not just miraculously 'happen'. Somehow we have to make the transition from what we were or are doing to doing it differently. So next we need to focus on how the crossover from existing to future ways of working is made.

The final deliverable in the deliver phase is the transition plan which creates the bridge between where we want to go and where we are now. All the plans, assessments and tools get us to the point where we have identified new roles and responsibilities (and those gaps with the 'as-is' stage). The most critical and sensitive task, that of role to skills matching,[2] is still to be done. Role to skills matching is the process of matching living, breathing individuals to future roles or jobs – literally putting people's names in the boxes of the new organisation chart. In addition, transition planning considers the degree of change that individuals will undergo and defines the policies and processes that will be used and relied upon for delivering the change. It should also anticipate support needs for individuals and define how this support will be provided.

As change manager, you do not own the transition plan or have responsibility for the transition activities unless you are an experienced and qualified HR practitioner *and* this has been specifically agreed as 'in scope' for your role. However, it is your responsibility to engage HR, preferably at the time impact assessments are conducted, so it can prepare and plan for the changes to people and jobs.

Key activities in transition planning are:

▌ conducting a capability assessment (of incumbent staff)

▌ making internal appointments

▌ identifying external recruitment needs

▌ identifying training and development needs

▌ monitoring performance indicators.

When defining your approach to transition, you will be influenced by the complexity of the change, the level of impact on people and the organisation culture. Some changes are instant, like switching off an old computer system one day and booting up a new system the next. Other changes are implemented incrementally, allowing people to get used to change one piece at a time or one group at a time.

2 This is *not* the same as job to role matching. Job to role matching is the process where roles (combinations of tasks) are allocated a user profile or 'job' type in an IT system which determines access to system areas or levels of security.

Some transformations even require the organisation to go through a series of interim stages before the future state can be operational.

In all types of transitions, you must make sure there is a detailed plan which includes all the HR activities. If it involves changes to roles (training, job descriptions and job evaluations), staffing levels, redundancies, terms and conditions or redeployments, it is critical that you get HR involved early and understand its capability and capacity to apply the procedures and policies. In addition, there are some potential derailment factors that you have to be familiar with.

▌ You cannot go faster than legislation or trade union agreements allow.

▌ Beware of recruitment lead times.

▌ Check, check and check again that senior management will support and follow through when the going gets tough.

▌ Make the biggest changes that the organisation can accept and avoid 'death by 1000 cuts'.

▌ Spend time on risk identification and mitigation.

CASE STUDY

Right people for the right job

I was working with a government agency faced with a review and restructuring of both frontline and back office services to achieve significant efficiency savings whilst meeting new performance targets. This involved the implementation of a new ERP system, new business processes, ways of working and behaviours. I joined the project after the design phase to implement and embed the new HR model, processes and e-HR technology.

When I joined the project the agency was not only implementing its change programme but also reducing headcount through a voluntary redundancy scheme. The scheme resulted in the loss of those staff with the most marketable skills. These were the skills that I needed to implement the change programme and support the new HR model and technology. This meant building a team with staff who did not have the right skills and whose motivation had been affected by the redundancy programme and the ongoing organisational change.

▶

The key lessons that I learnt were to:

▌ Identify key staff early and invest in their development so they are retained, take on new roles in the organisation and are role models for new ways of working and behaviours.

▌ Don't compromise on staff in the restructured service. Staff that have the right skills and behaviours are critically important – don't just accept people who are being redeployed.

▌ Use the performance management system to reward and recognise staff for actively using new systems, processes and adopting new behaviours.

Phil Lewis, Management Consultant

Considerations checklist for change planning

In your role as change manager, you will have several areas of responsibility that you will be required to manage simultaneously and on a daily basis. These are, broadly speaking: change leadership; project administration; delivery of change activities and products; team and change capability development; governance and process; and culture. When you are creating the change plan, you must remember that all of these elements will require attention and must be factored into the resource plan before you make any adjustments for capacity flexibility or contingency.

> make any adjustments for capacity flexibility or contingency

Project administration – a source of unplanned work

Understanding what else I would need to do, in addition to the actual change management plan activities I was in charge of, was a big lesson from a personal perspective. In my first project leadership role, I totally underestimated just how much of my, and my team's, time would be taken up to do project administration (PMO) type tasks. I had a nasty shock when I realised that the resource capacity I had requested and had approved would be significantly stretched if I tried to absorb all those tasks into the existing team. I will never forget having to go back to the programme board to request more resources, not because something had changed, but because of my oversight.

To help you avoid making such a basic and fundamental mistake, we have created a checklist to highlight some of the less-obvious time and resource considerations for your change plan, which we recommend you work through when you think you are ready to start developing solutions and delivering change.

Change management responsibility	Change plan/resource considerations	Included in plan (tick all that apply)	Reasons for not including in plan
Leadership	Change strategy: ▌ research and assessment ▌ presentation/delivery ▌ approval ▌ review process and frequency. Change sponsorship: ▌ sponsor management programme ▌ change leaders development. Change plan: ▌ tool/technique evaluation and selection ▌ requirement for specialist or limited skills (e.g. third-party providers) ▌ plan approval ▌ review process and frequency.		
Project delivery	Mobilisation: ▌ events planning and management. Workload planning: ▌ alignment of project plans ▌ tool licences and certification ▌ allocate tasks to named resources ▌ key resource availability/holidays. Measures and CSFs: ▌ define approach (e.g. balanced scorecard) ▌ availability/accessibility of data.		
Team and capability development	▌ Team meetings schedule ▌ Skills/competencies training ▌ Team building/development ▌ Performance reviews ▌ Coaching		
Governance and process	Decision making and approval: ▌ process leadtimes. Risks and issues: ▌ process management and review ▌ escalation and cascade leadtimes. Project administration and reporting Governance meeting schedule		

Change management responsibility	Change plan/resource considerations	Included in plan (tick all that apply)	Reasons for not including in plan
Transition planning	Leadtimes: ▌ legislation ▌ consultation ▌ recruitment. Job evaluation process: ▌ approvals.		

Your particular situation may not require you to include all the elements in the checklist, but will ensure you are making these omissions consciously and not because you've just forgotten about them.

CASE STUDY

Developing an organisational change practice

If you are thinking of building an organisational change practice or embedding people change into your projects, you may find this checklist useful. I created it for supporting large-scale technology projects, introducing new initiatives or restructuring.

At project start:

▌ Table all people-related impacts to avoid aspects being overlooked.

▌ Identify and engage stakeholders early – discuss roles and the business imperative for the change.

▌ Enable stakeholders to understand reasons for addressing people factors and challenges and ways to raise concerns.

▌ Discuss the cost of not surfacing and mitigating people risks proactively.

▌ Help others visualise the desired state.

▌ Articulate the benefits of having disciplined, repeatable, sustainable processes.

During the project:

▌ Show how focusing on the people and behaviour aspects of change helps deliver real, intended business benefits.

▌ Point out the cost of superficial change/adoption.

▌ Build advocacy and success by demonstrating what can be done.

▌ Keep leaders apprised of people not just technical risks.

▌ Provide education and coaching to increase understanding of change management.

▌ Create impetus for people or organisational change by building capability, becoming subject matter experts and 'go-to' people.

Towards the end:

▌ Build momentum and credibility by creating a centre of excellence – become custodians of the methodology, practices, and shared resources.

▌ Document and share your story/journey internally and externally to sustain momentum.

▌ Present and share your successes anecdotally and tangibly, widely and often.

Having a checklist helps me focus on effective implementation and provides ways to assess and track progress.

Nimira Harjee, Independent Change and
Organisational Development Consultant

Making change happen

UP TO NOW, WE HAVE EXPLORED many aspects of change – recognising the type of change, what can be anticipated and planned for, the scheduling and managing of activities and mitigating identifiable risks. In this chapter we explore the emotional engagement and responses from the people in the organisation that you will need to deal with, and the more personal aspects of being a change manager.

We have collected stories and case studies from our colleagues and fellow change managers with whom we have worked to illustrate or shed a different perspective on the different topics in this chapter. Change management is a personal and individual experience, so we wanted to share a variety of experiences, some positive and some negative, with you in anticipation that these messages will bring to life much of what change management is about and inform your own approach and style.

Orienteering in the change management space

So, you're a change manager on a project. You've met the programme team, you have a copy of the project goals and now what? At this point, you generally find yourself in one of two positions either:

1 the project is ramping up and the project team are embarking on the planning stage, or

2 the plan has been drawn up and somebody has realised that there is a gap regarding change management and you've been parachuted in and need to play 'catch-up'.

Joining a project halfway through

I joined a project as a consultant to provide the functional expertise that the client had requested. The project was an ERP implementation and change programme, of which I was to lead the latter. The project was late, over budget and characterised by mistrust between the client, technical and consulting teams. My first and immediate task was to visit the plethora of client personalities, understand their needs and current position and develop a forum through which change could be managed. This was easy. It was the 'extra-role' project needs that were the most taxing for me. As well as being the change lead I also had to make the project work more effectively due to the dire leadership in place. Basically, the change (my part) would not succeed unless the project governance was put right. This meant that I also had to become negotiator, team motivator, cleaner, nurse, governance designer and communicator. This was a lengthy and emotionally draining period and not one I remember with any affection.

The learning I gained was: (1) joining an existing project requires an immediate assessment and communication of your responsibilities as you understand them and the individual value you bring; (2) manage the scope and expectations of what you (one person) can physically do. If the project is badly run or under-resourced, get established before you grow your responsibilities beyond your formal role.

Fergus Smith, Independent Management Consultant

Once you know 'when' in the project you are, you can start to think about what needs to be done and subsequently, how actually to do it.

Championing the change

A journey of 1000 miles begins with a single step.

Ancient Chinese proverb

Before you can take that first step, you must have knowledge of a few vital decisions, such as where the organisation/business is going and why it wants to go there. But you also need to recognise that you are not just going to be a passenger on this quest, and that you will also be undertaking a personal journey. Before stepping aboard the transport, you should examine your own reasons and priorities – beginning with answering the following two questions:

1 Why am I doing this change?

2 Of all the changes we could be making now, is this the most important for the organisation, employees and myself?

> you will also be undertaking a personal journey

If you can't honestly answer these questions, you may not be personally committed enough to make the change successful. Your colleagues are being asked to trust you as their guide through upheaval and uncertainty, so you need to be sure you have the dedication and determination to take them to the finish line.

CASE STUDY

A change manager's questions

It's often easier to coach others through change than assess what's hindering you from achieving different results. Over the last three years, I've used the following questions to wrestle with significant personal and professional change.

- How am I reacting to my circumstances?
- What is straining, stressing, taxing me and sapping my energy?
- How is it showing up in my behavior and interaction with others?
- What interpretations and judgements am I making?
- When do I feel threatened and vulnerable?
- What is my habitual reaction?
- What is distorting my perspective?
- What's the issue at hand; what needs to be surfaced?
- What defenses do I need to overcome?
- What am I avoiding?

▶

- What is pushing me out of my uncomfortable zone and how am I reacting?
- What am I hanging on to and need to let go?
- Where do I get stuck and how can I get unstuck?
- What am I learning about myself through this?
- What is required of me at this moment?

Here is what I have found works:

- thinking ahead
- having an action plan
- being flexible, taking things in stride and trusting the outcome
- stepping back, reflecting and asking – where am I and is this where I want to be?
- shifting gears to regain momentum
- recognising the opportunity; being grateful for the lesson.

What do I need to remember?

- Change is about making a shift. When I shift, others shift. By not shifting, I stay stuck and frustrated.
- Change is difficult even when you understand it intellectually. Questions provided me with distance and perspective.

Nimira Harjee, Independent Change and
Organisational Development Consultant

Hearts and minds

Managing change is a major challenge for organisations. A common perception is that projects fail because people do not like undergoing and adapting to change. A more realistic version of reality is that projects fail because those running them avoid, do not plan for, or cannot deal with, the more emotive problems and issues.

CIPD (2005) research evidence shows that:

- employees are not necessarily hostile to change but major changes – particularly leading to redundancies – tend to cause negative attitudes

■ most people say change in their organisation is badly managed

■ employee trust in organisations has declined and this can make the process of managing change more difficult.

In the preface of *The Heart of Change*, John Kotter (2002) writes that the central issue for change is never strategy, structure, culture or systems. Although important, the core of the matter is always about changing the behaviour of people, and behaviour change happens in highly successful situations mostly by speaking to people's feelings:

> In highly successful change efforts, people find ways to help others see the problems or solutions in ways that influence emotions, not just thought. Feelings then alter behaviour sufficiently to overcome all the many barriers to sensible large-scale change.
>
> Kotter and Cohen, 2002

Employee perception and 'fair dealing'

Building effective people management policies and practices into the change management process at an early stage is helpful, but it is more important for a change manager to recognise shifts occurring in the relationship between people and organisations during business change. Key influencing factors on this relationship (also known as 'the psychological contract') are as follows.

■ **Process fairness**: people want to know that their interests will be taken into account when important decisions are taken; they want to be treated with respect; they are more likely to be satisfied with their job if they are consulted about change.

■ **Communications**: an effective two-way dialogue between employer and employees is a necessary means of giving expression to employee 'voice'.

■ **Managing expectations**: employers need to make clear to employees what they can expect from the change. Managers may have a tendency to emphasise positive messages and play down more negative ones, but employees can usually distinguish rhetoric from reality and employees' trust may be undermined. Managing expectations, particularly when bad news is anticipated, will increase the chances of establishing trust.

monitor employee attitudes on a regular basis

Breach of the psychological contract can seriously damage the employer–employee relationship. You will need to monitor employee attitudes on a regular basis as a means of identifying where action may be needed but only if you are ready and willing to act on the results. It won't always be possible to avoid a breach but employees are more likely to be forgiving if you can explain what has gone wrong and how the business or project intends to deal with it.

Managing resistance

One of the most important issues you will need to manage will be resistance to change. Effectively and constructively dealing with resistance is essential to building trust and relationships with colleagues, employees and clients. The employee is *not* always right, but the way you deal with them has to be. There are tools included in this book to help you, such as the resistance assessment and approach. Your approach or way you choose to deal with resistance may also have an impact on the resource levels you may need.

Resistance occurs among employees and managers because the impact of change projects on individuals can be personally as well as professionally significant. Resistance is not necessarily a negative reflection on the change stream or the project, and should not be viewed as isolated or a series of incidents but as part of the overall change process. The way we as change managers deal with resistance will be seen as a critical element of our effectiveness and professionalism.

People manifest resistance by what they say and do. Resistance usually take the form of 'rational' concerns or arguments, for example, and arises from:

 job loss
 a change in job role

▌not knowing what the future holds or your place in the organisation

▌a lack of understanding of where you are going and why.

Employees' real or underlying concerns may be totally different. In many cases these tend to be politically or emotionally motivated and down to:

▌lack of career or financial advancement

▌possible damage to relationships with superiors

▌territorial threat

▌loss of credibility or reputation

▌embarrassment/loss of self-esteem

▌fear of the unknown

▌threat to familiar contacts: customers, colleagues, managers, group membership.

Understanding the rational, political and emotional dimensions of change and resistance is the key to discovering the real underlying issues beyond what people express. Try to avoid the tendency to judge the validity of an individual's reason for resistance. Your role is to understand it and work to minimise negative impacts to the change programme.

So what does resistance look like? Peter Block (1999) identifies 13 different types of resistance:

1 avoidance of responsibility

2 flooding with detail

3 one-word answers

4 impracticality

5 attacking

6 compliance

7 confusion

8 changing the subject

9 I'm not surprised

10 silence

11 time

12 nit-picking

13 pressing for solutions.

Block also outlines a useful technique for managing resistance – AIR:

Acknowledge	Investigate	Reinforce
What they have said in a genuine way	Identify the main source of the resistance	Reinforce the positive aspects of anything you are proposing
	Encourage them to talk more about it – and listen	Calmly and clearly explain the reasons for change (again!)
	Isolate and work the separate issues	Look for acceptance

Surfacing resistance is quite positive, because if you know what the resistance is you can address it. From experience, if a change is too quiet we start to question if it is actually happening! Resistance will get noisier as the change becomes real to people, and you will become skilled at pinpointing when someone realises change is actually occurring. Help them through it, recalling your own reactions as you came to grips with the change.

Rolling up your sleeves

How we deal with any business change is influenced by our individual leadership style, experience and expertise. In this section we look at the different ways change managers have dealt with situations and share their experiences with you.

Get into the project mindset

Your first challenge will be to get your head around the business context and project. Draw on Chapter 13 for understanding the context, and Chapter 3 for the project management methodology. If you've not worked on a programme or project before, there is a lot to learn – including the language. Do your homework, read a good book or get a free masterclass from a project manager you know. The project plan document is usually held in a specialist application, such as MS Project. Make sure you get the right application installed and do a crash course on the basics.

anticipate and build alignment into your initial plan

There may be a project plan already, in which case you need to understand certain elements so that you can organise your change activities to 'align'. If you develop your change plan in isolation, you will have to 'retrofit' your plan with the other project streams. This is never a one-way activity and your project team colleagues may need to shift things in their areas of responsibility to accommodate yours. The more you can anticipate and build alignment into your initial plan, the less upheaval and rework you (and your project colleagues) will need to do.

Be prepared

Keep in your conscious mind that change is not fixed or linear, so solving one problem does not mean the end of problems. It actually helps to highlight others. Issues that had not been planned for, or even those which were expected, can manifest very differently to what you might expect.

CASE STUDY

Being prepared

I recently led a start-up project to create a Talent Strategy in an organisation of 25,000 which had moved from being one brand to eleven brands. My first priority was to update myself with current research, consolidate my knowledge for the task and prepare my view of the strategy, approach and plan. This thought process allowed me to formulate a clear viewpoint which helped me to shape the task re: what good looks like and the benefits so I would be ready for conversations with stakeholders. I built and managed stakeholder relationships and the end result was that two executive board members became sponsors.

Even though I had done my preparation (as an HR professional), starting stakeholder conversations with Talent was the wrong approach. I needed to learn what they thought the business challenges were and, subsequently, what were the people challenges.

My experience in the area of Talent did initially establish my credibility, but for me it was only 50 per cent of what I needed. I found it was my line manager, the Senior HR VP, I had to convince and build his confidence in me. This caused me a huge amount of frustration but my external mentor supported me through this time. The other 50 per cent was about having an approach that involved the main stakeholders in building and executing the solution, and having a great project plan that delivered measurable results.

My learnings were:

1. If your project is to have any credibility you will need to establish what the commercial benefits are, and engage leaders early on to gain sponsorship.

2. Reflect on your conversations, even those not focusing on your objective, as they may identify key issues.

3. A big lesson for me was that I should have made the executive sponsorship visible to my manager sooner. As soon as I did his confidence increased as these were his colleagues!

4. Project management experience is crucial.

Chantelle Edwards, Global Talent Director, Gategroup

Line up your resources – and know where you can go for help or expertise – mobilise your network, and engage with your mentor or coach. Keep everyone informed of your progress and issues, and share successes. Pragmatism is essential and you must also feel comfortable with a certain degree of ambiguity and flexibility in order to operate effectively.

Be clear about your role

Your next challenge will be to understand the complexity of your role. Change management is made up of several workstreams, which might or might not come under the ownership of the change manager (e.g. training and communications). There may be good reasons for those workstreams to report through another line, but be clear what that line is and who has the overall accountability for performance and deliverables.

Late stage role and responsibility changes

I joined a project to implement a customer-relationship management (CRM) system into the company's sales force well into the develop phase. My role had been explained to me by the project manager and the focus was very much on communications and stakeholder management. A couple of weeks in, and just six weeks before roll-out, I asked what user training would be delivered so that I could plan the communications to employees. My lead-team colleagues told me the IT developers were 'writing a manual'. There was no training strategy, no plan and no resources in the budget for developing or delivering training to employees. Subsequently, I found myself with the added responsibility for end-user training. However, I was prepared for this possibility (before raising the question in the first place) and was able to leverage this crisis to negotiate the required training resources and integrate process and behaviour change sessions into the training programmes as conditions for my taking on this responsibility.

Once your remit is clear, if you just expect to deliver what's in your plan, you will fail. As well as delivering the change plan, you will have a role to build and manage your team and develop change capability in the organisation, as well as being a full, role-modelling member of the project leadership team.

manage your team and develop change capability

Your remit and responsibilities will intersect across other project and business disciplines. Be sure you and they know the limitations of your responsibilities and that instances of handover or accountability are clear and well understood. Make sure you have agreed your role KPIs and objectives and share them with others.

Get to know the people and personalities

A massive 98 per cent of managers across the UK said they come into contact with difficult work colleagues on a regular basis, according to a 2005 survey by training company PTP Training & Marketing. A study of more than 250 senior professionals found that half said they encountered difficult people on a daily basis. Despite the scale of the problem only 15 per cent of managers admitted to confronting the member of staff who is being difficult.

The way a team or project works can be quite complex. There are often subtle balances between personalities and work responsibilities to be maintained. Personalities can exert a very strong influence in the workplace and yet it is not always easy to predict how employees will express their feelings when they are upset or angry, and how they may change their behaviour in difficult or stressful situations.

CASE STUDY

Working with difficult personalities

When I was starting out as a consultant, I was taught that people's resistance to new ways of working was not aimed at me but at the process of change. This was due to perfectly natural concerns, such as the impact of the programme on their future power base or relationships.

On one particular project I found the reverse to be true. Resistance was concentrated in two key staff, the Operations and HR directors. Their resistance was quite definitely personal and aimed at me, as the agent of change. Their behaviours were frequently focused on undermining my position in the eyes of my employer and the project sponsor. What helped me survive was the realisation that the people who struggle most with change are usually seriously uncomfortable with themselves as people. Change forces introspection and an evaluation of personal needs, wants and the ability to operate more effectively in a 'new' organisation. For those lacking in self-confidence or ability, looking inside themselves reveals their own inadequacy or what they are afraid others may see.

For change to truly work in an organisation, every person has to change – encouraged, led or coerced – or leave. The key learnings from this project for me were:

1 there are no easy ways to deal with this

2 to ensure subsequently that I was emotionally prepared and able to deploy strategies to protect myself against such personal and vicious attacks in the future.

Fergus Smith, Independent Management Consultant

Getting to know the personalities or traits of your team and key stakeholders can minimise the risks of conflict or resistance. There are well known tools, such as the Myers-Briggs Personality Type Indicator (MBTI), that can help provide a framework and language for people to discuss their strengths, weaknesses and preferences, which promotes empathy and understanding.

The following three areas crop up frequently (ACAS, 2007) and are ones you should be aware of.

1 The 'personality mix' within a team can be upset when a new member of staff joins or if two colleagues suddenly fall out. If individuals are upset or unhappy they are more likely to become frustrated. Individuals may also respond to difficult or challenging situations in a stereotypical way, such as avoidance or aggression. This can be a result of 'learnt behaviour'. Learnt behaviour is often a mixture of:

– the way people have been taught to behave

– the behaviour people have copied from others

– a strategy people adopt to cope with problems.

2 Most people have very clear ideas about what they think is fair. These are partly a reflection of personal values, but partly societal or shared values. For example:

– to give someone a fair hearing

– to explain the reasoning behind a decision

– to be impartial

– to hear an appeal against a decision.

3 If personalities and values are ignored or neglected, conflict can arise between personalities, or between teams. This can often take the form of:

- rivalry between colleagues

- disagreements over a team's goals or shared values

- resentment that one team is not pulling its weight.

Change managers should be alert and able to spot which personality types are likely to clash and use their skills to defuse situations. It is also essential that you have the necessary people skills to deal effectively and constructively with difficult personalities who can be a considerable barrier to the harmony, motivation and performance of a project.

> I have always found that the big things that cause organisations to get into difficulties have more to do with personalities than policies. I would say that, first, you must be very aware that personalities are important; they're more important the bigger the business, and they're more important the more senior people get. Secondly, personalities can be dealt with, but if they can't, you have to get rid of one of them. Organisations can get into difficulties if personalities are allowed to get in the way of the business interest. The higher you go up the corporate ladder the more important personalities and egos become, increasing the risk of disputes.
>
> Sir Peter Middleton, former chairman of Barclays Group, Harvard Business School Press, 2007

Believe in what you're doing

Few, if any, organisations have 'courage' in their list of essential competencies. Change management in particular is mostly about courage: the courage to fail, the courage to try something new and to take risks. For many managers, the fear of getting it wrong means they do nothing – they freeze, like a rabbit caught in car headlights. Being a change manager requires personal and interpersonal courage (part of emotional intelligence – EQ) to say what needs to be said and to deal directly, quickly and effectively with emotionally stressful situations.

> being a change manager requires personal and interpersonal courage

Taking the bull by the horns

A large investment bank launched a project to embed new ways of working in an internal consultancy whose highly charismatic leader was effective and successful. He was also verbose and had a tendency to stifle debate and new ideas from his senior team. From my observations of meetings and workshops, it was clear that the senior team in the business unit exhibited a high degree of frustration. They perceived that their ideas for improvement of the unit were (a) not given due consideration and (b) not welcome. However, nobody was willing to challenge the leader directly on this issue. It was apparent that the project would fail if this situation was not resolved.

I learned that attrition in the senior levels of the unit was running at over 25 per cent and used this information to persuade the individual to try a new mode of operating as leader in this project. I employed a two-step approach to make the leader aware of the unanimous feelings of his team and persuaded him to absent himself for particular meetings. We agreed that the recommendations would be presented to him after the event. The next step was for him to attend meetings, but be restricted to giving a yes/no approval to suggestions after discussion was complete (if 'no' then reasons had to be given). Escalating his level of involvement to settling disagreements in the team and keeping true to the strategy gave him a clear role and accountability.

My learnings from this were:

1. evidence can be a strong argument for changing behaviour
2. focus on changing roles and accountabilities, not personal style
3. a change manager must have the courage to tell it how it is – i.e. articulate the issues that others shy away from.

Dr Howard McMinn, Vice-president, Deloitte Consulting

If you don't believe in the value of what you are doing, not only will you have to deal with your own crises of confidence as well as juggling a challenging workload, but others will also recognise this failure in confidence and your credibility will suffer. Your enthusiasm and passion will go a long way in conveying the value of change in a project. However, be careful that you don't get carried away....

The enthusiastic consultant

In a client kick-off event, the lead consultant stated that this project (an ERP implementation) would be the 'hardest thing the group had done in their working lives'. A question came from the floor: 'Is it harder than fighting fires underground? 'Cos that's what I used to do!'

The learning – never overstate.

Dr Howard McMinn, Vice-president, Deloitte Consulting

Recognising when your job is done

The nature of projects is that they are finite. There is a huge amount written about the start-up and management of projects, but one area that is less well-documented is the signing-off stage. Unlike many other project roles, there are important responsibilities for the change manager beyond the implementation or 'go-live' phase in making sure the new processes, behaviours, etc. are transitioned from project accountability to business-as-usual. Change, and especially culture change, does not stop at the end of the project life cycle or when the programme has been delivered. You may well have completed a project successfully, on time and on budget, but if people don't know that or aren't made aware of exactly what you have achieved, then you may end up with dissatisfied stakeholders.

There are also emotional and political factors that you may need to deal with. We have both experienced a sense of dependency, 'What will we do without you?' and 'I don't know if we can do this without your help again'. People can be fearful of personal failure but also of a loss of face that may come with it. Some projects can last months or even years and you become part of the fabric of the teams you are working with. It can be an emotional wrench, or even generate a sense of betrayal in those left behind when you move on. Part of helping provide closure for the project, sponsors and team members is to hold 'wrap-up parties', give out awards or recognition letters to the team, and decide on the final date that the stream closes.

There are no clear-cut criteria to say exactly when this is, so how do you know when your role is done? If you can answer 'yes' to the questions below, this will give you a good indication that your role has finished.

Questions

Has the project achieved its desired outcomes?

Has the change stream delivered its objectives?

Does feedback show that people are aware of and understand the changes made?

Do people have the capabilities required to be successful?

Do people understand the new ways in which they can apply their new skill and knowledge in a working context?

Are performance measures showing improvement?

Are managers taking responsibility for the new processes and behaviours?

Have the activities, monitoring and feedback tasks been handed over?

Have you planned your exit and managed stakeholder expectations?

Have you identified and agreed on-going support (e.g. coaching or follow-up reviews)?

CASE STUDY

Lessons learned

One typical exercise at the end of a project or work stream is to hold a session on lessons learned. This is when you gather your project or change team and capture what went well, what could have been better, and where/who the lessons should be passed on to. One way to know if you are at the end of your job as change manager is to float the idea of a lessons learned session with your project manager or sponsor. Once people stop freaking out that it's 'too soon!', you know your role is nearing completion. Be aware, you will probably be asked to facilitate lessons learned across the programme, and be accountable for ensuring they are taken into consideration by other projects or change teams.

Role-modelling the culture of change

Woven throughout this book is the theme of self-awareness. It is not by accident and we cannot emphasise the importance of this enough. Your awareness of your personality, preferences, prejudices, values, strengths and blind spots will shape how the change unfolds and even its level of success.

The process you choose to follow for completing activities in your change plan, and even the activities you choose to complete, will be influenced by culture. As you are reading this book, you are probably saying to yourself at some point: 'That would never work here.' That's culture. If you want to change it, you need to be ready to role model the desired culture yourself.

> you will be able to shift how people think about change

That means demonstrating courage to surface tough issues and confronting behaviour that is not supporting the change. You will find yourself proposing plans that involve employees from the bottom-up as well as top-down, role modelling good reporting and documentation, and encouraging and influencing others to do the same. If you can show it works, with evidence, you will be able to shift how people think about change, and have a greater chance of success.

You will have an influence on culture at many levels:

▌ at the strategic level, in clarifying and driving organisational behaviour

▌ at the leadership level, in coaching others how to manage and drive change

- at the project level, in setting the tone for how the change is carried out in the organisation
- at the team level, in setting the expectation for how your team members interact with each other and the organisation as you move through the 4D process.

There will be many opportunities daily where you will knowingly or unknowingly influence culture. It is worth spending some time reflecting on this, and a simple exercise for you is to start watching for moments of daily decision making within your role. Decisions unfold every minute, so start asking yourself some questions about how the decision was made, who was involved, what the environment was and what happened afterwards. Was it a 'telling' decision, or 'co-created' (see Chapter 13)? Where was it done – over coffee or in a boardroom? Was there a committee? How did people know what to do afterwards and how was it followed up? This knowledge will help you understand what is acceptable and tolerated (the norm) in your organisation, team or project.

This norm will be the support or bane of your existence. If the norm is successful in driving change, then you will have an easier time completing change activities, capturing decisions, implementing plans and realising benefits. If the norm is not successful, then you have to determine for yourself what is possible to make the change successful. When change comes up against established culture, culture wins. Be careful of taking on behaviour that is too counter-culture.

For example, if the norm is 'telling' and what happens is that people listen, then ignore the message and go back to their business, you will need to work with leadership to help them understand what has to change in their behaviour. You may need to design activities that allow two-way communication to occur, as this will facilitate the acceptance of change. Look for current examples of where that happens, and learn from them. Is videoconferencing used often? What about using face-to-face meetings or workshops, or is it an e-mail/chat culture? Find the cultural norms and use them to your advantage.

Culture change project

My client was a public sector body that wanted to engage and motivate staff, building trust with management. There were barriers between the upper, middle and lower echelons of the organisation and very poor communication between each band. Management had attempted to build a values set but had not engaged sufficiently with the staff to make the values meaningful. A programme was developed; the intention being to change the culture through formalising how decisions were made and how these decisions were communicated. The aim was to provide visibility and clarity of the direction the organisation needed to take.

The issues the project team faced were that culture could not be changed without behavioural change at the very top of the organisation. In four months, only a partial buy-in had been achieved at this level and this was reflected in the various departments. The second issue was that behavioural change is very personal and the greatest resistance to change came from the board members who were the least confident or comfortable with themselves. The third issue is that culture work requires extensive dialogue between management and staff. If there is no vertical engagement, there will be no change.

The key learning point from this project was that culture change takes time, at least a year, to start to bear fruit. The implication is that this needs to be understood at the programme decision or planning stages so that expectations are properly managed.

Fergus Smith, Independent Management Consultant

If the project is about culture change, and by that we mean creating a deep, sustainable shift in organisational values and behaviours, you must know your own values first and be able to describe them comfortably in lay terms. You will find yourself in situations where you are working with the organisation to define what trust looks like day-to-day. You will need to be confident that trust is something you value, that you can describe what it looks and feels like to you, and that you act in alignment with that description. You will be challenged on your values and have to role model the desired values of the organisation, reminding others of them if they do not.

your behaviour will be observed very closely

Being a change manager, in many ways, means being prepared to be under a microscope. Your behaviour will be observed very closely by those around you, and your influence will be deeper and more far-reaching than you anticipate. It is a very powerful role. If you are a comic book fan, this line will be familiar: 'With great power there must also come great responsibility' (Lee, 1967).

People can tell if your heart is not in something. As a change manager, be prepared to give your heart to the change. Others will take their cue from you.

Making change stick

MOST PROJECTS ARE DISBANDED after implementation is completed, but change management does not end there. Once the change is live, the change management emphasis shifts from effecting the change to sustaining it. What most organisations and projects fail to recognise/plan/budget for is the time and effort required for the change to become embedded and 'business-as-usual'.

Organisation effectiveness

Different ways of approaching and perceiving change will influence how change is to be embedded. The key to sustainable change is an effective organisation. The new processes, structures and behaviours must all be aligned to the strategy of the organisation in order to deliver the change, and this is covered in detail in Chapters 5 to 15. At the end of a project a retrospective look or review of the changes implemented is a good safety check that all the different elements are working effectively and in harmony, producing the successful business outcome every change manager strives for. Organisation effectiveness is made up of two main factors: strategic alignment and management alignment.

Strategic alignment

There are four levers available to reinforce the change and encourage the required change in behaviour:

1. operational support
2. motivators

3 systemic compliance

4 process reinforcement.

Figure 16.1 shows the relationship between strategy, behaviours and, ultimately, organisation culture. Strategy is delivered by the business performing well and achieving its operating objectives. Progress against objectives and the contribution required is monitored by metrics, which in turn direct the activities and effort of the workforce. How well those activities are performed, and the quality of outcomes from those activities, is dependent on the behaviour and attitudes of employees.

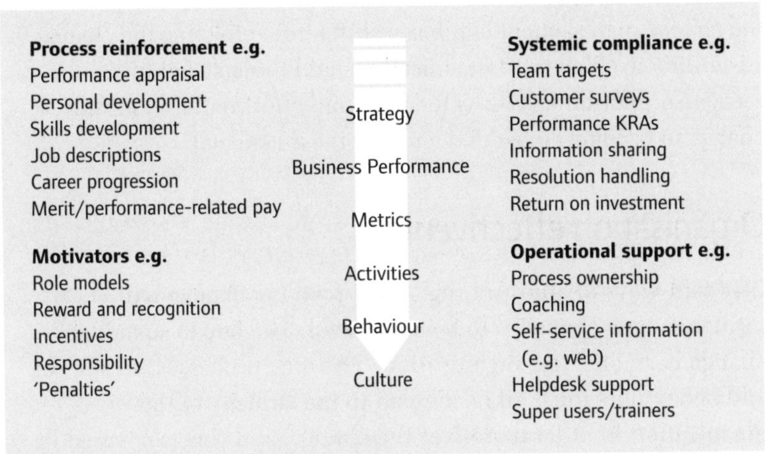

Process reinforcement e.g.
Performance appraisal
Personal development
Skills development
Job descriptions
Career progression
Merit/performance-related pay

Motivators e.g.
Role models
Reward and recognition
Incentives
Responsibility
'Penalties'

Strategy

Business Performance

Metrics

Activities

Behaviour

Culture

Systemic compliance e.g.
Team targets
Customer surveys
Performance KRAs
Information sharing
Resolution handling
Return on investment

Operational support e.g.
Process ownership
Coaching
Self-service information
  (e.g. web)
Helpdesk support
Super users/trainers

FIGURE 16.1 Strategic alignment cascade

These levers will come into play at different times in the process of sustaining change, but they must all be considered and addressed for the change truly to stick.

The most significant group of factors in sustaining change relate to pay and benefits, and the most significant person in this decision making is the employee's line manager.

Management alignment

Our experience shows that the single most influential factor in sustainable change is the engagement of business line managers and developing managers as agents of change. It is comparatively easy to change business processes and structures, but to lead change, managers need to challenge and support their people in doing new things in new ways and confront poor performers. Change provides the catalyst, but it is people who take the opportunities and shape the results.

Change triggers decision making for the employees: Is this what I want? Is there a future or career? What's in it for me? Respect, trust and a personal understanding or connection between the employee and their line manager has deep repercussions on the acceptance and sustainability of the new ways of working. The employee–manager relationship is also highly influential on employee attrition, retention and performance.

As we have established earlier in the book, change is about people. Technology does not rewire itself (yet), processes are not conducted or improved on their own, and developing a vision for the future is not something that draws itself on paper. The top motivators for people to stay and contribute to an organisation are: achievement, recognition, the work itself, responsibility and advancement (Herzberg, 1999).

As the change becomes 'business as usual', managers will be responsible for making it align to those motivators by:

- giving people stretch responsibilities incorporating the change
- integrating the change with the current work and making it meaningful
- recognising those who are doing well
- enforcing consequences for those who are not
- continually evaluating roles and responsibilities to provide opportunities for development and advancement.

We know that change works best when there is a foundation of commitment and collaboration, but cooperation is not enough. Winning the hearts and minds of line management is the biggest challenge you are likely to face.

From project to 'business-as-usual'

After implementation, there are a number of project-related activities to complete if the change is to have a chance of sticking. These include diagnosing bottlenecks, barriers or gaps in processes, systems and resources that will need troubleshooting to resolve. Many of these fall under the category of 'operational support', for example:

- Do people know where to go for more information on the project or the change? (Websites, floorwalkers, superusers, managers, help desks and the change network should be kept up to date on all developments until transfer to business as usual.)
- If the change is technology based, when the technology breaks (we guarantee something will fall over in the first week) does everyone on the project team know the emergency or back-up procedures and any manual workarounds?
- Are the emergency and contingency communications in place to help users?
- How frequently will you gather employee feedback about how effective the change is or the level of employee acceptance?
- Who has the responsibility for acting on the immediate feedback?
- What mop-up training will be available to cover any unplanned gaps?

These areas of 'operational support' are often the first to feel the effects of the change and are also good indicators of potential problems further down the system or process.

Closing project activities and handover to the business

Once the project objectives have been delivered and the new systems and processes have stabilised, it is time to transfer ownership into the business. When you are handing over a project to the business, there are two types of activities to consider – those that will cease with the end of the project, and those that will be maintained and enhanced by the business going forward.

It is essential to map all the activities that will end, and those that will be passed to the business. To do this, we recommend holding a workshop with representatives from across the project and the impacted business areas. During the workshop, you will need to identify collectively the activity, owner, date of closedown and, if applicable, business owner and date the handover will be complete.

For activities that end the project, choose a closedown date based on final acceptance of the last deliverable. Plan for any post-closedown wash up such as:

- organising and backing up project's shared drives
- filing or archiving any project-relevant materials
- conducting lessons learned workshops
- completing final project gateway and audit reviews
- submitting the closedown report to the sponsor and steering committee.

For project activities that are being handed to the business, work with the identified business owner to plan the handover. As you have just implemented the 'to-be', this is the new 'as-is'. Handover should include:

- passing on electronic and paper files of materials and documents
- meetings scheduled in the future with stakeholders to review and maintain anything related to process, technology, people, performance and benefits measures
- documented maintenance process for updates and improvements to change (quarterly reviews, etc.)
- documented roles, responsibilities and KPIs for maintaining process/technology/performance – this should be done as part of the transition plan but if that was not completed during the project it should be reviewed now and added to the business owner's job description and performance criteria

▌ knowledge transfer or training sessions to up-skill future owners

▌ sharing tips and lessons learned from the project owner to the business owner.

Project closure and recognition

Once the closure and handover activities are complete, it is time for project closure. A closure ritual is important, as during a project the work is very intense, and ownership and team bonding can be very strong. That sense of investment does not dissolve overnight, nor should it. People's efforts should be recognised through an event such as a closedown party and include rewards and recognition. Some ideas are:

▌ hold a final lessons learned session for each group

▌ provide personalised letters/cards of recognition from the executive sponsor

▌ create a slideshow of photographs that chart the journey from beginning to end

▌ distribute small packs of the 'top five' materials created over the course of the project, with 'how to' guides.

As the project closes down, those involved will probably leave the project on different days. Schedule all the leaving events, lessons learned and parties well in advance, so people will be able to attend.

a closure ritual is important

Separate to any event, all project team members will need to complete or have interim performance reviews. This is especially true of those who were part of change governance – the change leaders and change network. While it may seem obvious to do performance reviews for the change team and change manager, feedback should be provided, at the very least, to the change sponsor, change leaders and change network. It is important that people are recognised for their effort, not only by the project, but also by the line manager for the role they are returning to post-project.

As change manager, your team will be redeployed over time. You will probably be the last one there to turn off the lights, which means that all the tasks left undone will need to be done, by you! Don't overload yourself at the very end, keep at least one project or team colleague to help you with the documentation, reporting and closure activities. Once the project closure activities or deliverables are completed, you will need to manage a 'mini-handover' between you/your team member and the business.

Summary, themes and tips

ORGANISATIONAL CHANGE IS INCREASING, yet the high levels of failure indicate that effective management of these changes is still lacking (CIPD, 2007). Such a gap tells us that there is much to learn about how to manage change more effectively. We know that a lack of project management discipline can lead to slippages in timings, in achievement of desired outcomes or in ensuring that projects do deliver as planned. An integrated, project management approach to change directly addresses risks to successful change implementations, ensuring that interventions are both effective and sustainable in the long term.

The art of being a change manager

In this book we have tried to capture our experiences of being change managers – and it is a combination of being and doing, science and art. This book is intended to help a change manager set up, plan and manage a successful change project stream, but it won't deliver it. That's your job – you have to be great at managing meetings, driving outcomes, following up on next steps, and doing the work. A change manager requires a distinct set of skills and characteristics:

- problem identification
- professional credibility
- creating conditions for change
- personal courage and confidence
- judgement
- selection and analysis
- generating commitment
- building and sustaining relationships.

The change prism provides a structure and a discipline for diagnosis, planning and measurement of change interventions. But you need to have an analytical mind and systems thinking to link the data you gather from deploying the tools and executing the activities to outcomes and deliverables. The data yielded by the tools can be overwhelming, but asking yourself, 'What action can I take for this information to drive the change?' will help you figure out if the data are actually useful. It's about constantly looking at the end point of the journey (the 'to-be') and selecting your most effective and efficient means of getting there.

> the change prism provides a structure and a discipline

It's not a role for people who like to sit back and relax during a work day, it's full-on and intensive. The good news is that it is never dull.

Lessons learned

If we were to try and summarise the key points from our learnings about what makes a good change manager, they would be something like this (in no particular order).

- 360-degree relationships – manage up, down and across the project stakeholders, and manage up, down and across the stakeholders receiving the change in the business. Invest in creating relationships of trust and mutual respect. Report often to each on progress and involve others in building recommendations and implementation.

- Challenge yourself constantly to learn and be open to others' opinions. Project managing change does not mean you have the answers.

- Control – change managers are the ultimate control freaks. We like to think that if we put enough Post-its® and plans together we can somehow control the outcome. There is so much out of your control, do your best and let go of the rest. If you have set everything up for success it may still not reach the absolute best outcome. Accept that sometimes good is good enough.

- Early warnings – if things look as if they are going to be late or fail, let your project manager and sponsor know as soon as you can. The worst you can do is allow the failure to occur without letting anyone know it's coming – especially your sponsor. No-one likes to be blindsided.

- Mistakes are inevitable. The way to gain experience is by making mistakes, these are all opportunities to learn and grow. Not trying again is where you really fail.

- Timing is a massive factor you can't control. Sometimes the organisation leadership gets ahead of the rest of the people. It is their job to be thinking in the future and over long time spans, but that doesn't mean the organisation (internal employees and external customers) are ready for it.

- Ride out the troughs. There will be lulls when things aren't working or nothing is moving as quickly as you'd like. Go with it, as there will be times when it picks up and takes off too.

- Powerful pauses – when it feels like lots of things aren't working at the same time, stop pushing or fixing on all fronts. Sometimes the best thing you can do is nothing, just let things work themselves out.

- Be a good manager and leader yourself.

- Sponsor commitment comes and goes, and priorities change. Keep the change you are project managing as far up the priority list as possible. This is especially challenging in long-term projects.

- Push back on scope and responsibilities – as a change manager, you can gain the reputation that you should be involved in everything. That is not the case – push accountability and responsibility to those who should have it.

- When to say 'no'. Some change management work is bad business. If there is no visible commitment from leadership/sponsors, and no pull from the business for the change, do not be tempted to fill their roles for them. Raise the problem, do what you can to fix it, and if it's unfixable, walk away.

▌ The right amount of change. Don't try to force more change than the business can absorb and take on as business as usual. Things must come off the plate, too. This is sometimes hard to see downstream, as there will be unintended consequences from the change you introduce that are total blind spots. Do your best to understand the ripples the change will create, and be prepared to challenge the sponsor to scope and scale it back if needed.

▌ Courage and humbleness – you will need to manage this dichotomy within yourself. Courage is to step into the unknown, take risks, confront issues and stand up for what you know, and the humbleness to realise you never have the full picture or all the answers.

▌ Unplanned change – although change can be project managed, change can also be unplanned. Being an effective change manager is also about your ability to respond to and resolve those unexpected issues and having the capacity and capability to do so.

Change management themes

Regardless of the change model and approach, a number of key themes emerge that are present in all change projects.

▌ Addressing fears and concerns – fear is a barrier to change as it prevents action. If there is fear, acknowledge it, but do not accept it. Once it is identified do your best to eliminate it. Engage with employees' feelings and provide a safe environment for them to discuss their concerns. Employees should be taken through the commitment curve and encouraged to think of change as a journey, breaking the whole into bite-sized chunks.

▌ Communication – this is the greatest single factor that influences whether a project or change is successful. Lack of or poor communication is often quoted (or blamed) for why change fails. We communicate because we want something to change: a perception; understanding; information that someone holds. The purpose of communication is, ultimately, to change behaviour.

▌ Enabling behavioural change – new goals, whether corporate or individual, require behavioural change. For people to change their behaviours and work in new ways, the environment must be created for that change to happen. Behavioural change must be managed and co-ordinated to minimise any negative impact on performance or output. The business case will determine the corporate or project objectives that must be translated into targets devolved through key result areas (KRAs) and team objectives. If, for example, new behaviours are not aligned to the activities in PMM documents, or if employees cannot link their activities back to the strategy, people will revert to the old way of doing things.

Training and education – for people to change, it is necessary to ensure that employees have the necessary tools, understanding and skills to carry out the new ways of working. Training not only needs to provide the skills and know-how but also instil a level of confidence for the employee to change. Training needs must be identified for each group or individual and role-specific training programmes developed for each employee or group. Any training must be directly linked to capability improvement as defined in the corporate, regional or affiliate strategy. Training is often the last change or communications intervention available to deliver messages about the change.

Removing barriers before implementation – it is people's natural inclination to work around issues rather than attempt to solve or remove them. One of the most powerful ways to identify potential barriers and remove them is to involve employees in the change before it is implemented. Employee involvement also has the two-fold benefit of hearing what employees are concerned about but also creating a level of understanding or advocacy (or for systems, power users) for the change or project.

what gets rewarded gets done

Supporting behavioural change – once the change has been implemented, it must be sustained or people may revert back to old ways. What gets rewarded gets done. This is most likely to occur if the changes are perceived to be 'too difficult' or 'don't make sense'. These views are reinforced if any of the levels in the strategic alignment cascade are not aligned and mixed messages about expectations and performance are generated.

Implementation of a structured project management approach to change can create transparency and will communicate to employees that their concerns regarding the change are being addressed. This will improve the levels of comfort and confidence in the employees regarding the change and project teams.

Our three favourite top 10 lists

On our travels, we have felt both elation and heartache as we project managed change. This section gives you our best personal and professional tips, lists, and some things to remember when you can't quite recall why on earth you signed up for this journey.

The top 10 reasons why transformation programmes fail

1. Not establishing a great enough sense of urgency
2. Not creating a powerful enough guiding coalition
3. Lacking a vision
4. Under-communicating the vision by a factor of 10
5. Not removing obstacles to the new vision
6. Not systematically planning for creating short-term wins
7. Declaring victory too soon
8. Not anchoring changes in the corporation's culture
9. Lack of a measurement system
10. Failure to involve people.

(Kotter, 1995)

The 10 things every change winner does

1. Gains commitment from the management chain
2. Celebrates successes
3. Creates a single direction

4 Undertakes necessary changes only

5 Takes time to plan

6 Communicates well and continually

7 Listens to people's issues and concerns

8 Stays personally involved

9 Protects people's self-worth

10 Works with resistance, not against it.

(Evard and Gipple, 2001)

The 10 barriers to successful change

1 Employees feel treated like robots

2 Change has a 'flavour-of-the-month' track record

3 Resistance goes undercover

4 Employees are saying 'I don't know how this affects me'

5 The culture is different to the change

6 HR policies are different to the change

7 Your employees are stressed out

8 Turf battles occur

9 Employees believe change is not needed

10 Leader lacks credibility.

(Evard and Gipple, 2001)

Our favourite websites

The internet is a marvellous tool, and you can find great change management guidance, resources and thinking. Be discerning, and use what's best for you. The websites we have found most useful, and go back to again and again are: www.change-management.com; www.businessballs.com; www.beingfirst.com/changeresources/; www.cipd.co.uk; and www.ogc.gov.uk.

If you want to learn more about the approach, methods and tools in this book, go to www.uncommonexpertise.co.uk for more information.

Closing remarks

Change is about people, relationships and personal values. There is no substitute for expertise and experience, and the concepts, principles and tools in this book should provide you with a firm grounding which we hope will be a foundation for you to build your understanding and expertise. You are now armed with the tools to project manage change. Add to that your own style and a strong belief in what you are doing and you will be successful.

Appendix 1 Strategic (SWOT) analysis template

Please note that these criteria examples relate to assessing a new business venture or proposition. Many listed criteria can apply to other quadrants, and the examples are not exhaustive. You should identify and use any other criteria that are appropriate to your situation.

Stengths	Weaknesses
Criteria examples Advantages of proposition? Capabilities? Competitive advantages? USPs (unique selling points)? Resources, Assets, People? Experience, knowledge, data? Financial reserves, likely returns? Marketing – reach, distribution, awareness? Innovative aspects? Location and geographical? Price, value, quality? Accreditations, qualifications, certifications? Processes, systems, IT, communications? Cultural, attitudinal, behavioural? Management cover, succession? Philosophy and values?	**Criteria examples** Disadvantages of proposition? Gaps in capabilities? Lack of competitive strength? Reputation, presence and reach? Financials? Own known vulnerabilities? Timescales, deadlines and pressures? Cashflow, start-up cash-drain? Continuity, supply chain robustness? Effects on core activities, distraction? Reliability of data, plan predictability? Morale, commitment, leadership? Accreditations, etc? Processes and systems, etc? Management cover, succession?
Opportunities	**Threats**
Criteria examples Market developments? Competitors' vulnerabilities? Industry or lifestyle trends? Technology development and innovation? Global influences? New markets, vertical, horizontal? Niche target markets? Geographical, export, import? New USPs? Tactics: e.g., surprise, major contracts? Business and product development? Information and research? Partnerships, agencies, distribution? Volumes, production, economies? Seasonal, weather, fashion influences?	**Criteria examples** Political effects? Legislative effects? Environmental effects? IT developments? Competitor intentions – various? Market demand? New technologies, services, ideas? Vital contracts and partners? Sustaining internal capabilities? Obstacles faced? Insurmountable weaknesses? Loss of key staff? Sustainable financial backing? Economy – home, abroad? Seasonality, weather effects?

Appendix 2 Example process diagram

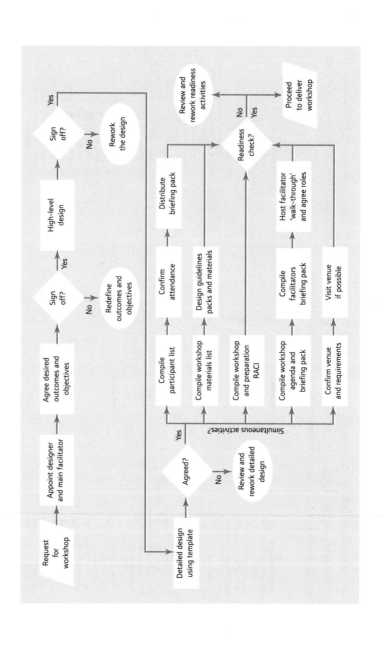

Appendix 3
McKinsey 7S model

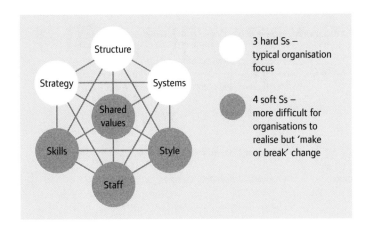

Appendix 4

Alternative scope descriptors

Depth of change	How it affects the organisation
Graze	Fine-tuning; focus on efficiency
Surface	Restructure; reallocate resources
Shallow	Improve/change planning; slight change in thinking or emphasis
Shift	Change of CEO/MD; leadership style; strategy
Penetrating	Change in definition of success, targets, goals
Deep	Change of vision, philosophy and mission
Deepest (transformational)	Paradigm shift; change in how you think; how problems are solved; how we do business

Source: Based on Huczynski, A. and Buchanan, D. (2007) *Organizational Behaviour: An Introductory Text*, 7th Edition, Harlow: Financial Times Prentice Hall, page 592. Reprinted with permission.

Appendix 5 The RACI process

The RACI process provides a clear basis for defining accountabilities and structure.

Definition

R Who is RESPONSIBLE? — The person who has to do it (the doer)

A Who is ACCOUNTABLE? — The person who makes the final decision and has ultimate ownership

C Who is CONSULTED? — The person who must be consulted *before* a decision or action is taken

I Who is INFORMED? — The person who must be informed that a decision or action *has* been taken

Sample RACI Matrix:
PROCESS: Making a process change

Functional roles

Activities	Process Facilitator	Line Facilitator	Setter	Operator
Plan activities	I	A	A	I
Prepare detail		C	A/R	I
Change process document	A	R		I
Perform change	I	A	R	R

RACI Analysis

RACI Analysis

If you find:

Horizontal

Lots of Rs	Too many people involved?
No Rs or As	Why do it? Is the job getting done?
More than one A	Confusion, indecision?
Lots of Cs	Does everyone consulted add value?
Lots of Is	Do they all need to know?

Vertical

Lots of Rs	Too much work?
No empty space	Too much work? Too much consultation?
No Rs or As	Can the function be eliminated?
Too many As	Is accountability at the right level? Is the organisation too hierarchical?

Appendix 6

Team temperature questionnaire

1 Strongly disagree	2 Disagree	3 Neutral	4 Agree	5 Strongly agree				

	1	2	3	4	5
1. Amongst us, we all know who is responsible for activities and deliverables	1	2	3	4	5
2. We understand the strengths and weaknesses of our team.	1	2	3	4	5
3. We have a team charter.	1	2	3	4	5
4. We help each other learn.	1	2	3	4	5
5. We are clear about our competency strengths and gaps.	1	2	3	4	5
6. We have the right skills in the team.	1	2	3	4	5
7. We regularly review our progress.	1	2	3	4	5
8. We are confident about meeting the challenge we have set ourselves.	1	2	3	4	5
9. We value the differences within the team.	1	2	3	4	5
10. We regularly give feedback to each other.	1	2	3	4	5
11. We have the right people in the team.	1	2	3	4	5
12. Team members actively apply their skills.	1	2	3	4	5
13. We have effective meetings which are well facilitated.	1	2	3	4	5
14. We are genuine with each other.	1	2	3	4	5
15. Depending on the task at hand, the leadership role is rotated within the team.	1	2	3	4	5
16. We walk the talk.	1	2	3	4	5
17. Against our key performance indicators (KPIs), we have produced some exceptional work.	1	2	3	4	5
18. Depending on the skills requirements, we rotate team members and occasionally involve additional members to support.	1	2	3	4	5
19. Overall, everyone really works together.	1	2	3	4	5
20. We rely on each other.	1	2	3	4	5
21. We have spent time on developing team competencies (e.g. meeting management)	1	2	3	4	5
22. We help each other be successful.	1	2	3	4	5
23. We spend as much time doing things as we do reviewing what we have done.	1	2	3	4	5
24. So far, we have exceeded our performance expectations.	1	2	3	4	5

25. Do you believe our team has made progress since January 2008?
☐ Yes ☐ No

If yes, could you please outline areas of greatest change. If no, could you please let us know what in your opinion has prevented this change.

_____

_____

26. In moving forward, the best thing that we could work on as a team would be (please complete this statement) …

_____

_____

Key to criteria

Accountability: Q1 Q15 Q20	Valuing others: Q2 Q9 Q14	Competencies: Q5 Q11 Q21	Common approach: Q13 Q19 Q23
Commitment: Q3 Q8 Q16	Feedback and learning: Q4 Q10 Q22	Technical skills: Q6 Q12 Q18	Measurement: Q7 Q17 Q24

Glossary

Activity Transforms the inputs through a series of tasks, actions, analysis or synthesis into a refined product or output

Advocates People who want the change and are supportive

Affiliate Division, business unit or site within a company

APM Association for Project Management

Benefits case Key element of a business case; identifying the expected benefits, how they will be measured and when they are likely to be achieved

BPR Business process re-engineering

BU Business unit

Business case Outlines the strategy and objectives (business reasons) for undertaking a change project or programme

Change agent The local, on-the-ground voice of the executive sponsor. Agents do not have the authority to make decisions about the change, but do provide day-to-day clarity and work closely with the change leader to implement change

Change leader Change leaders are the local sponsors of change, the line managers that people look to immediately when wondering whether or not to take a change seriously. A change leader has all the same attributes and skills as a sponsor, and has the additional tough task of making it work locally

Change management Change management is the process, tools and techniques to manage the people-side of business change to achieve the most successful business outcome

Change manager Change managers are responsible for identifying, driving and completing the activities to manage the change

Change management strategy A change strategy is the first deliverable in the change management work stream. A change strategy answers three main questions: 'What are our reasons for doing this?, What do we want to achieve?, How will we get there?' It acts as both the baseline and anchor point for the change management plan, setting boundaries for the 'as-is' and the desired 'to-be'

Change network In large-scale change, there may be many change agents or change leaders working together, (sometimes called change champions) forming a change network, completing activities on the change plan

Change plan The change plan defines what you need to do (the activities, order and resources) to complete the change strategy. It provides the structure so that work streams for each of the lenses in the change prism are integrated and aligned to the overall project plan

Change prism A copyrighted model containing eight lenses that acts as (1) a checklist for what is likely to change and what the level and type of impact the change is likely to have and (2) a framework for planning

Change team The change team are charged with implementing the change plan

CIA Change impact assessment

CIM/CIPS/CMI/CIMA UK professional bodies – various chartered institutes of marketing, patents, accounting and management

CIPD Chartered Institute of Personnel Development, based in the UK

CRA Change readiness assessment

CRM Customer relationship management

CRP Conference room pilot. Workshops are the key milestones/deliverables in the design phase and are called CRPs to distinguish them from any other workshop activity

CSF Critical success factor

Deliverables Tangible or intangible products (documents, services, decisions) that are identified and agreed to as part of the project plan

Dependency A dependency is a reliance on one piece of work finishing before the next can begin

EQ Emotional intelligence

ERP Enterprise resource planning

FELA Federal Employers' Liability Act

FPOC First point of contact

Hot-desking A work area that can be used by any employee at any time, resulting in several employees using a desk over the course of a day. If there is a reservation system for the desk, it is called 'hotelling'

HPT framework A set of criteria that makes up a high-performance team

Input The materials, capital, resources and information that a process receives and acts upon in order to generate an output

Issue An issue is a risk that has reached its due date, when what you anticipated might happen actually happens

KPI Key performance indicator

KRA Key result area

Lenses (eight) Each lens in the change prism looks at a sequential set of activities that could be performed at certain stages of the project

M&A Mergers and acquisitions

MBTI Myers-Briggs Type Indicator

Methodology A standardised and repeatable way of doing or process

Milestone A scheduled event that signifies completion of a deliverable or a set of related deliverables. It has no duration and no effort; it is a flag in the project plan to signify the work is done

MIS Management information systems

OA Organisation alignment

OD Organisation design

OGC Office of Government Commerce (UK)

Output Documents, information, plans or decisions produced by the application of activities on inputs that deliver value to the organisation

PD Planned description

PDR Plan-do-review, refers to a cycle of task execution

PMI Project Management Institute

PMM Performance management and measurement

PMO Project management office

PRINCE2 UK Government project methodology

Programme A programme is a set of related projects, sometimes called a portfolio, and requires different handling and skills in its management than a project

Project A temporary endeavour undertaken to create a unique product, service or result

Project/change stream The group of activities that work in alignment with other project streams, such as process or technology, to make up the overall project plan

Project plan Project plans are generally organised in phases with the number of phases dependent on the complexity and scale of the project. The plan sets out the work or 'work packages' to be completed during the project, with their start and finish dates, the resources required and a cash flow profile which will show at what stages of the project money will be spent

RACI Device for identifying levels of ownership and roles relating to activities and tasks. Stands for: responsible, accountable, consulted, informed

RAG Red, amber, green

RFP Request for proposal

Risk A risk is an unplanned event or situation that may occur but has not yet occurred *and*, if it does occur, would have an impact on the project/programme's ability to achieve its objectives: cost, benefits, timescale or quality

SBU Strategic business unit

SCM Supply chain management

Six Sigma Six Sigma is a methodology that seeks to eliminate defects in any process

SME Subject matter expert

Span of control The number of resources (people, financial, technical) that are within one person's responsibility. Usually refers to number of people reporting directly into someone (such as 25:1, 10:1 etc.)

SPOC Single point of contact

Sponsor (change) The change sponsor is the 'go-to' executive for the change manager, and will provide day-to-day assistance, guidance and escalation in completing the change strategy. This may be the same person as the executive sponsor in smaller scale change

Sponsor (executive) The sponsor is the *one* person within the business who has the power to stop and start a change. This person is usually a manager of managers, sits high up the organisation, and/or has the power to direct others to allocate resources to a change (financial, technical and human). This person has the scale of the change within their remit and will set the tone of the change

Stakeholder Any individual or group who is affected by a change, or has a 'stake' in it

SWOT analysis Strategic analysis of an organisation's strengths, weaknesses, opportunities and threats

Target Large groups of people or individuals who, as a result of the change initiative, project or programme, will do something different. Part of their job will change, the technology they use will change, or relationships in the organisation will change. They will sell new products, use new processes or adapt to a different location

Team Group of individuals sharing common purpose and objectives

Theme Recurring subject or topics linked by a common factor or root cause

TNA Training needs analysis

TOM Target operating model

Toolkit Collection of methods and devices to execute activities and accelerate outcomes

ToR Terms of reference

Tort Tort law defines what constitutes a legal injury, and establishes the circumstances under which one person may be held liable for another's injury

TQM Total quality management

Vanilla Used in describing standard IT systems, meaning 'non-customised'

WIIFM What's in it for me?

Workgroup More than one person with common or similar tasks

Bibliography

ACAS (2007) *Managing Conflict at Work*, Advisory, Conciliation and Arbitration Service

Ackerman-Anderson, L. and Anderson, D. (2002) *Defining Your Key Change Leadership Roles And Responsibilities – A Being First Change Tool*, www.Changeresources.com

American Institute of Stress (2003) http://www.stress.org/job.htm

Anderson, V. (2007) *The Value of Learning: A New Model of Value and Evaluation*, Chartered Institute of Personnel and Development

Beer, M. *et al.* (1990) *The Critical Path to Corporate Renewal*, Harvard Business School Press

Belbin, M. (1993) *Team Roles at Work*, Butterworth Heinemann

Block, P. (1999) *Flawless Consulting: A Guide to Getting Your Expertise Used*, Pfeiffer

CIPD (2004) *Reorganising for Success: A Survey Of HR's Role In Change*, Chartered Institute of Personnel and Development

CIPD (2005) *Managing Change: The Role Of The Psychological Contract*, Chartered Institute of Personnel and Development

CIPD (2007) *Change Management Factsheet*, Chartered Institute of Personnel and Development

Darwin, C. (1859) *On the Origin of Species by Means of Natural Selection, or the Preservation of Favoured Races in the Struggle for Life*, 1st edn, John Murray

Evard, B.L. and Gipple, C.A. (2001) *Managing Business Change for Dummies*, Hungry Minds Inc.

Furnham, A. (2002) 'Managers as Change Agents', *Journal of Change Management*, 3(1): 21–9

Gagne, R. (1965) *The Conditions of Learning*, Holt, Rinehart & Winston

Goold, M. and Campbell, A. (2002) *Do You Have a Well Designed Organisation?*, Harvard Business Review

Harkins, P. (1999) *Powerful Conversations: How High Impact Leaders Communicate*, McGraw-Hill Professional

Harvard Business School Press (2007) *Lessons Learned series: Managing Conflict*, Harvard Business School Press

Herzberg, F. (1999) 'Frederick Herzberg: The Hygiene-Motivation Theory', *Thinkers*, Chartered Management Institute

Hiatt, J. and Creasey, T. (2008) 'The Definition And History Of Change Management', Change Management Tutorial Series, http://www.change-management.com/tutorial-definition-history.htm, Prosci Research

Hiatt, J. *et al.* (2004) *Employee's Survival Guide to Change*, rev. edn, Prosci Research

Higgs, M. and Rowland, D. (2003) *Is change changing? An examination of approaches to change and its leadership,* Henley working paper 313, Henley Management College

Holmes, T.H. and Rahe, R.H. (1967) 'The Social Readjustment Rating Scale', *Journal of Psychosomatic Research*, 11(2): 213–18

Huczynski, A. and Buchanan, D. (2006) *Organizational Behaviour: An Introductory Text*, FT/Prentice Hall

Humphrey, Watts S. (1989) *Managing the Software Process*, Addison-Wesley Professional

James, J.W. and Friedman, R. (2003) *The 'Hidden' Annual Costs of Grief in America's Workplace, 2003 Report*, The Grief Recovery Institute Educational Foundation, Inc.

Johnson, G. and Scholes, K. (1993) *Exploring Corporate Strategy*, Prentice Hall

Katzenbach, J. R. and Smith, D. K. (1994) *The Wisdom of Teams: Creating the High-Performance Organization*, HarperBusiness

Kelly, M. *et al.* (2003) *Managing Change With Personal Resilience: 21 Keys For Bouncing Back & Staying On Top In Turbulent Organizations*, Mark Kelly Books

Kirkpatrick, D.L. (1959) 'Techniques for Evaluating Training Programs', *Journal of the American Society of Training and Development*, 33(11): 3–9

Kotter, J. (1995) 'The Top 10 Reasons Why Transformation Programmes Fail', *Harvard Business Review*, March–April

Kotter, J. (1996) *Leading Change*, Harvard Business School Press

Kotter, J. and Cohen, D. (2002) *The Heart of Change*, Harvard Business School Press

Kübler-Ross, E. (1969) *On Death & Dying*, Simon & Schuster/Touchstone

Lee, S. (1967) *The First Spiderman*, Marvel

Lewin, K. (1951) *Field Theory in Social Science*, Harper and Row

Bibliography

Lukac-Greenwood, J. *et al.* (2006) *Team Assessment Questionnaire*, unpublished

Moss Kanter, R. (1999) *The Enduring Skills of Change Leaders*, Leader to Leader, No. 13, Drucker Foundation and Jossey-Bass, Inc.

Newton, R. (2005) *The Project Manager*, FT/Prentice Hall

Nokes, S. and Kelly, S. (2007) *The Definitive Guide to Project Management*, FT/Prentice Hall

ODR (1998) *Fundamentals of Change Management*, Conner Partners

PMI (2000) *A Guide to the Project Management Body of Knowledge* (PMBOK Guide), Project Management Institute

PTP Training & Marketing Ltd (2005) *Where are the difficult People?* www.ptp.co.uk

Russell-Jones, N. (2003) *Managing Change Pocketbook*, Management Pocketbooks

Saratoga Research (2001) *Saratoga Institute Workforce Diagnostic System Benchmarking Reports 2001*, Price Waterhouse Coopers

Schein, E.H. (1992) *Organizational Culture and Leadership*, Jossey-Bass

Senge, P. *et al.* (1994) *The Fifth Discipline Fieldbook*, Doubleday Business

Sholtz, C. (1987) 'Corporate Culture And Strategy – The Problem Of Strategic Fit', *Long Range Planning*, Vol. 20, Issue 4, pp. 78–87

Siebert, A. (2005) *The Resiliency Advantage: Master Change, Thrive Under Pressure, and Bounce Back from Setbacks*, Practical Psychology Press

Simmons, A. (2006) *The Story Factor*, Basic Books

Smith, J. M. (2002) *'It' Happens! How to Become Change-Resilient*, Lifepath plc

Tamkin, P. (2005) *The Contribution of Skills to Business Performance*, Institute of Employment Studies

Trompenaars, F. and Hampden-Turner, C. (1997) *Riding the Waves of Culture: Understanding Cultural Diversity in Business*, Nicholas Brealey Publishing Ltd

Tuckman, B. (1965) 'Developmental Sequence in Small Groups', *Psychological Bulletin*, 63: 384–99

Waterman, R. Jr, Peters, T. and Phillips, J.R. (1980) 'Structure is not Organisation', *Business Horizons*, 23: 14–26

Wilkinson, D. (2006) *The Ambiguity Advantage*, Palgrave Macmillan

Williams, T. (2008) *Managing Projects Factsheet*, Chartered Institute of Personnel and Development

Index

Terms in bold indicate glossary items.

FINANCIAL TIMES

Think big for less